Lecture Notes
in Business Information Processing

411

More information about this series at http://www.springer.com/series/7911

David Aveiro · Giancarlo Guizzardi ·
Robert Pergl · Henderik A. Proper (Eds.)

Advances in
Enterprise Engineering XIV

10th Enterprise Engineering Working Conference, EEWC 2020
Bozen-Bolzano, Italy, September 28, October 19
and November 9–10, 2020
Revised Selected Papers

 Springer

Editors
David Aveiro ⓘ
University of Madeira
Funchal, Portugal

Robert Pergl ⓘ
Czech Technical University
Prague, Czech Republic

Giancarlo Guizzardi ⓘ
Free University of Bozen-Bolzano
Bozen-Bolzano, Italy

Henderik A. Proper ⓘ
Luxembourg Institute of Science
and Technology
Esch-sur-Alzette, Luxembourg

ISSN 1865-1348   ISSN 1865-1356   (electronic)
Lecture Notes in Business Information Processing
ISBN 978-3-030-74195-2   ISBN 978-3-030-74196-9   (eBook)
https://doi.org/10.1007/978-3-030-74196-9

This Springer imprint is published by the registered company Springer Nature Switzerland AG
The registered company address is: Gewerbestrasse 11, 6330 Cham, Switzerland

Preface

This book contains the revised papers of the 10th Enterprise Engineering Working Conference, EEWC 2020, held September 28, October 19 and November 9–10, 2020, (online) in Bozen/Bolzano, Italy, as part of BOSK 2020. It was organised by the CIAO! Enterprise Engineering Network (CEEN), a community of academics and practitioners who strive to contribute to the development of the discipline of enterprise engineering (EE), and to apply it in practice. The aim is to develop a holistic and general systems theory-based understanding on how to (re)design and run enterprises effectively. The ambition is to develop a consistent and coherent set of theories, models, and associated methods that enable enterprises to reflect, in a systematic way, on how to realize improvements, and assist them, in practice, in achieving their aspirations.

In doing so, sound empirical and scientific foundations should underlie all efforts and all organizational aspects that are relevant should be considered, while combining already existing knowledge from the scientific fields of information systems, software engineering, and management, as well as philosophy, semiotics, and sociology, among others. In other words, the (re)design of an enterprise and the subsequent implementation of changes should be the consequence of rationalized decisions that take into account the nature and reality of the enterprise and its environment, and respect relevant empirical and scientific principles.

Enterprises are considered as systems whose reality has a dual nature by being simultaneously, on the one hand, centrally and purposefully (re)designed, and, on the other hand, emergent in a distributed way, given the fact that its main agents, the humans that are the "pearls" of the organization, act with free will in a creative and in a responsible (or sometimes not) way. We acknowledge that, in practice, the development of enterprises is not always a purely rational/evidence-based process. As such, we believe the field of EE aims to provide evidence-based insights into the design and evolution of enterprises and the consequences of different choices irrespective of the way decisions are made.

The origin of the scientific foundations of our present body of knowledge is the CIAO! Paradigm (Communication, Information, Action, Organization) as expressed in our Enterprise Engineering Manifesto and the paper "The Discipline of Enterprise Engineering". In this paradigm, organization is considered to emerge in human communication, through the intermediate roles of information and action. Based on the CIAO! Paradigm, several theories have been developed, and are still being proposed. They are published as technical reports.

CEEN welcomes proposals of improvements to our current body of knowledge, as well as the inclusion of compliant and alternative views, always keeping in mind the need to maintain global systemic coherence, consistency, and scientific rigor of the entire EE body of knowledge as a prerequisite for the consolidation of this new engineering discipline. Yearly events like the Enterprise Engineering Working Conference and associated Doctoral Consortium are organized to promote the presentation of EE research and application in practice, as well as discussions on the contents and current state of our body of theories and methods.

Since 2005, CEEN has organized the CIAO! Workshop and, since 2008, its proceedings have been published as *Advances in Enterprise Engineering* in the Springer LNBIP series. From 2011 onwards, this workshop was replaced by the Enterprise Engineering Working Conference (EEWC).

This volume contains the proceedings of EEWC 2020, which received 23 submissions. Each submission was reviewed (double-blind) by three Program Committee members and the decision was to accept eight full papers and two short papers, which were carefully reviewed and selected for inclusion in this volume. Following the spirit of a working conference, we decided to publish post-proceedings after the event, where the papers that were presented and made available to conference participants were revised and extended by the authors taking in account the discussions that happened at the conference, the feedback of the reviewers, and new developments that might have taken place in the research during/after the conference. This year's online format enabled also several interesting keynotes, of which three are included in this proceedings.

EEWC aims to address the challenges that modern and complex enterprises are facing in a rapidly changing world. The participants of the working conference share a belief that dealing with these challenges requires rigorous and scientific solutions, focusing on the design and engineering of enterprises. The goal of EEWC is to stimulate interaction between the different stakeholders, scientists, and practitioners, interested in making enterprise engineering a reality.

We thank all the participants, authors, and reviewers for their contributions to EEWC 2020 and hope that you find these proceedings useful to your explorations on current enterprise engineering challenges.

January 2021

David Aveiro
Giancarlo Guizzardi
Robert Pergl
Henderik A. Proper

Organization

EEWC 2020 was the tenth working conference resulting from a series of successful EEWC events over the past few years. These events are aimed at addressing the challenges that modern and complex enterprises are facing in a rapidly changing world. The participants in these events share the belief that dealing with these challenges requires rigorous and scientific solutions, focusing on the design and engineering of enterprises.

This conviction has led to the effort of annually organizing an international working conference on the topic of enterprise engineering, in order to bring together all stakeholders interested in making enterprise engineering a reality. This means that not only scientists are invited, but also practitioners. Moreover, it also means that the conference is aimed at active participation, discussion, and exchange of ideas in order to stimulate future cooperation among the participants. As such the EEWC events contribute to the further development of enterprise engineering as a mature discipline.

The organization of EEWC 2020 and the peer review of the contributions to the conference were accomplished by an outstanding international team of experts in the fields of enterprise engineering. The following is the organizational structure of EEWC 2020.

Program Co-chairs

David Aveiro   University of Madeira and Madeira Interactive
                                Technologies Institute, Portugal
Giancarlo Guizzardi   Free University of Bozen-Bolzano, Italy
Robert Pergl   Czech Technical University in Prague, Czech Republic
Henderik A. Proper   Luxembourg Institute of Science and Technology,
                                Luxembourg

Program Committee

Alberto Silva   INESC and University of Lisbon, Portugal
Carlos Mendes   University of Lisbon and DIGIPRISE Lda, Portugal
Carlos Páscoa   University of Lisbon, Portugal
Christian Huemer   TU Wien, Austria
Eduard Babkin   Higher School of Economics, Nizhny Novgorod,
                                Russia
Florian Matthes   Technical University Munich, Germany
Frederik Gailly   Ghent University, Belgium
Geert Poels   Ghent University, Belgium
Graham McLeod   University of Cape Town and Inspired.org,
                                South Africa

Hans Mulder   University of Antwerp, Belgium
Jan Dietz   Delft University of Technology, the Netherlands
Jan Verelst   University of Antwerp, Belgium
Jens Gulden   University of Duisburg-Essen, Germany
Julio Cesar Nardi   Federal Institute of Espírito Santo, Brazil
Marcello Bax   Federal University of Minas Gerais, Brazil
Martin Op 't Land   Capgemini, the Netherlands; University of Antwerp, Belgium
Mauricio Almeida   Federal University of Minas Gerais, Brazil
Miguel Mira Da Silva   INESC and University of Lisbon, Portugal
Niek Pluijmert   INQA Quality Consultants, the Netherlands
Petr Křemen   Czech Technical University in Prague, Czech Republic
Pnina Soffer   University of Haifa, Israel
Renata Guizzardi   University of Twente, the Netherlands
Robert Lagerström   KTH Royal Institute of Technology, Sweden
Rony Flatscher   Wirtschaftsuniversität Wien, Austria
Sérgio Guerreiro   IST and INESC-ID, Portugal
Steven van Kervel   Formetis, the Netherlands
Stijn Hoppenbrouwers   HAN University of Applied Sciences, the Netherlands
Tatiana Poletaeva   Higher School of Economics, Nizhny Novgorod, Russia
Ulrik Franke   Swedish Defense Research Agency, Sweden

Contents

Enterprise Engineering Practice

Keynote Papers

Radical Digitalization: Challenges and Opportunities for Enterprise Modeling

Kurt Sandkuhl[1,2]([⊠])

[1] Institute of Computer Science, University of Rostock, Rostock, Germany
kurt.sandkuhl@uni-rostock.de
[2] Jönköping University, Jönköping, Sweden
kurt.sandkuhl@ju.se

Abstract. Digitalization and digital transformation have been an important topic for a lot of industries and application domains during the last years. In many enterprises, the result is a long list of digitalization projects – some of them completed, many still ongoing - and doubts about long-term benefits. Where are the disruptive effects of digital transformation? Radical digitalization is a way of (re-)focusing on innovation opportunities with strategic and long-term effects for an enterprise. In practice, this requires definition of problems and goals, changes in business models, design of new processes and services – and much more that can be supported by enterprise modeling. The resulting challenges and opportunities for enterprise modeling are discussed in the paper. The perspective taken is the practice of enterprise modeling rather than new theoretical approaches.

Keywords: Enterprise modeling · Radical digitalization · Digital transformation

1 Introduction

Radical digitalization, the main topic of this paper, is a methodical approach to support enterprises in focusing on digitalization activities most significant for their long-term development. Digitalization and digital transformation have been important topics in many industrial domains since several years (cf. Sect. 2) . Many enterprises made substantial investments in digitalization projects, which sometimes resulted in success stories presented to the public and discussed in the media. Examples are fully automated processing of loan requests in banking[1], shops without any cashier in retail industry[2], elevators displaying interactive advertisements while you are waiting[3] or lawn mower robots prepared for third party services[4].

However, motivation for the work presented in the paper is the observation that a lot of enterprises struggle to create business value from digitalization and others hesitate to

---

[1] An example is easyCredit (https://www.easycredit.de/).

[2] For an example, see Amazon go (https://www.amazon.com/go) and [1].

[3] See https://www.schindler.com/com/internet/en/mobility-solutions/products/digital-media-services/doorshow.html and [2].

[4] See https://www.husqvarna.com/ca-en/products/robotic-lawn-mowers/ and [3].

© Springer Nature Switzerland AG 2021
D. Aveiro et al. (Eds.): EEWC 2020, LNBIP 411, pp. 3–21, 2021.
https://doi.org/10.1007/978-3-030-74196-9_1

invest into digitalization efforts because they have difficulties to decide where to start. We argue that these enterprises could have benefits from exploring digitalization options by questioning established operational procedures or product features, even outside current limits of feasibility. This is what we call "radical digitalization". Our experience shows that many enterprises focus too much on solving known problems and additionally are not aware of the state of the art. What to them at first sight seem to be extreme or radical changes in their business and "impossible to implement" turns out, after closer investigation, to be feasible on a mid-term perspective if the right strategy is selected.

Enterprise modeling as a discipline offers many methodical approaches to support digitalization projects (see Sect. 3), but many enterprises do not consider EM as relevant for digital transformation and, as a consequence, do not systematically use EM techniques. However, to find and implement radical digitalization options requires methodical guidance. The resulting challenge for the EM community is how to support enterprises and at the same time bring our knowledge into operation?

This paper is more a combination of a position paper and a report on practices and experiences than the development of a new methodical approach or theoretical contribution to enterprise modeling. The aim of this paper is twofold: (a) to elaborate on the meaning of and motivation for radical digitalization and (b) to provide recommendations how to apply techniques from enterprise modeling for radical digitalization.

The rest of the paper is structured as follows. Section 2 introduces the field of digital transformation (DT) and proposes the dimensions operation, product/services and organizational scope to define the focus of radical digitalization activities. Section 3 gives an overview to existing method support from enterprise modeling for DT. Section 4 defines the term radical digitalization (RD), shows an illustrative example and proposes a procedural approach. Section 5 presents application examples for RD. Section 6 focuses on challenges and opportunities for enterprise modeling (EM). Section 7 summarizes our work.

2 Digitalization and Digital Transformation

Digitization, digitalization and digital transformation are terms frequently discussed in research and industry without a clear differentiation of their meaning. *Digitization* basically refers to transforming analog representations into computer-readable (digital) representations. In an enterprise context, digitization often is a precondition for optimizing processes and making operations more efficient and includes, for example, replacing printed forms or documents by digital ones. *Digitalization* can be described as a general term for activities transforming information, processes, products or services into a form that can be handled, supported or processed by information and communication technology [4]. Examples for such activities are the optimization of work and business processes (including automation of internal workflows), electronic data exchange with customers and suppliers; introduction of electronic commerce or support websites for products, customer communication and sales channels via social media, etc. [4]. *Digital transformation* is concerned with the changes digitalization and digital technologies can bring about in a company's business model [5], including the transformation of existing products or services into digital variants that offer advantages over tangible products

[6]. The focus here is on the disruptive potential of digital technologies and the resulting substantial change in markets and social and economic consequences [7].

Digitization and digitalization have to be considered as well researched topics. The focus in current research is more on digital transformation, i.e. when emerging changes in customer needs, competitive constellations, potentials for new service offerings or new partner structures affect both the value offering (i.e. the products or services) and the value creation processes (i.e. manufacturing or service delivery) of a company [8]. Berman and Bell [9] proposed to distinguish between transformation of the value proposition and the value creation when analyzing and planning digital transformation. Our work refines these two "dimensions" into several transformation stages and adds the dimension of organizational scope. The dimensions all are divided into different steps, which form the prerequisite for the next step.

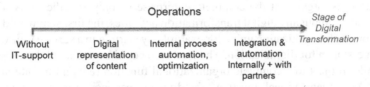

Fig. 1. Operations dimension of digital transformation

In the operations dimension, illustrated in Fig. 1, the lowest level is characterized by the usage of non-digital representations (i.e., without IT support) for information, for example forms on paper, folders with printed documents or assembly instructions on paper. There is probably hardly any company without some kind of IT-support but there are many companies where some task or activity still is performed using non-digital means. Here, the first step towards digital transformation would be digitization, i.e., to replace the analog with digital representations of the content, e.g. documents as PDF or forms to be filled in on a computer. With digital representations, automated processing of data would be possible, which is the next step. For this step, the usage of information systems or process technology is necessary to achieve an automation of process steps and end-to-end coverage of the process under consideration. The last step would be an integration of processes within the own enterprise or with partners, suppliers and clients, if desirable. Such integration aims at avoiding re-entering the same data in other IT systems for other processes.

In the product/service dimension, illustrated in Fig. 2, the most basic step are physical products without any built-in IT or services delivered without IT support. The first step is to complement the product/service with IT-based information but without actually changing the product/service. An example would be maintenance information for products or information about services on the web. The next step is to extend functionality and value proposition of products by integrating IT-components, for example to allow for monitoring the status of a product based on sensors and control units in the product connected it to a computer network. For services such an extension could be monitoring via Internet how much of the service has been completed. The third step is redefinition of the value proposition of a product or service which leads to a completely new value offering and requires connecting to the Internet and managing the behavior and functionality with IT. An example is to sell the functionality of the product instead of a physical device, measured in operation hours or performance delivered – which practically would not be possible without the sensors and Internet connection.

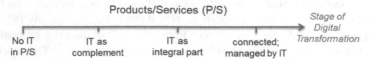

Fig. 2. Product/Service dimension of digital transformation

In the organizational scope dimension, illustrated in Fig. 3, we address if the digital transformation is targeted at the complete enterprise or only specific units. From an initial situation without any digital transformation activities, the first step would be pilot activities for single organization units, for example by starting in a service unit with staff and customers open for digitalization. The next step could be to extend the experiences from the pilot project to a complete organizational function (e.g., all maintenance and repair units) or organizational unit (e.g., the division responsible for a certain product line). The third step would be to include the whole organization.

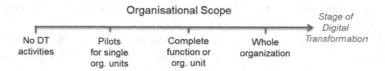

Fig. 3. Organizational Scope dimension of digital transformation

For the radical digitalization discussed in Sect. 3, the above dimensions of digital transformation serve as an aid to define the scope and focus of "radical" activities: what radical innovation options exist for operations?; what options for the products/services?; what organizational scope has to be included?

3   Method Support from Enterprise Modeling for Digital Transformation

The introduction to the field of digital transformation in Sect. 2 showed that DT potentially concerns business models, processes, products and services, organization structures and capabilities, i.e., all aspects of an enterprise. It also showed that DT basically is an organizational change process that needs to be anchored in knowledge about the current situation in an enterprise and has to include the systematic design of the future situation. The field of enterprise modeling offers a large number of different methods to support DT that address, for example, the various aspects of an enterprise (business process modeling, product modeling, service modeling, goal modeling, etc.) or different transformation phases (analysis of current situation, development of DT options, design future situation, etc.). There are only a few methods addressing digital transformation specifically, for example DITP [10]. An overview and description of EM methods is given in textbooks on conceptual modeling [11] and enterprise modeling [12].

For the purpose of this paper, it is useful to group existing EM methods along two viewpoints:

- the level of granularity addressed by existing methods: is the focus of a method to analyze or design "in the large", i.e., overall structures and processes or general architectures and components? Or is the focus more on exact details and specifics, i.e. analysis/design "in the small"? Analysis and design in the large is more important for phases of scoping, idea generation and discussion of potential DT alternatives, whereas "in the small" is required for identifying change needs in detail or designing details of implementation.
- the dimensionality of the method: is the focus on modeling one specific aspect (e.g., goals, processes, products, etc.) or on integrating multiple aspects into the same model?

Table 1 uses these viewpoints and proposes to group existing EM methods accordingly. In particular in the first row (i.e., methods with focus on one selected aspect), the table only contains some examples of the many existing methods.

Table 1. Enterprise modeling methods to support digital transformation

Dimensionality	Granularity	
	Analysis and Design "in the large"	Analysis and Design "in the small"
Focus on one selected aspect	Service blueprinting; Feature Modeling; Value Modeling; Goal/Problem Modeling; Business Process Maps; [...]	Information Modeling; Business Process Modelling; Product Modeling; Software Modeling; [...]
Focus on integrating multiple aspects	Modeling Business Models; Enterprise Modeling; Enterprise Architecture Modeling; Capability Modeling	Enterprise Modeling

As radical digitalization mostly is addressing the identification, evaluation and selection of DT options, we argue that mainly analysis and design *in the large* is required with a focus on *various aspects* of the enterprise relevant for the business model and the future enterprise design. Thus, we will shortly describe the EM method categories in the lower left quadrant of Table 1 in the following, as they are considered the most relevant ones: modeling business models; enterprise modeling; enterprise architecture modeling and capability modeling.

Modeling Business Models

In general, the business model of an enterprise describes the essential elements that create and deliver a value proposition for the customers, including the economic model and underlying logic, the key resources and key processes [13]. Most approaches for analyzing and developing business models include several dimensions or perspectives of an enterprise, which typically include the value proposition, value creation activities, customers and competitors, capital model and supplier or partners. Examples for frequently used approaches are the business model canvas [14], business model innovation [15] and business model management [16, 17]. In the business model management approach, six partial models are recommended [17]: the *capital model* is subdivided into financing model and revenue model. The *financing model* describes the sources of the capital that is necessary for business activity. The revenue model provides means to generally systemize business models by four dimensions: direct or indirect generation of revenue, as well as the transaction-dependent and the transaction-independent generation of revenue. The *procurement model* describes production factors and their sources. Here the distribution of power between suppliers and demanders is an important aspect. The *manufacturing model* covers the combination of input factors to new goods and services. Demand structures as well as the competitive situation are described by the respective sub-models of the *market model*. The *service offer model* defines which services are provided to the customers, while the *distribution model* focuses on the channels that are used to make the services available to the specific customer groups.

Enterprise Modeling

EM is the process of creating an enterprise model that captures all the enterprise's aspects or perspectives required for a given modeling purpose, like modeling the "as-is" or "to-be" situation in digitalization or digital transformation. An enterprise model consists of a set of interlinked sub-models, each of them focusing on a specific perspective, like processes, goals, concepts, actors, rules, information systems (IS). EM is performed with the help of enterprise modelling methods [12] used for capturing, communicating, and sharing enterprise knowledge [18]. Depending on the way and extent of involvement of enterprise stakeholders in modelling, some EM methods can be characterized as *participatory*, i.e., EM *involving users or enterprise stakeholders* is called *participative modelling* [19]. Participatory enterprise modelling includes collaboration activities between enterprise stakeholders and modelling experts during joint modelling sessions. The aim with a participative approach for EM is to simultaneously work with different stakeholders in a collaborative way to avoid conceptual deviations (misalignment) between the stakeholders and their different perspectives.

Enterprise Architecture Modeling

The field of Enterprise Architecture (EA) [20, 21] has been developed for more than a decade as a discipline that aims to model, align and understand important interactions between business and IT [22]. Enterprise Architecture Management (EAM) is a management approach that establishes, maintains and uses a coherent set of guidelines, architecture principles and governance regimes that offer direction and support in the design and development of an architecture to realize the enterprise's transformation objectives. An effective architecture management approach for digital enterprises supports the digitalization of products and services [23].

EAM, as defined by several standards such as ArchiMate [24] and TOGAF [25], uses a relatively large set of different views and perspectives for managing and documenting the business-IT-alignment. According to TOGAF the enterprise architecture is divided into four partial architectures [25]: Business Architecture defines the business strategy, governance, organization and the most important business processes; Data Architecture describes the structure of logical and physical data elements and data management resources in the organization; Application Architecture defines a design for the individually used application system and its relationship to the core business processes of the organization; Technology Architecture describes the software and hardware functions required to support the development of business, data and application services. This includes IT infrastructure, middleware, networks, communication, processing and standards.

Capability Management
Capability management promotes an organizational mindset that puts capabilities in focus of business model, organizational design and information systems development. The definition of capability is the ability and capacity that enables an enterprise to achieve a business goal in a certain context [26]. Implementation of capability management has to address the perspectives of enterprise strategy and vision (e.g. goals and key performance indicators), enterprise designs such as processes and IS architectures, the anticipated deployment contexts of capabilities and their effects on enterprise designs, as well as best practices (e.g. process variants and patterns) for dealing with context changes.

In [27] a method to capability management is introduced, which describes a systematic way to plan, design, develop, deploy, operate, and adjust capabilities. This method, the capability-driven design and development (CDD), consists of a number of method components each focusing on a specific task of the capability cycle, such as Capability Design, Context Modeling, Patterns and Variability Modeling, Capability Adjustment Algorithm Specification, as well as method extensions for dealing with certain business challenges such as supporting business process outsourcing and managing service configuration with the support of open data [28].

4   Radical Digitalization

Based on the background information presented in Sect. 2, this section introduces our view on radical digitalization (RD). In Sect. 4.1, we define the term and discuss what enterprises are likely to have benefits from working on radical digitalization options. In Sect. 4.2, an application case from manufacturing is presented to illustrate the need for RD. Section 4.3 introduces a procedural approach for RD in enterprises.

4.1   Definition and Target Groups

As already discussed in the introduction, our position is that many enterprises do not fully exploit the potential of digitalization because they stay in the limits of current products and services and focus on solving known problems instead of aiming at far-reaching innovations. Such enterprises could have benefits from investigating what potential for severe or "extreme" changes in their business models, products and operations exists. They should be encouraged to think "radical" as this might help to find opportunities (and sometimes threats) and support identification of the most promising DT ideas. We propose to call this approach "radical digitalization" with the following definition:

Radical digitalization is concerned with fundamental and far-reaching changes digital technologies can bring to an enterprise's operations and products. The search for radical digitalization options should be deliberately detached from current limits of feasibility in order to focus on digitalization options with potential for significant and long-term competitive advantages.

Much literature on DT considers digital innovation and disruption as element of DT (see, e.g., [29]), which also positions radical digitalization within the field of DT as fundamental and far-reaching changes often are disruptive. It is important to notice that the term "radical" relates to the enterprise under consideration and not to the general state-of-the-art. What might be an extreme and radical innovation for a certain enterprise, could be the established practice in another company.

The approach of radical digitalization is not relevant and suitable for all enterprises. Enterprises already successful in digital transformation or in domains not affected by digitalization obviously do not need an approach supporting DT. The most promising target groups from our experience are

- enterprises with some history in digital transformation, for example manifested in digital innovation projects, but expecting more potential and value creation from innovations with digital technologies, and
- enterprises that investigated digitalization, are aware of the need for digital innovations, but did not start any activities yet. Often, such enterprises seem to be lost in the "forest" of advices presented in digital transformation guide books and by DT experts.

4.2 Application Case for RD from Manufacturing Industries

As an illustration for the need of radical digitalization, we use an application case from manufacturing industries. The company under consideration is part of a major automotive group and producing tools that are used in manufacturing processes at the automotive group's production sites and at production facilities of other car makers. The construction, production and maintenance of the tools is the main business of the case company.

The case company is operating largely independently of the automotive group and has own decision rights regarding the internal organizational structures, business processes, IT infrastructure, information systems and technology selection. In 2017, when the automotive group started a major digitalization strategy, the case company also started to invest in own digitalization activities. As a result, a portfolio of digitalization projects was defined with the aim to increase the effectiveness and efficiency of operations of the case company. In bi-monthly steering meetings, the projects of the portfolio are discussed and the status is updated. Figure 4 shows an excerpt of the visualization of the portfolio, the project map, at the end of Q2 2020. The project map includes four of the nine departments (blue columns) and the ongoing (upper part) and planned projects (lower part) in these departments. Figure 5 explains, what information is included for every project in the map.

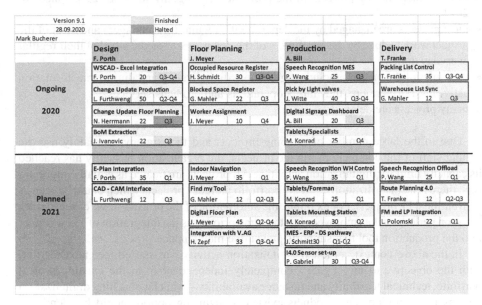

Fig. 4. Project portfolio of the case company (Color figure online)

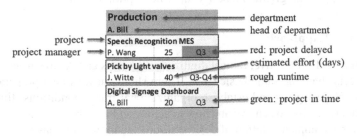

Fig. 5. Explanation of information in Fig. 4

The CEO and the management group of the case company are not fully satisfied with the digitalization results achieved so far. Although a lot of activities and projects were successfully completed and contributed to the aim of more efficiency and effectiveness, there is the general impression that these projects did not result in a better market position or increased competitiveness of the case company. In the management group, there was an ongoing discussion and disagreement whether to start a new digitalization initiative or not. The supporters argued that some important aspects of digitalization haven't been investigated yet. The opponents argued that the majority of the ongoing projects should be completed before starting new ones because they already consumed some efforts and there is no additional capacity available in the organization.

An analysis of the project portfolio in September 2020 revealed some facts that helped to explain this disagreement:

- in total, there are 67 projects in the portfolio (38 ongoing in 2020, 29 planned for 2021),
- most projects are managed by the department's regular line managers and most of the project work is done by the employees of the department "on the side" of their regular everyday duties,
- the topics of the projects include digitization, digitalization and digital transformation activities. Furthermore, they target operations and products/services,
- many projects are delayed.

Due to the large number of ongoing projects and the strategy, to mainly use the regular staff of the company to run the projects, the organization basically has reached its capacity limit for digitalization activities. All projects are treated as equally important (i.e., there is no prioritization), and the portfolio includes projects which could be seen as conventional IT projects. For example, the automation of the process flow for registering vacation periods of the employees has the same priority as the integration of a new sensor into the production tool that supports preventive maintenance.

In the above context, a radical digitalization activity was started (see next section) with the objective to investigate - completely independent from the existing project portfolio, technical feasibility and resource availability – what far-reaching digitalization options for operations and products exist. If convincing options could be identified, the plan was to revisit the project portfolio in order to free resources by canceling or postponing projects and giving the newly identified option priority.

4.3 Procedural Approach

From a methodical perspective, radical digitization projects and "conventional" digitalization projects share the same basic steps. There should always be a preparation step to define the project goals and establish organizational frame conditions (time frame, budget, staff, etc.); what to achieve and how to achieve it has to be specified in sufficient detail; and for the implementation of desired future situation, there has to be an implementation roadmap and projects to realize the solution accordingly. All these steps can be supported by the EM methods introduced in Sect. 3.

The most significant difference of radical digitalization projects and conventional ones lies in the first step. As the aim is to find digitalization options with potential for significant and long-term competitive advantages – which even might be seemingly drastic or unrealistic – well prepared idea generation workshops with strong participation from the enterprise side and careful preparation are recommendable. Based on our experience from RD projects, a participatory way of working involving all relevant stakeholders in the enterprise, i.e., different enterprise functions and hierarchy levels, not only the management, is strongly recommended. This increases the diversity of radical ideas and the available knowledge from the inside of an enterprise. The exact knowledge of the current situation in the enterprise is not absolutely necessary, but knowledge about technological trends, market changes inspiring ideas from related areas is very useful (see also Sect. 6.1).

Such workshops should include the exploration of digitalization options, selection of the most promising one(s), initial evaluation of these options with respect to feasibility, required efforts and effects on business model and organization, and definition of the next steps towards an implementation roadmap. Table 2 shows typical steps for preparing and conducting such a workshop.

Table 2. Procedural steps for radical digitalization workshops

Phase	Step	Activity
Workshop preparation	Preparation for application domain	• Explore trends in the domain • Relevant technological innovations • Innovations in related industries
	Preparation on management level	• Meeting with Top Management to motivate/get resources and mandate • Select participants from all relevant departments
	Preparation on participant level	• Inform all participants about purpose of the workshop • Encourage them to bring unusual ideas
RD workshop	Idea generation	• Collection of digitalization options • Divided into "products" and "operations" (see Sect. 2) • Joint clustering and identification of "top" priorities
	Evaluation	• Evaluation of top priority options, possibly in smaller groups or parallel working streams • Composition of groups depending on topic
	Selection	• Presentation of results of all groups • Joint decision on priorities
Implementation planning	Implementation roadmap	• Define implementation roadmap • Secure organizational commitment, funding and staff
	Project start	• Initiate first projects

The application case described in the previous section used this procedural approach for preparing radical digitalization. A radical digitalization workshop was planned to investigate the potential for drastic changes and innovations, like, reduction of production time to 10%, elimination of setup time of the production system, or fully automated internal logistics. Preparation and execution of the workshop included several steps: together with the management, participants were selected representing all relevant departments of the company (design, production, logistics, procurement, human resources, economics, service and customer care), mostly represented by the heads of the unit. All participants were informed beforehand about the purpose of the workshop, the need to think "out-of-the-box" and the importance of their participation. The workshop consisted of three major steps:

Step 1 encompassed the collection of proposals from the participants for the radical digitalization of products and of operations. The facilitator of the workshop guided sorting of the ideas into groups. Step 2 aimed at joint clustering the collected options and definition of priorities. The purpose was, essentially, to agree on a joint understanding and a clear separation of all clusters. The clusters the participants agreed on were marked with different colors. The definition of priorities was done using a voting approach. In Step 3, an initial evaluation of the top three options for radical digitalization of products and the top three transformations in operations was done. For this purpose, the workshop switched from a joint session with all participants to parallel sessions in two groups. Each group started with one option and had the task to elaborate the essentials of the option. After having completed all options all participants gathered and selected the top priority to be implemented.

After the workshop, an implementation roadmap was developed by a group of department heads and the top management. The implementation projects included the definition of the business model changes in more detail using a method for modelling business models (see Sect. 3). With the future business model defined, the required changes in the enterprise architecture were determined and the development of an enterprise model for the future situation started.

5 Application Examples of Radical Digitalization

In addition to the illustrative example discussed in Sect. 4.2 and 4.3, this section provides some more application examples for radical digitalization. The examples originate from the application sectors industrial services (ventilation/air condition facilities), hospitality services (restaurant) and manufacturing (producer of pumps).

Service Provider of Ventilation/Air Condition Facilities
The case study company offers services in the field of ventilation, air conditioning, refrigeration and clean room technology. Business units are construction, production of ventilation components, engineering service, and maintenance and repair. The focus of the digitalization activity was in the area of maintenance and repair, i.e., the scope of the digitalization was the maintenance department. The major service offered is inspection and maintenance of ventilation/clean room facilities, which often consist of several hundred components, various control units and many filters and fluids to change during maintenance. Documentation of all maintenance steps is important due to existing

regulations and high quality requirements. The project was initiated because the service technicians and maintenance manager complained about too many printed documents, forms to fill in and time required to do the paper work.

Radical digitization objective in this project was to **"reduce administrative effort for the maintenance process to 20% of the initial amount"** – which the management group of the company considered as very ambitious and difficult to reach. In this context, the administrative tasks include arranging appointments, creation & checking of orders, creating checklists & protocols, instructing technicians, procurement of spare parts and consumable supplies, writing invoices etc. The status of the processes was captured and modeled, all relevant roles identified and the existing information and document flow determined.

The company managed to reduce the effort to roughly 30% by replacing all printed documents and folders by electronic representations and by automating many process steps: The service technicians were equipped with a mobile device and the maintenance department with an additional software package that allowed for digital assignment of orders to technicians and provision of all documentation. During maintenance the technicians can use QR codes for identification of components in the facility, access to technical specifications, data capturing and the maintenance protocol. As soon as the technicians define the order as completed, the invoice to the customer is automatically generated in the back-office and the procurement of spare parts and consumables for the next maintenance is generated.

Restaurant Group

The second example is a restaurant group at the German Riviera. The motivation for digitalization is increasing popularity among tourists and locals, and at the same time problems to recruit more staff members to meet the growing demand. The owners of the restaurant considered digitalization as possibility to increase efficiency in operations and at the same time improve the image as "modern" location. The overall goal was to have more time for excellent food and service for the guests. To reach this goal, the radical idea emerged to **take no more phone calls during opening hours.** This basically meant that communication with the customers by phone, for example for booking a table, had to be replaced by a digitized process acceptable and with added value for the customers.

An analysis of the established IT infrastructure in the restaurant showed a point-of-sale cashier system (POS), an accounting system and content management for the website and social media. Booking of tables in the restaurant was made by calling or visiting the restaurant. The staff would write this into a large book with separate pages for every day. When leaving the restaurant, the customers received a printed sales slip; formal invoices were sent on request some days later.

In the digitalization project, one step taken was to substitute the physical "reservation book" by digital booking of tables. For this purpose, the new booking process was designed from customer and staff perspective, the booking function in the POS was activated and a booking link was added on the web-site and in social media. The next activity was to implement "one step check-out" for the customers, which basically addressed digitalizing the payment process. This included the possibility to register payment data when booking the table, and an extension of the POS for customer management. As a result, the customers only had to sign the bill and the restaurant would initiate the payment and send an electronic invoice by e-mail. From a technical perspective, the restaurant case transformed into digital on-boarding and off-boarding of customers including integration with back-office processes.

Producer of Pumps
The third example is a medium-sized manufacturer of different kinds of pumps and pumping technologies, e.g. swimming pool pumps, sewage pumps, industrial pumps for heavy environments or ship pumps. After-sales services are also part of the business, which include maintenance and repair. Although its business is stable and developing well, the management decided to explore digitalization as possibility to create new service opportunities and business models. One of the core ideas of the company's product management was to integrate sensors into the pumps, equip them with a data communication device and send sensor information to the back-office. In this context, the radical idea emerged to have **no more business trips for the maintenance staff**. This basically meant that maintenance of the pumps had to be possible without visiting the location where the pump is installed.

The digitalization project implemented a "digital twin" of the pumps by, for example, integrating additional sensors for measuring throughput, energy consumption, soiling, and providing a real-time visualization of the pumps' status for the maintenance staff in the back-office. Furthermore, changes in the organization structure were made: the maintenance department was extended with a "monitoring and control" unit and agreements with regional service providers were made. Although the resulting new service of "remote monitoring" was not meant to replace the established maintenance service, it provided the foundation for a new service offer as an alternative to buying the pump as such: pumping-as-a-service. Pumping as a service aims at selling the functionality of the pump instead of the pump as physical device, which would lead to a service agreement where the company is paid for pumped cubic meters or hours of pumping.

6   Challenges and Opportunities for Enterprise Modeling

Radical digitalization projects offer many opportunities for applying enterprise modeling techniques, but also provide some challenges for the enterprise modelers working in such projects. The opportunities essentially have already been described in Sect. 3 when discussing the existing EM methods for digital transformation: enterprise modeling offers a large number of different methods to support digitalization projects in general, and also radical digitalization projects. As illustrated in the application case in Sect. 4, method support is available for all essential aspects of radical digitalization. Thus, enterprise modelers should actively offer participation in radical digitalization projects or develop such projects in cooperation with enterprises.

One of the challenges to address is how to make companies realize the usefulness and value of EM and start to apply the existing methods. The key to this question probably is that "modelling is not an end, i.e. a purpose on its own, but a means to an end" [30]. For companies interested in digitalization, digitalization is the "end" and EM a means to reach this end. This basically means that a company's problems or challenges have to be the starting point for any EM project.

When it comes to the challenge of "value creation by digitalization" the employees and stakeholders of an enterprise probably are the key to identify the right digitalization option, but in order to motivate their participation in digitalization projects and to convince the management, there must at least be a basic understanding of the situation in the enterprise or in the industrial domain of the enterprise. The resulting challenge from enterprise modelers is to either develop the necessary knowledge or to team up with an expert in the domain under consideration.

The other challenges discussed in this section are related to the actual modeling tasks in the radical digitalization projects. The aim is to provide advice and practices.

6.1 Find the Most Promising Digitization Option

As explained in Sect. 4, the digitalization workshop at the beginning of a radical digitalization project is probably the most important step. It is essential for the project that the workshop is considered as successful by the participating employees and stakeholders and that it results in a convincing digitalization option with the potential to create long-term competitive advantages. Thus, preparation of the workshop is very important which holds the challenge for the enterprise modelers and facilitators of the workshop to define a strategy for conducting the workshop and activating the participants. In addition to the recommendations in Sect. 4.3, this section addresses the challenge how to act if the enterprise stakeholders do not bring innovative ideas to the workshop and collection of "radical" options is slow or not progressing at all.

In this situation, i.e., when entering radical digitalization projects as an enterprise modeler or an external consultant who aims at supporting the enterprise, it usually makes sense to have some examples or guiding questions available, which can provide inspiration to the stakeholders in the enterprise. These examples or questions should only be used if the creative part of the workshop (see Sect. 4.3) does not result in sufficient ideas. If the stakeholders come up with own proposals, no inspiration is needed and should be used.

Table 3 presents a selection of objectives that many enterprises would consider as radical. If the objective contains percentage values (e.g., reduce [...] to 10%), these values are examples. When confronted with the objectives, the stakeholders in an enterprise will often consider them as impossible to reach, which is part of the approach. If reaching the objective would mean an important and long-lasting strategic advantage for the enterprise, it is important to explore how close the enterprise can get to reaching the objective. Often, the stakeholders are not aware of technical and organizational possibilities.

For each objective, possibilities for organizational or technical ways to reach the objective are given in Table 3. These possibilities stay on a very general level because they only can be elaborated in more detail for a concrete enterprise and the situation in this enterprise. Enterprise modelers should prepare such a list of questions or even a similar table for the workshop and also have a set of real-world examples available who worked with similar objectives.

Table 3. Examples for radical digitalization objectives

Dimension	Digitalization objective	How to achieve the objective?
Operations	Reduce the duration of a business process to 10%	• Provide all inputs to the process machine-readable
Operations	Reduce the effort of a business process to 10%	• Automation of process steps as far as possible • Eliminate exceptions from process flow as much as possible • Investigate outsourcing of process steps to more efficient partners • Remove process steps not contributing to core value creation
Services	Only self-service for certain customer groups	• Create digital processes and IS-support for all customer services • Switch all customer-related communication to digital channels • Revise customer journey and touchpoint concept
Products	All product variants can be produced on the same production line	• Integrate control unit into products that can be configured during assembly • Implement modular product structure that allows for adding/removing components based on customer order • Connect production line to manufacturing execution system that allows for individual configuration/composition of products • If necessary, change variants of products offered to customers to what can be produced on the production line
Services	Fully automatic performance of defined services	• Define inputs, outputs and interfaces for services • Transform all supporting business processes and applications to digital ones • Define decision logic for services
Products	Substitute all products by service	• Re-design products to include actuators and sensors for all essential functions and information • Design customer services and market offers for "product-as-a-service" • Design preventive maintenance and reliable operation services
Products	Reduce number of components to 20%	• All products have to use the same components, i.e., strict modularization and defined interfaces • Implement customer demands only by configuration of components

6.2 Make Sure the Best Option Actually Is Implemented

Of utmost importance in radical digitalization projects is the identify the most promising digitalization option that is accepted by the key stakeholders in the organization as the option to pursue and that is expected to result in long-lasting competitive advantages. When this option has been identified, for example by using the procedure presented in 4.3 and supported by the questions in 6.1, the next challenge is to **carefully plan the implementation** of this option.

Planning the implementation has at least two aspects: (1) the technical and organizational implementation roadmap, including design and development process of future operations and/or products and services, and (2) sufficient funding, staff and organizational commitment from top management and company owners for the implementation roadmap. The former to a large extent can be prepared and supported with EM methods (e.g. for detailing the business model, enterprise architecture, product/service details or business process changes), whereas the latter requires experience in organizational change management and often also innovation management.

To avoid that great digitalization ideas developed and supported by various stakeholders in an enterprise never reach the implementation phase, the innovation readiness and possibilities for implementation should already be discussed in the preparatory meetings with the management. This includes aspects such as willingness for strategic investment, risk tolerance, previous experience in innovation projects or availability of competences and staff capacity [31].

6.3   One EM Approach Might Not Be Sufficient

Many enterprise modelers will be able to name their favorite and most frequently used EM method – and this probably will be the method with their highest level of expertise and experience. Specialization on one or a small number of EM methods makes perfect sense in conventional EM projects, in particular because this also has to include knowledge about supporting tools, established practices, reusable models, etc. However, for radical digitalization projects this this might not be sufficient.

In RD projects the application domain under consideration and/or the different phases of the digitalization projects often require a spectrum of different methods. A number of industrial application domains have established practices or de facto standards when it comes to modeling which can be useful when exploring digitalization options. Examples are—Furthermore, early phases of elaboration RD options often are better supported by business model approaches, whereas later phases require enterprise architecture or capability modeling.

In this context, it often makes sense to have an enterprise modeling team with different competences that performs the RD project. Among the team members should always be someone with expertise in the application domain under consideration and an expert in participatory modeling. Furthermore, knowledge in analyzing and designing business models and "architecture thinking" often are required.

7   Summary

The core topic of this paper is how to help enterprises to find promising digitalization options with far-reaching effects – and how to apply enterprise modeling methods for this purpose. We propose the approach of "radical digitalization" that builds on the mindset that thinking in drastic changes or setting seemingly unrealistic goals help enterprises to look beyond established practices and products and to identify valuable future digitalization options. Radical digitalization basically is a special way to approach digital transformation, which applies participatory modeling in the early phases of digital transformation projects and includes modeling the changes DT will require from different viewpoints (e.g., business model, enterprise architecture, capabilities) and in different perspectives (processes, organization structures, products, IS/IT) of an enterprise.

One aim of our work also is to encourage the enterprise modeling community to take a stronger stake in digital transformation. The field of enterprise modeling offers many modelling methods valuable for digital transformation. Section 3 discusses some of these approaches; Sects. 4 and 6 discuss possibilities to apply them; and Sect. 5 provides examples.

References

1. Grewal, D., Roggeveen, A., Nordfält, J.: The future of retailing. J. Retail. **93**(1), 1–6 (2017). https://doi.org/10.1016/j.jretai.2016.12.008
2. Sandkuhl, K., Smirnov, A., Shilov, N., Wißotzki, M.: Targeted digital signage: technologies, approaches and experiences. In: Galinina, O., Andreev, S., Balandin, S., Koucheryavy, Y. (eds.) NEW2AN/ruSMART-2018. LNCS, vol. 11118, pp. 77–88. Springer, Cham (2018). https://doi.org/10.1007/978-3-030-01168-0_8
3. Kaidalova, J., Sandkuhl, K., Seigerroth, U.: Challenges in integrating product-IT into enterprise architecture–a case study. In: International Conference on ENTERprise Information Systems, CENTERIS 2017, International Conference on Project MANagement, ProjMAN 2017 and International Conference on Health and Social Care Information Systems and Technologies, HCist 2017, Barcelona; Spain, 8–10 November 2017, vol. 121, pp. 525–533. Elsevier (2017)
4. Zimmermann, A., et al.: Leveraging analytics for digital transformation of enterprise services and architectures. In: El-Sheikh, E., Zimmermann, A., Jain, L.C. (eds.) Emerging Trends in the Evolution of Service-Oriented and Enterprise Architectures. ISRL, vol. 111, pp. 91–112. Springer, Cham (2016). https://doi.org/10.1007/978-3-319-40564-3_6
5. Hess, T., Matt, C., Benlian, A., Wiesböck, F.: Options for formulating a digital transformation strategy. MIS Q. Exec. **15**(2), 6 (2016)
6. Gassmann, O., Frankenberger, K., Csik, M.: The Business Model Navigator. 55 Models that will Revolutionise Your Business. Pearson, London (2014)
7. Hirsch-Kreinsen, H., ten Hompel, M.: Digitalisierung industrieller Arbeit: Entwicklungsperspektiven und Gestaltungsansätze. In: Vogel-Heuser, B., Bauernhansl, T., ten Hompel, M. (eds.) Handbuch Industrie 4.0 Bd.3, pp. 357–376. Springer, Heidelberg (2017). https://doi.org/10.1007/978-3-662-53251-5_21
8. Ivanov, D., Dolgui, A., Sokolov, B.: The impact of digital technology and Industry 4.0 on the ripple effect and supply chain risk analytics. Int. J. Prod. Res. **57**(3), 829–846 (2019). https://doi.org/10.1080/00207543.2018.1488086
9. Berman, S.J., Bell, R.: Digital transformation: creating new business models where digital meets physical. IBM Institute for Business Value (2011)
10. Wißotzki, M., Sandkuhl, K., Wichmann, J.: Digital innovation and transformation: approach and experiences. In: Zimmermann, A., Schmidt, R., Jain, L.C. (eds.) Architecting the Digital Transformation. ISRL, vol. 188, pp. 9–36. Springer, Cham (2021). https://doi.org/10.1007/978-3-030-49640-1_2
11. Karagiannis, D., Mayr, H.C., Mylopoulos, J. (ed.): Domain-Specific Conceptual Modeling. Springer, Cham (2016). https://doi.org/10.1007/978-3-319-39417-6
12. Sandkuhl, K., Stirna, J., Persson, A., Wißotzki, M. (ed.): Enterprise Modeling. Tackling Business Challenges with the 4EM Method. The Enterprise Engineering Series. Springer, Heidelberg (2014). https://doi.org/10.1007/978-3-662-43725-4
13. Zott, C., Amit, R.: Business model design: an activity system perspective. Long Range Plan. **43**(2–3), 216–226 (2010). https://doi.org/10.1016/j.lrp.2009.07.004

14. Osterwalder, A., Pigneur, Y.: Business Model Generation: A Handbook for Visionaries, Game Changers, and Challengers. Wiley, Hoboken (2010)
15. Schallmo, D., Williams, C.A., Boardman, L.: Digital transformation of business models—Best practice, enablers, and roadmap. Int. J. Innov. Manag. **21**(08), 1740014 (2017)
16. Wirtz, B.W.: Business model management: design process instruments. In: Textbook for the Digital Society, 2nd edn., Speyer (2016)
17. Wirtz, B.W.: Business model management. Design–Instrumente–Erfolgsfaktoren von Geschäftsmodellen. Gabler (2011)
18. Vernadat, F.: Enterprise modeling and integration. Boom Koninklijke Uitgevers (1996)
19. Stirna, J., Persson, A., Sandkuhl, K.: Participative enterprise modeling: experiences and recommendations. In: Krogstie, J., Opdahl, A., Sindre, G. (eds.) CAiSE 2007. LNCS, vol. 4495, pp. 546–560. Springer, Heidelberg (2007). https://doi.org/10.1007/978-3-540-72988-4_38
20. Ahlemann, F. (ed.): Strategic Enterprise Architecture Management. Challenges, Best Practices, and Future Developments. Springer, New York (2012). https://doi.org/10.1007/978-3-642-24223-6
21. Lankhorst, M. (ed.): Enterprise Architecture at Work. Modelling, Communication and Analysis. The Enterprise Engineering Series. Springer, Heidelberg (2017). https://doi.org/10.1007/978-3-662-53933-0
22. Winter, R.: Architectural thinking. Bus. Inf. Syst. Eng. **6**(6), 361–364 (2014)
23. Zimmermann, A., Schmidt, R., Sandkuhl, K., Wißotzki, M., Jugel, D., Möhring, M.: Digital enterprise architecture-transformation for the internet of things. In: 19th International Enterprise Distributed Object Computing Workshop, pp. 130–138. IEEE (2015)
24. The Open Group: ArchiMate® 3.0.1 Specification, 1st edn. Van Haren Publishing, Zaltbommel (2017)
25. The Open Group: The TOGAF Standard, Version 9.2. TOGAF Series. Van Haren Publishing, Zaltbommel (2018)
26. Bērziša, S., et al.: Capability driven development: an approach to designing digital enterprises. Bus. Inf. Syst. Eng. **57**(1), 15–25 (2015)
27. Sandkuhl, K., Stirna, J. (eds.) Capability Management in Digital Enterprises. Springer, Cham (2018). https://doi.org/10.1007/978-3-319-90424-5
28. Kampars, J., Zdravkovic, J., Stirna, J., Grabis, J.: Extending organizational capabilities with Open Data to support sustainable and dynamic business ecosystems. Softw. Syst. Model. **19**(2), 371–398 (2019). https://doi.org/10.1007/s10270-019-00756-7
29. Skog, D.A., Wimelius, H., Sandberg, J.: Digital disruption. Bus. Inf. Syst. Eng. **60**(5), 431–437 (2018). https://doi.org/10.1007/s12599-018-0550-4
30. Sandkuhl, K., et al.: From expert discipline to common practice: a vision and research agenda for extending the reach of enterprise modeling. Bus. Inf. Syst. Eng. **60**(1), 69–80 (2018)
31. Yen, H.R., Wang, W., Wei, C.P., Hsu, S.H.Y., Chiu, H.C.: Service innovation readiness: dimensions and performance outcome. Decis. Support Syst. **53**(4), 813–824 (2012)

Human-Centred Design as the Way Forward for Organization Design and Enterprise Engineering

Rodrigo Magalhaes(⊠)

Instituto de Engenharia de Sistemas e Computadores, Investigação e Desenvolvimento, Lisbon, Portugal
Rodrigo.Magalhaes@inov.pt

Abstract. In this paper, human-centred design is put forward as an intellectual framework that can benefit both organization design (OD) and enterprise engineering (EE) research. The paper starts with a very brief summary of the main ideas contained in the book *Designing Organization Design: a human-centred approach* [18], where the principles of human-centred design have been applied to organization design. The paper suggests that while integration between OD and EE may not be a feasible proposition as part of the modelling exercise, the human-centred organization design (HCOD) framework can provide the contextual background in which EE researchers can/should situate, conceptualize, develop, and test their abstracted process models. Moreover, HCOD can provide important conceptual hooks to link separate projects in the areas of OD and EE. Two suggestions are put forward: the first concerns the modelling of meaning and sensemaking in the interaction of human actors, and the second refers to the use of the notions of causal and narrative design trace to keep track and analyze multifarious aspects of the organization's self-awareness.

Keywords: Human-Centred Organization Design · Principles · Meaning · Sensemaking

1 Introduction

In 2005–6, I was approached by my friend Jose Tribolet of the University of Lisbon with a research project on organizational engineering. I had never heard of organizational engineering and it sounded almost like a contradiction in terms, but it was certainly a challenge, especially because of the opportunity to put to work some of my doctoral research in the information systems discipline. In responding to Jose, I had to decide how I might contribute to the project and my almost immediate reaction was to say: "organization design seems to the be the right match for organizational engineering"! And so, the project *Organization Design and Engineering* was born, later to be renamed *Organization Design and Enterprise Engineering*.

As the project got under way, I become increasingly (and alarmedly) aware of the limitations of organization design as a topic represented in most textbooks of management

© Springer Nature Switzerland AG 2021
D. Aveiro et al. (Eds.): EEWC 2020, LNBIP 411, pp. 22–37, 2021.
https://doi.org/10.1007/978-3-030-74196-9_2

or organization. Firstly, in spite of its name, there is hardly any design in organization design. While for engineers, the word "design" is part of a process of building something, for us in management and organization, organization design was the same as establishing the macro structure of the organization, wholly silent about the micro level. Secondly, while engineers are very interested in the modeling of organizational processes, for us in management and organization processes are not part of the concerns of organization design at all. Organization design seemed to be reserved only for discussions about vertical workflows, but never horizontal ones. Thirdly, most engineers expect organization design theory to have something to say about behaviour, however in management and organization textbooks, organization design is mostly portrayed as an activity characterized by "cold cognitive scripts and rules" rather than "hot emotional attitudes and beliefs" [7].

Thus, I had to concede that organization design was not only underspecified as a field of study but was also not very useful as practical management tool. Meanwhile, the research literature had been spawning several very interesting pieces containing new ideas and alternative directions for organization design; however, attempts at bringing the pieces together could not be found anywhere… Beyond contingency theory, no common thread could be discerned to keep organization design together as a coherent body of knowledge. Yet, among the emerging trends, there was one that showed particular promise – design, with particular reference to human-centered design, applied to organization design. Design principles seemed to apply naturally to the design of organizations or, at least, to the design of a new conception of organizations. Both are/should be:

- Systemic
- Interactive and network-based
- Service-oriented
- Normative/Ethics-oriented
- Desiderata/Innovation-oriented
- Meaning-oriented

Hence, if design and organization design share fundamental principles, the design discipline might conceivably be a key source and a uniting thread for organization design. This was the working hypothesis that set me off on a long journey of academic research, which resulted is an entirely new approach to organization design – Human-Centred Organization Design – recently published in a book by Oxford University Press [18].

In parallel, the issue of the integration of Organization Design (OD) and Enterprise Engineering (EE) research was always a target of my research efforts and over time I had the privilege of contributing towards several initiatives aimed at tackling this issue. However, the macro nature of OD approaches dealing with structural or behavioural aspects of the organization, and the micro focus of EE research aimed at the modelling of processes abstracted from parts of the organization, makes integration a real challenge. The proof of the difficulties faced by various integration attempts is the relative lack of success of the two journals, which I helped to launch in the period 2010–18: *International Journal of Organization Design and Engineering* (Inderscience) and *Organization Design and Enterprise Engineering* (Springer).

So, how can Human-Centred Organization Design (HCOD) contribute to the advancement of EE research, as well as joint EE and OD research projects? In this paper I propose that HCOD can play an important role in providing an integrated contextual background in which EE researchers can/should situate, conceptualize, develop, and test their abstracted process models. In addition, the paper suggests two more areas where interesting joint OD-EE research could be developed. The first involves the key principle of HCD – design as meaning – which can provide a semantic foundation for projects in both EE modelling and OD qualitative research. The second hinges on the concept of design (or interactive) trace, which can bring together EE and OD researchers, each group working on one of the perspectives of the concept – causal trace and narrative trace.

2 Human-Centred Organization Design(ing)

Human-Centred Organization Design (HCOD) stands as an alternative to Contingency-Based Organization Design, the traditional academic school of thought for organization design research. HCOD is founded upon the aims and principles of design as a discipline, while remaining keenly aware of the roots of organizations as social constructions. More specifically, the new organization design paradigm is inspired by the human-centred design movement and follows the notion put forward by Krippendorff [14] and others that design should be defined as creation of meaning. According to this trend and its cognitive underpinnings, the worth of any design is judged in accordance with the perceptions and meanings that the artifact's stakeholders attribute to the design. HCOD is driven by design logics and guided by values of democratic participation, while placing meaning making and meaning taking at the center of organizational life.

2.1 What is the Difference Between Design and Human-Centred Design?

Simon [23] proposed the introduction of a new field of study, distinct from the natural sciences and the social sciences, a field applicable to professional schools of thought, such as medicine, engineering or management. He called it "science of design", a "body of intellectually tough, analytic, partly formalizable, partly empirical, teachable doctrine about the design process" (Ibid, p. 113). As the cornerstone of this new theory, Simon advocated the solution of "design problems". A solution is given in the form of a combination of values qualifying a set of key variables, representing the artifact under study in its own environment. Although very popular among the engineering and management communities, Simon's decision-making model now begins to be questioned as a method for approaching problems in the real world of people and organizations.

The criticism about the Simonion conception of design marks the launch of the notion of human-centred design. In expounding upon the realm of the sciences of the artificial or the sciences of design, Krippendorff [13] claims that design is primarily about "making sense of things". He states:

As soon as I move beyond the engineering of functional products, I need to be concerned with what the artefacts of design could possibly *mean* to users and interested parties, with the multiple rationalities that people can bring to bear on them [15].

Compared with Simon's [23] stance on design science, Krippendorff's [14] human-centred design (HCD) reverses the relation between the design object and its intention. For Simon the artefact is at the core, while for Krippendorff meaning is the core of the design process and the artefact becomes a medium for communicating the meanings intended by the designer and perceived by the user. According to Krippendorff [14] "design constitutes being human", a statement that is explained as follows:

- DESIGN is a way to understand things, to make them meaningful, to feel at home with them and to make them part one's life
- DESIGN is intrinsically motivating. Making something or having a hand in creating something is always inherently satisfying
- DESIGN occurs in everyday life (…) when people are prevented from deciding who they are or how they want to live their life they are essentially reduced to appendices of systems, machine parts, anonymous and interchangeable (Ibid, pp. 73–74).

The label of human centred design denotes a democratic and humanistic orientation aimed at developing "viable emancipative proposals in the form of material and semiotic artifacts" [2]. The acknowledgment of human centred design principle as the intellectual foundation for a new organization design framework has enormous consequences. First and foremost, meaning is constitutive of the human being, with identity emerging as the primordial set of meanings, defining who the person is. If applied to organization, identity is established as the superordinate attribute of its design, ruling over everything that the organization is and does, including its image, reputation, quality of relationships with employees or customers and its overall ethical stance.

2.2   Grouping Organizational Meanings as Processes of HCOD

In order to make sense of the types of organizational meanings that can be found in organizations, I submit Davidson's [4] triangular theory of meaning as the intellectual underpinning. I suggest that Davidson's three categories of meaning – objective, subjective and intersubjective – can be metaphorically adapted and be made to fit three levels of meaning-making in organizations: managerially-generated, organizationally-generated and stakeholder-generated, to include internal and external stakeholders. Davidson's philosophy heralds *intersubjectivity* as a new turn in the study of knowledge. Intersubjectivity is one of three varieties of knowledge, alongside subjectivity and objectivity. Objective knowledge is about what I know about the world around us, the locations, the shapes and sizes, as well as many of the causal properties of the objects in the world. Subjective knowledge is about our own knowledge of our sensations, our thoughts, desires and intentions. Intersubjective knowledge is about our knowledge about other people's knowledge.

In order to adapt Davidson's triangular theory to organizational meaning-making, I suggest that the organization can be split into three broad categories of practice, which would then correspond to different categories of meaning-making. Considering that all organizations exit to provide a service, the first level includes all those who are involved in the service provision, but do not have managerial responsibilities. Let us call it the "organizational" level. The second group includes all those who are affected by the service provision, which includes not only customers or users of the service, but also suppliers and shareholders who stand to gain from the service provision. The last level of practice is made up by those who have the responsibility of managing the service provision and receiving the feedback from those being affected by the service; this group is made up by the managerial staff. Next, when placing these three levels of meaning-making in organizations side by side with Davidson's three types of knowledge – subjective, objective and intersubjective –some interesting similarities emerge. Figure 1 shows the proposed three levels of meaning-making in organizations.

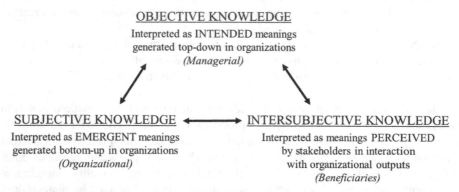

Fig. 1. Davidson's [4] Triangle of knowledge interpreted as three broad categories of organizational meaning-making

1. Managerially generated intended meanings (objective)

The first category of meaning-making in organizations is the managerial category. An interesting similarity can be established between this category and *objective* meaning from Davidson's triangle, in the sense that the meaning-making that is to be expected from managerial staff is based on facts and therefore believed to be "objective". A key component of managerial responsibilities entails finding reliable and trustworthy information about the world around the company, as well as about many of the causal connections between the organization's business and the objects and events in the world. Such information is meant to be as objective as possible. As part of their jobs, managers need to issue instructions derived from the uncovered information and make decisions, in the best interests of the organization. In this sense, the type of meaning generated at the managerial level can also be labelled as *intended*.

2. Organizationally generated emergent meanings (subjective)

The second general category of organizational meanings are those generated in a bottom-up manner by members of the organization while going about their daily activities. In order to better explain this category, I resort to the metaphor of "silent design" proposed by Gorb and Dumas [11]. They suggest that much of the design in any organization originates from the myriad of local, micro initiatives taken by subordinates often deviating from the original intention are the outcome of meanings that emerge as and when participants come into contact with their tasks and with the organizational artefacts made available to them. Such meanings are part of *subjective* knowledge, in the sense that while taking decisions at the local level, organizational members are often not fully aware of all the information about constraints or opportunities that management has at its disposal. Thus, in acting on the basis of first impressions and personal preferences, participants make use of subjective knowledge, that is, the knowledge that is based on one's sensations, thoughts, desires or intentions.

3. Beneficiaries generated perceived meanings (intersubjective)

The third category originates from the outside of the organization, to include the meanings generated by the very large group of stakeholders who can be called the "beneficiaries" of the service the organization provides. They concern the meanings that emerge from the interactions of customers, users and other external stakeholders with the organization and its outcomes, such as products or services. The label *intersubjective* is metaphorically relevant in view of the importance of the "knowledge of others" to the successful operation of any organization, while recognizing the challenges inherent in any attempt to access, capture and process other people's knowledge.

2.3   Organization Design-As-Is and Organization Design-To-Be

Once created, organizational artefacts join the organization's historical legacy of artefacts, which determine most of what the organization accomplishes in terms of its results. In parallel, new artefacts and modified existing artefacts are always in the process of being developed. The first group constitute organization design as a noun, and the latter organization design as a verb. The category of perceived design/meaning relates to the conception of organization design as a noun, i.e., organization design "as-is" or organization design as historical legacy. The other two categories relate to the notion of organization design as a verb, i.e., organization design as "to-be" or organization design as dynamic change.

So, there is constant interplay between the two meanings of organization design – noun and verb. The concept of organization design as noun might be metaphorically explained as a snapshot of the designing process (verb) as perceived by internal and external stakeholders, as and when they come into contact with the organization and form judgements about what they perceive. By external stakeholders I mean anybody interested in the workings of the organization, including media reporters, government officials or organizational researchers collecting data for a case study. Organization designing, on the other hand, denotes the processes behind the organization's growth and development. Hence, the crux of the problem of managing the organization's design is in the *bridging between the two modes*: organization design as historical legacy (design-as-is) and organization design as dynamic change (design-to-be).

2.4   The Logics of Human-Centred Design

Finally, organization design processes do not exist in a vacuum. Whenever an organization, for-profit or not-for-profit, is designed or re-designed there is an unquestioned set of logics or assumptions always at play. For example, it is always assumed that an organization must have a hierarchical structure, with job descriptions and a pay scale. If the organization is for-profit there is an assumption that profit-maximizing is one of the key goals and that the investors have more rights over the organization's business that any other stakeholder. These assumptions, beliefs or logics coming from external bodies, such as management consultants, other organizations, especially the larger and more successful ones and the academic community, constitute a powerful layer of influence on organization designers.

In any given institutional field, there is a prevailing logic or received wisdom, which is absorbed in a semi-conscious fashion by the practitioners of that field. Organization design has also developed its own "logic", which has changed over the years, but which has never been guided by what I may call a human-centred design perspective. Organization design logics affect all organizations in the same field of activity through forces of isomorphism and conformity. In guiding organization designers about the way organization *should be* designed, organization design logics set the tone of managerial discourse and obviously constitute a major facilitator or obstacle for any attempt at changing the status quo.

And while there have been a variety of logics or ways of thinking about organization design over the years, there have not been as many theories that can explain organization design in an integrated way. In this paper, I suggest that the design discipline can provide a comprehensive theory or at least an epistemological half-glue that can coherently bind together many of the existing contributions from both management/organization studies and design. In pursuing this line of thought, I propose five organization design logics, which are derived from a matching of design principles, traditional organization design logics and a few selected themes from management/organization studies expressing current and future trends and concerns. The five new organization design logics are:

1. The logic of identity and identification. Inspired by the notion of *design as superordinate meaning and ambition*, this logic is informed by the literatures on the economics and sociology of identity. Its starting point is the semantic relationship between the concepts of "design", "meaning" and "identity". Thus, if "to design" means "to create meaning" and if identity is defined as the "meanings perceived and shared by a collective", then "to design an organization" means, primarily, "to create an identity".

2. The normative logic. Supported by the ethical principles of design and in line with stakeholder theory, the normative logic holds that (i) enterprises have a moral duty to ensure the welfare of all their stakeholders, not only that of stockholders; (ii) by acting in a socially responsible manner toward all their stakeholders, firms can enhance their performance and gain business advantage through more motivated employees, loyal customers, innovative products and processes, improved reputation, as well as supportive communities [12].

3. The logic of service. Service is one of the key tenets of design, however, in the traditional logics of organization design, service has not been considered as a dimension. Instead, organization design has been guided by a logic of markets and price mechanisms. However, according to the new Service-Dominant view, service precedes the market as the foundation of economic exchange and all businesses are service

businesses [28, 29]. For this reason, service is one of the logics of organization design.

4. The logic of effectual designing. In design theory, the design process starts with the expression of *desiderata*, to mean a hope, a wish, an ambition, an aspiration, a call or a will towards something. In management lingo, this is equivalent to effectuation, an alternative to the paradigm of causation or business planning [22]. Thus, unlike conventional wisdom in organization studies, in designing organizations with an effectual logic, goals and objectives are not in place when the design process begins, making action become exploratory in nature, rather than exploitative.

5. The logic of interactive structure. One of the consequences of the exponential rise in interactivity in organizations is that the traditional hierarchy is beginning to look more and more like a heterarchy. It can be said that hierarchy represents the formal side of the organization, while heterarchy refers partly to the informal organization and partly to the formal structure. While heterarchy creates a lot more room for improvisation and creativity, hierarchy will continue to play a role in maintain a degree of stability in rules and procedures. Thus, the logic of interactive structure deals with ensuring an appropriate balance between connect-and-communicate (heterarchy) and command-and-control (hierarchy).

Figure 2 shows the relationship between the processes and the logics of organization design.

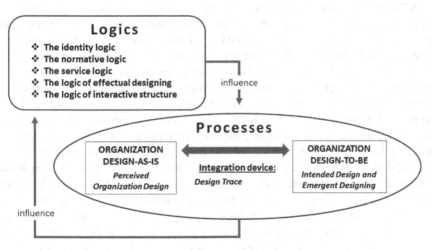

Fig. 2. The logics and process of organizational design

Having provided a very brief summary of the main ideas contained in my book, I will now move to the realm of Enterprise Engineering (EE) research and offer three suggestions about how human-centred design might provide a way forward for joint EE and OD research projects.

3 Human-Centred Organization Design as the Way Forward for EE and OD: Three Suggestions

3.1 Suggestion 1: HCOD Offers EE Researchers a Principle-Based Framework of Organization upon Which to Abstract and Model Enterprise Processes

Before I move to the recommendation itself, I will briefly outline the relevant trend from Enterprise Engineering (EE) research. In the case of this first suggestion, it is worth outlining some of the foundations of this field. The Society of Enterprise Engineering, based in the USA, defines enterprises as "systems of processes that can be engineered both individually and holistically" [16]. In Europe, the DEMO (Dynamic Essential Modelling of Organizations) methodology has prominence and has been presented as one of the foundations of the discipline of EE [5]. DEMO was originally triggered by a dissatisfaction with the state-of the-art in requirements determination in the 80s and 90s and is currently about Enterprise Ontology. However, the ambition is for DEMO to include also other EE theories, namely Enterprise Architecture and Enterprise Management and Governance [6].

In the past, there have been suggestions that the DEMO methodology might also cover organization design. I disagree because even with the inclusion of Enterprise Architecture and Enterprise Management & Governance, DEMO is not suitable as an all-encompassing framework for OD. DEMO is an enterprise engineering modelling methodology and as explained above the level of analysis of the "enterprise" is not the same as the level of analysis of the "organization". The "enterprise" is about organizational processes, and the foundations of enterprise engineering methodologies cannot simply be carried over to the organizational level. Enterprises are "systems of processes" and they cannot be treated as being the same as organization through an "aggregation of processes". Also, it must be understood that there are limits to the modelling of organization, for example, how to model customer emotions or leadership behaviours?

Having said this, it must be acknowledged that the processes that constitute the aim of EE methodologies are part of the building blocks of organization. The organization is made up by myriad types of building blocks – finance-related, management-related, marketing-related, design-related, etc. In this paper, I am concerned with the design-related building blocks. Unfortunately, organization design has traditionally been defined very narrowly in both the academic and managerial worlds, and in most textbooks, it is still considered to be the same as the organization's structure. For this reason, organization design is not associated in the minds of managers or academics with other characteristics, such as image, reputation or the quality of relationships with employees or customers, nor with ethics and the organization's role in society. However, organization design cannot be divorced from the social ills caused by organizations, a point that is acutely made by Buchanan [3], a scholar from the design discipline:

[Management] theories have been employed with varying degrees of practical success in creating and developing the for-profit, not-for-profit, and governmental organizations that surround us today, and I recognize many of the benefits of organizations that have yielded our social and cultural world. Yet, paradoxically, there is widespread dissatisfaction with organizations and what they do to affect the thought and behavior of human beings, as if the designs are flawed in one way or another (...) I do not yet understand the full effect of organizations on our lives but, increasingly, I are aware of negative effects on human experience.

Principled Organization Design

In his writings about human-centric design, Krippendorff makes a special reference to his ambitious mission of creating a societal role for design. In his book [14], he states: "the semantic turn acknowledges design as a fundamental human right, the right to construct one's own world, interact with fellow beings in theirs and make contributions to the ecology of human accessible artifacts. (Ibid, p. 322). Such desiderata are part of a wider trend of design humanism focused on the reduction of domination of the powerful over the powerless, the excluded and the economically less favored [2]. Hence, if design is inherently democratic, in a scenario where organization design is governed by design values and principles, organization design would also be construed as being essentially democratic. As I argue in my book, there is a growing recognition that organization design needs to *leave its agnostic comfort zone* and embrace an approach closer to the concerns of contemporary society.

The framework of organization design logics discussed above is derived from the principles of contemporary design culture and is intended as a change platform for the status quo in organization design thinking. Thus, as EE researchers go about their investigations, which involve abstracting, evaluating, judging and modelling enterprise processes, they are invited to reflect upon the HCOD guidelines discussed in this paper. In other words, in their role of builders of organizations and despite intervening at a very low level of analysis in terms of the overall picture, EE researchers have an opportunity to contribute to a change in the paradigm of organization design. Seen in this light, HCOD can accommodate different types of methodologies, including DEMO.

3.2 Suggestion 2: HCOD Offers Meaning and Sensemaking as Mediators Between Organization Designing and the Abstracting and Modelling Activities from Enterprise Engineering Research

In the research effort into EE there are several examples of work addressing meaning-related issues. For example, in the agent-centric perspective of EE, human actors represent actual individuals and groups rather than roles, since the aim is to capture the behaviour (i.e., the meanings) of organizational members [32]. It has also been pointed out that enterprise architectures are *boundary objects* due to their distinctive ability to influence perspective making and perspective taking in the process of *organizational sensemaking* [19]. Along the same line, in a model-enabled approach to EE models must be acknowledged as boundary objects in the communication among the different parties involved in organizational design [20]. A boundary object is any object that is part of different social worlds and is aimed at facilitating communication between them, for example a map. In addressing the topic of *domain modelling*, Proper and Guizzardi [17] talk about its semiotic foundations and communicative stance. Thus, models can *enable* informed interactions and become part of the continuous dialogue that defines organizational design.

Sensemaking Theory

Weick took the study of sensemaking beyond the individual experience and into the realm of organizations, but with special emphasis on organizing, proposing that sensemaking and organizing are mutually constituted as phenomena [31]. In the context of the human-centred orientation of this paper, an important accomplishment of his work is the turning of attention from organization as the outcome of decision-making to organization as the result of meaning-making and meaning-taking activities. Sensemaking, simply defined as "the making of sense" [30], is an all-encompassing epistemological position inspired on social constructionism. It is about the structuring of unknown contexts or actions and assigning them with meaning.

In explaining sensemaking as the organization of flux and in choosing a definition of organization as "an attempt to order the intrinsic flux of human action (…) through generalizing and institutionalizing particular meanings and rules" [27], Weick [31] concurs with the proponents of human-centred design about the role of meaning. Meaning is the engine that brings order to the ever-changing flow of human action, while sensemaking is the analytical tool that allows us to deal with meaning. Sensemaking is distinguished from other explanatory processes such as understanding or interpreting by seven characteristics succinctly described below. Weick explains that some of the characteristics may become more pivotal than others, according to the sensemaking event [31].

The seven properties explain how an individual develops a sense (and later a meaning) of any situation and strongly influence the way the individual will update and develop their perception of the situation for future action. In other words, sensemaking lies at the foundation of a consciousness or awareness that organizational actors develop of the organization and of their place in it. Sensemaking is:

1. Grounded on identity construction
2. Retrospective
3. Enactive
4. Social
5. Ongoing
6. Focused on and by extracted cues
7. Driven by plausibility rather than accuracy

Grounded in Identity Construction. Sensemaking starts with identity. This means that all our meaning-making activity starts with the meanings associated with ourselves as individuals. Who I am, what academic degree I hold, what type of job I do, who my friends are, are all factors that shape our identity and influence how we perceive and act in the organization. Our identity is continually being redefined as a result of experiences and contact with others.

Retrospective. Sensemaking can be seen as a process of comparison that we rely on to interpret current events. Thus, in order to give meaning to the "present" we compare it to similar or familiar event from our past. The properties of retrospection and identity construction interact, in the sense that when individuals construct their understandings of organizational events by including or omitting past information, they do so based on their self-image, which includes their self-esteem and self-confidence. Thus, all new information is filtered through the lenses of past experiences, which include who we are and how we perceive ourselves.

Enactive. This property explains that sensemaking is always associated with action and that the sense is created through the individual's acting upon on his/her environment. In other words, sense does not exist "out there" but is always created "within". Thus, enaction also implies that we create the environments we meet and that future sensemaking can be either constrained or enabled by the very environment that we have created, like in a self-fulfilling prophecy. Enactment works though the stages of noticing, bracketing, and labelling. Noticing entails interpreting something that has already occurred during the organizing process but has not yet been named or acknowledged. This requires providing the new event with a provisional name (or bracketing). Finally, labelling is explained in the following way: "in organizing, functional deployment means imposing labels on interdependent events in ways that suggest plausible acts of managing, coordinating, and distributing [31].

Social. This property acknowledges that the sensemaking process is contingent on our interactions with others, whether physically present or not. Also, the organization's rules, routines and symbols have a powerful influence in shaping the individual's sensemaking criteria, as well as providing routines or scripts for the individual's appropriate conduct. If routines or scripts do not exist, the individual will always rely on her social environment for her sensemaking activity.

Ongoing. Weick maintains that we are constantly making sense of what is happening around us and that moments and cues are extracted from this ongoing flow of events to make sense of the current situation. If there is a breakdown in a routine our focus is diverted, and the flow may be temporarily halted.

Focused on and by Extracted Cues. The sensemaking process involves focusing on certain elements, while completely ignoring others, in order to support our interpretation of an event. Since sensemaking is retrospective, past experiences dictate what cues we will extract to make sense of a situation. The process involves noticing, bracketing and labeling. In organizing, "functional deployment means imposing labels on interdependent events in ways that suggest plausible acts of managing, coordinating, and distributing [31].

Driven by Plausibility Rather than Accuracy. This principle implies that we do not rely on the accuracy of our perceptions when we make sense of an event, but instead we presume and look for cues that make our perceptions seem plausible and on the basis of past experience. In the process, we run the risk of eliminating what is accurate and instead rely on incomplete or faulty information in determining the best way forward.

Weick's conceptualization of sensemaking is entirely dependent on language and the notion that sensemaking and organizing are mutually constituted highlights the role of communication. Communication, in the form of conversations and texts preserved in social structures, brings organizations into existence through patterns of organizing, which, in turn, are located in patterns and modes of sensemaking. This together with the seven properties of sensemaking can be built into a methodology that can be used in analyzing models as boundary objects. One example of such a methodology is the organizational rules theory proposed by Mills and Murgatroyd [21], offering an analysis of the organizational rules that lie behind the ways in which individuals organize and the manner in which they interact in the organization.

3.3 Suggestion 3: HCOD Offers Design Trace (or Interaction Trace) as a Bridge between OD and EE Research

Going back to the research into EE, Tribolet and colleagues take a more applied perspective focusing on the need to deal with the challenges faced with today's exploding complexity of organizational environments, increasing speeds of interactions and gigantic volumes of information flows. These challenges create the need not only for a shared, up-to-date and coherent view of the organization at all times, but also for a shared record of the history of changes to organizational self. Tribolet [25] has proposed the notion of *organizational self-awareness* as both the cause and the consequence of the ever-growing potential afforded by information technologies to represent the organization and its activities. The more organizational members know about their organization's activities, the more efficient in reaching its objectives the organization will become. In other words, the more we are able, through modelling techniques, to represent the organization, the sharper the need to keep track of the organization's self-awareness [1].

A parallel concept that has been put forward by this research team is *enterprise cartography*. Enterprise cartography deals with the dynamic design and production of architectural views which depict the components of an organization and their interlinkages [26]. This project entails (1) collecting sensory data and (2) feeding it into semantic organizational models, aimed at facilitating the communication and analysis of enterprise artefacts by means of constantly updated model-based views of the enterprise's digital architecture. Apart from the obvious connections with Suggestion # 2 above (Meaning and Sensemaking), this conceptual development can also be supported by the notion of design (or interaction) trace, which is being developed as part of the HCOD framework.

Design Trace

All organizational interactions leave a trace that can be harnessed and used to help manage the organization's design. There are two types of design trace or interaction trace: causal and narrative [8]. The causal type is mostly enabled by technological means and provides data and information about past interactions or past designs. The narrative type is associated with qualitative human-centric approaches and relies on people and people's recollections of past events. Both types can be used in tandem as tools of organization design management.

In their study of two software-based companies as examples of organizations whose designs need to be in a permanent state of flux – Linux and Wikipedia – Garud et al. [8] focus on the causal trace. In the case of these two companies, the design trace is a software-based record of the changes introduced in the content of Wikipedia and in the software code of Linux, which serves not only as a locus of coordination but also as the link between organization design as a noun and organization design as a process. The authors explain that the challenge for preserving the value propositions that the designs of Linux and Wikipedia offer to customers is to devise a governance system that does not stifle innovation but at the same time provides some stability. These authors explain: "the design trace both chronicles and initiates generative engagement with an article [of Wikipedia] (...) it serves as a locus of coordination as well as a point of departure, allowing an article to remain in a state of perpetual change" [8].

The other type of trace – narrative – operates on the basis of the internal and external coherence of a narrative with the listener's existing knowledge. One of the possible types of narrative trace is affectual trace, investigated by Gherardi [10]. Rather than studying affect as a content, the authors investigate affectual traces in communication, through "the choice of words, the pitch of the voices, the crescendo in the verbal interactions, the mimicking of other (absent) voices, the broken language and the rhetorical figures of speech" (Ibid, p. NA), as well as the traces kept in the researchers's own memories, as well as in annotations made in logbooks.

Thus, if we consider that the organization's design is a sociomaterial network made up of practices and if practices as embodied know-how contain an important component of affect, then it can be reasonably assumed that the practices within the network leave behind a significant affectual trace. Affect operates as a "shadow organizing" force [9] and acts as a "conveyor belt", in terms of activity and movements within a situated practice, keeping all its elements together. Affect works within and in-between bodies, however it does not only refer to human, individual bodies but also to any other living and non-living ones. Affects are also collective and atmospheric forces operating externally to the body [24].

To conclude, the enterprise's digital architecture provides the technological infrastructure for the organization's designing activities, which means that increasingly organizations will rely on technology-based (i.e., causal) traces. However, organizations will continue to greatly depend on people, people's memories and people's relationships, which leads us to suggest that the future of linkage between organization design "as-is" and organization design "to-be" will depend on a blend of technology-based tools and narrative-based tools. Moreover, if we consider design trace as a continuum, the affectual trace and other forms of narrative trace would stand at one end of the continuum, whereas the rational-technical types of causal trace would stand at the other end. Thus, as a new research stream within Organization's Self-Awareness and Enterprise Cartography, I suggest that work can be developed to combine causal-types of trace with various forms of qualitative narrative trace to provide comprehensive feedback about the transitions between design-as-is and design-to-be.

4   Conclusion

In this paper, my key aim has been to put forward human-centred design as a powerful intellectual framework that can benefit both organization design (OD) and enterprise engineering (EE) research. Having suggested three ways in which HCOD can contribute either to EE research or to joint EE-OD research, all that is left to do is to reassert that whatever the approach, EE research is always about developing the best way to abstract and model processes which exist in real-life organizations. On the other hand, organizations are social entities and no matter the level of abstraction or the methodology used, intervention in organizations should always be aimed at contributing towards achieving organizations that are humanely managed, commercially viable, sustainably developed, highly innovative and firmly stakeholder aligned. These are the aims of human-centred organization design, which are offered to EE researchers as reference points about the direction of travel for any intervention in organizations.

References

1. Aveiro, D., Silva, A.R., Tribolet, J.M.: Towards a GOD-theory for organizational engineering: continuously modeling the continuous (re)generation, operation and deletion of the enterprise. In: Proceedings of the 2010 ACM Symposium on Applied Computing (SAC), Sierre, Switzerland, 22–26 March 2010 (2010)
2. Bonsiepe, G.: Design and democracy. Des. Issues **22**(2), 27–34 (2006)
3. Buchanan, R.: Worlds in the making: design, management, and the reform of organizational culture. She Ji: J. Des. Econ. Innov. **1**(1), 5–21 (2015)
4. Davidson, D.: Subjective, Intersubjective, Objective. Oxford University Press, New York (2001)
5. Dietz, J., et al.: The discipline of enterprise engineering. Int. J. Organ. Des. Eng. **3**(1), 86–114 (2013)
6. Dietz, J., Hoogervorst, J.: Foundations of Enterprise Engineering. Technical report. https://www.researchgate.net/publication/320353420_Foundations_of_Enterprise_Engineering. Accessed 10 Jan 2021
7. Elsbach, K.D.: Intraorganizational institutions. In: Baum, J.A.C. (ed.) The Blackwell Companion to Organizations. Blackwell, Malden (2002)
8. Garud, R., Jain, S., Tuertscher, P.: Incomplete by design and designing for incompleteness. Organ. Stud. **29**, 351–371 (2008)
9. Gherardi, S., Jensen, K., Nerland, M.: Shadow organizing: a metaphor to explore organizing as intra-relating. Qual. Res. Organiz. Manag. **12**(1), 2–17 (2017)
10. Gherardi, S., Murgia, A., Bellè, E., Miele, F., Carreri, A.: Tracking the sociomaterial traces of affect at the crossroads of affect and practice theories. Qual. Res. Organiz. Manag.: An Int. J. (2018). https://doi.org/10.1108/QROM-04-2018-1624
11. Gorb, P., Dumas, A.: Silent design. Des. Stud. **8**(3), 150–156 (1987)
12. Harrison, J.S., Barney, J.B., Freeman, R.E., Phillips, R.A. (eds.): The Cambridge Handbook of Stakeholder Theory. Cambridge University Press, Cambridge (2019)
13. Krippendorff, K.: On the essential contexts of artifacts or on the proposition that "design is making sense of things." Des. Issues **5**, 9–39 (1989)
14. Krippendorff, K.: The Semantic Turn: A New Foundation for Design. Taylor and Francis, Boca Raton (2006)
15. Krippendorff, K.: Principles of design and a trajectory of artificiality. J. Prod. Innov. Manag. **28**, 411–418 (2011)
16. Liles, D.H., Johnson, M.E., Meade, L.M., Underdown, D.R.: Enterprise engineering: a discipline? In: Proceeding of the Society for Enterprise Engineering Conference. Society for Enterprise Engineering, Kettering, Ohio (1995)
17. Proper, H.A., Guizzardi: on domain conceptualisation. In: Proceedings of the 10th Enterprise Engineering Working Conference (2020)
18. Magalhaes, R.: Designing Organization Design: A Human-Centred Design Approach. Oxford University Press, Oxford (2020)
19. Magalhães, R., Zacarias, M., Tribolet, J.M.: Making sense of enterprise architectures as tools of organizational self-awareness. J. Enterp. Archit. **3**(4), 64–72 (2007)

20. Magalhães, R., Proper, H.A.: Model-enabled design and engineering of organisations and their enterprises. Organiz. Des. Enterp. Eng. 1(1), 1–2 (2016). https://doi.org/10.1007/s41 251-016-0005-9
21. Mills, A.J., Murgatroyd, S.J.: Organizational Rules: A Framework for Understanding Organizational Action. Open University Press, Milton Keynes (1991)
22. Sarasvathy, S.: Causation and effectuation: toward a theoretical shift from economic inevitability to entrepreneurial contingency. Acad. Manag. Rev. 26(2), 243–263 (2001)
23. Simon, H.A.: The Sciences of the Artificial, 3rd edn. MIT Press, Cambridge, MA (1996)
24. Seyfert, R.: Beyond personal feelings and collective emotions: toward a theory of social affect. Theory Cult. Soc. 29(6), 27–46 (2012)
25. Tribolet, J.M.: Organizations, people, processes and knowledge: from the reification of the human being as a component of knowledge to the organizational "self-awareness". In: Amaral, L., Magalhães, R., Morais, C.C., Serrano, A., Zorrinho, C. (eds) Sistemas de Informação Organizacionais. Sílabo Editora, Lisboa (2005). (in Portuguese)
26. Tribolet, J.M., Sousa, P., Caetano, A.: The role of enterprise governance and cartography in enterprise engineering. Enterp. Model. Inf. Syst. Archit. 9(1), 38–49 (2014)
27. Tsoukas, H., Chia, R.: Organizational becoming: rethinking organizational change. Organ. Sci. 13(5), 567–582 (2002)
28. Vargo, S.L., Lusch, R.F.: Evolving to a new dominant logic for marketing. J. Mark. 68, 1–7 (2004)
29. Vargo, S.L., Lusch, R.F.: Service-dominant logic: continuing the evolution. J. Acad. Mark. Sci. 36, 1–10 (2008)
30. Weick, K.E.: Sensemaking in Organizations. Sage, Beverly Hills (1995)
31. Weick, K.E., Sutcliffe, K.M., Obstfeld, D.: Organizing and the process of sensemaking. Organ. Sci. 16(4), 409–421 (2005)
32. Zacarias, M., Pinto, H.S., Magalhães, R., Tribolet, J.: A context-aware and agent-centric perspective for the alignment between individuals and organizations. Inf. Syst. 35(4), 441–466 (2010)

Framing Enterprise Engineering Within General System's Theory: Perspectives of a Human Centered Future

José Tribolet[1,2] and Sérgio Guerreiro[1,2](✉)

[1] INESC-ID, Lisbon, Portugal
jose.tribolet@inesc.pt
[2] Instituto Superior Técnico, University of Lisbon, Lisbon, Portugal
sergio.guerreiro@tecnico.ulisboa.pt

Abstract. This paper frames the enterprise engineering body of knowledge within the scope of the general system's theory to challenge researchers and practitioners working in this field. Understanding that an organization is a living being that exist, acts and interacts, the goal of the paper is to narrow the discussion on how to observe, represent and act the enterprise in real-time. To that end, the following set of core elements are conceptualized and discussed: the organization, the actor, the observation, the time and the Kalman's dynamic control. Afterwards, those elements are combined to describe the duality that exists between the Human-self/organization-self dynamic control mechanisms including the time-delay concerns.

Keywords: Actor · Control · Enterprise Engineering · General systems theory · Observation · Organization

1 Introduction

Organizations, namely enterprises, are socio-technical entities that co-exist with Humans in the physical world. Moreover, an enterprise possess materials and virtual individuality. The purpose of this paper is to claim that by fully embedding the body of knowledge (BoK) of General System's Theory (GST) [2] at the core concepts of Enterprise Engineering (EE) [6,7] knowledge it is possible to potentiate the means of provide dynamic steering mechanisms to drive the behavior of an enterprise. At the same time, we preserve the respect to the freedom of the human actors and preserve the essential ethical principles that must obeyed by any engineering activity.

To address such an endeavour, this paper starts with a review of the explicit conceptual basis of any organization, of its actions and its behaviors. Then, the topics of enterprise steering and dynamic control [1], both from a systemic and holistic approaches, as well as an operational [8] and a design point of view [3,4], are argued. The GST BoK is applied to the fundamental engineering principles of dynamic system's control using the Kalman's state space control paradigm. This

© Springer Nature Switzerland AG 2021
D. Aveiro et al. (Eds.): EEWC 2020, LNBIP 411, pp. 38–45, 2021.
https://doi.org/10.1007/978-3-030-74196-9_3

solution allows the representation and understanding of how to design real-time systemic control mechanisms in an Enterprise. A particular emphasis is given to the need to provide the sufficient sensorization of an Enterprise [5], capable of assuring the adequate level of observability to achieve the desired level of controllability capable of ensuring the intended level of operational risk level in real-time [11].

This paper uses EE BoK to address all the phases of an enterprise life cycle: from conception [12], to design and construction, until operation, control, and finally, audit [10], adaptation and its maintenance. All of these stages include the multiple dimensions of management. The EE BoK is essential to assure that Humanity will retain the ultimate control on the technological tools we use and incorporate in the enterprise-self, namely the machines, in particular the *"silicon actors"* that are progressively equipped with powerful artificial intelligence (AI) and Autonomous Learning capabilities and in the near future other types of technological actors with attributes that are several orders of magnitude more powerful that individual humans and even the entire Humanity. The challenge to combine the "innovative" ontological foundations of EE with the *"hard"* capabilities to design and steer complex systems as provided by system's theory and dynamic systems control is open. If we do not *"engineer"* our Enterprises to be ultimately always leaded and controlled by Humans, we will, with all probability, be massively controlled by machines in a not so distant future.

For short, this paper raises the following research question: *"How can EE contribute to assure the means and the techniques to promote the desired behavior of each and all the actors, to enable that the resulting systemic organizational orchestration follows the desired prescribed trajectories?"*

The paper is organized as follows. Section 2 defines, and discusses, the core elements identified when framing EE within GST. Then, Sect. 3 combines the previous elements to organize a set of refined future research questions. Finally, Sect. 4 concludes the paper.

A full presentation of this paper is publicly available at https://youtu.be/qpJO22TIPMQ?t=2484. The content was presented in the scope of the author José Tribolet farewell lesson.

2 Elements to Frame EE Within GST

The following core elements are presented to frame EE within GST: the *Organization* (Subsect. 2.1), the *Actor* (Subsect. 2.2), the *Observation* (Subsect. 2.3), the *Time* (Subsect. 2.4) and the *Kalman's Dynamic Control Paradigm applied to Organizations* (Subsect. 2.5).

2.1 Organization

An organization is a living being, something that exists, acts and interacts. It is an entity that coexists with Humans in the physical world. An Organization has a physical as well as a socio-technical reality, which interacts, dynamically and continuously, with its physical and virtual environment, transforming it and being transformed by it. An organization is a reality built by Humans, whose emergent unique attributes are the result of its intrinsic systemic interactions and of the dynamic effects of its extrinsic relations.

Considering the detailed question: *an organization is made of what?* We consider that an organization is formed by active elements: the actors. Those elements have autonomous capabilities to act on the world as well as on themselves, in real-time, and along multiple concurrent networks. However, the actions of each individual actor never is 100% predictable.

And, considering the detailed question: *What does an organization do?* We consider that an organization does is simply the sum total of what its actors do when performing their actions along time. Organization is simply the sum of what its actors do through time. Therefore, an organization is a dynamic system. It is a complex network of networks of agents, whose end results are the organization's outputs as a response to the organization's inputs, along time. Consequently, it may thus be modelled as a gigantic state machine.

2.2 Actor

In the XXI century it is appropriate to say that organizations are bionic entities since its actors are physically of two types built either on a *"carbon base"* (Humans) or a *"silicon base"* (Computers). In this context, using a computer science paradigm, one may say that an organization is a complex *"semantic web"* of *"carbon and silicon servers"* operating continuously in real-time, each *"server"* acts, *"autonomous and freely"*, under the control of its own operating System, running the applications (*Apps*) it has downloaded.

As a consequence, an organization, as a bionic entity, is a unique *"persona"*, with its own degree of *"self-awareness"* [13] and its *"own will"*.

As a physical entity, an organization becomes a *bone fides*[1] specific subject of Engineering, whose study must be based on the scientific method. This is the field of Enterprise Engineering [6, 7]. The objects of study of EE are therefore the physical socio-technical entities that are not mechanical or electrical or chemical or biological systems, but are bionic living entities.

2.3 Observation

A necessary condition for the adequate operation of the dynamical organization system's control mechanisms is the degree of *"observability"* of the *"organizational's states"*, at any point in time, and the knowledge of the intended or prescribed states it should try to be in the future. Therefore, a key question for EE is how to provide the organization with the capabilities needed to know *"its state"* at any given point in time?

These capabilities will only exist if the organization is *"fully sensorized"*, i.e., is provided with sensors that register the elementary acts performed by each and all its carbon and silicon actors at any point in time. If those capabilities are

---

[1] It is a latin language expression meaning "good will", with loyalty, with honesty, in compliance with given word, also used with meaning of genuine.

not met then we cannot steer the organization. In other words, controlling the organization is only possible if fully sensorized exists.

2.4 Time

The organization' dynamics depends on the time element. If the delay between collecting the sensor's data, its interpretation in terms of the overall organization's state and the update of the control's available on each actor's cockpits is smaller then the dynamics of the organization's trajectory, then it is possible to condition in real-time the organization's behavior, according to previous determined trajectories, and within reasonable risk margins.

2.5 Kalman's Dynamic Control Paradigm Applied to Organizations

An organization obeys the laws of GST (which have been developed in the last 60 years) in particular the BoK on dynamic systems. These concepts are fully applicable to design, analyze, monitor and steer organizations. A relevant question for EE is how to *"steer"* the behavior of an organization, *i.e.*, how to condition the actions and interactions of its actors for it to achieve desirable and admissible trajectories? In systems engineering terms the existent BoK to achieve this goal is known as dynamic system's control. Engineering has a proven record of designing, building, operating and maintaining complex systems whose behavior is dynamically controlled in real-time to follow prescribed paths [8,9]. Many of these systems are *bona fides* socio-technical systems. Figure 1 depicts a conceptualization of the Kalman's dynamic control paradigm applied to organizations.

The degree of steering of any system, in our interest: an organization, is constrained by the degree of its observability capabilities. An organization without systemic observability capabilities is not capable of systemic steering its behaviour. However, given that each actor ultimately acts according to its *"free will"* and so is never *"fully controlled"*, one may conclude that the ultimate goal of steering the organization behavior is a lost cause. In this line of reasoning, how can EE contribute to assure the means and the techniques to promote the desired behavior of each and all the actors, to enable that the resulting systemic organizational orchestration follows the desired prescribed trajectories? Moreover, since Humans are the "core" organizational actors, how is Kalman's model applicable (Fig. 2) when there are *"Carbon Based Servers"*? As a partial answer for this question, this is achievable by incorporating best practices of modern control theory, namely by taking full advantage of feedback mechanisms and adding to the existing action cockpits of each actor the proper actuators that help conditioning their future acts.

In the context of actors *"free will"*, Fig. 3 depicts that each Human has its own persona and is autonomous, after *"observing"* and modelling *"it's reality"* at a given point in time, and given its own goals, the person's *"controller"* decides what actions the *"actor"* is gone do in the next instant of time. As introduced in Subsect. 2.4, in time concept, it is also noted that each agent actions is enforced in the instant $t+1$, whereas the controls are prescribed in instant t. Meaning a delay that could hinder the effect of control.

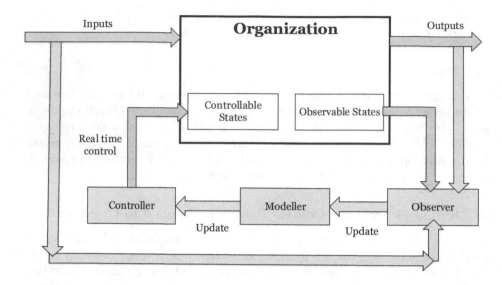

Fig. 1. Conceptualization of the Kalman's dynamic control paradigm applied to organizations.

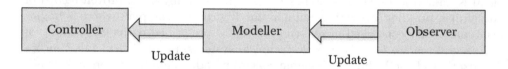

Fig. 2. Kalman's model.

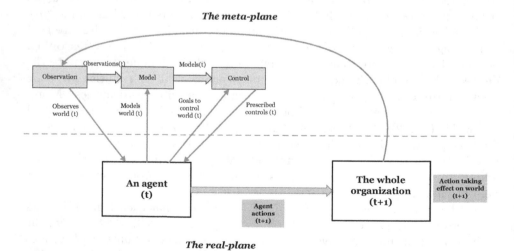

Fig. 3. Human Self Dynamic Control Mechanism with the timing concern.

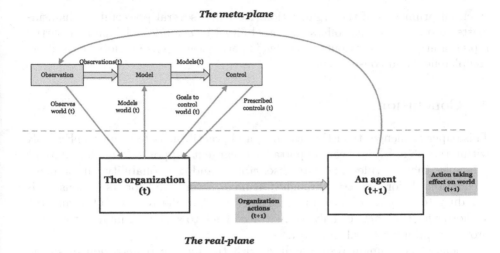

Fig. 4. The Organization Self Dynamic Control Mechanism with the timing concern.

Broadening this analysis, Fig. 4 depicts how Kalman's model is applicable to the *"organization"* entity as a holistic system.

3   Reflection Questions

The ontological foundation of EE is an essential framework to provide solid basis for answering the following indicating questions. These are grounded on the essential acts performed by the actors while executing their various commitments [6].

Question #1 – How does the "Organization" act, following the decisions made by its Kalman Controller?

Indicating answer #1 – The Organization acts through its actors. The actors act to pursue their own goals, in the context of their perception of reality, which includes their view of the enterprise-self, and of its goals at a given point in time.

Question #2 – How can EE contribute to enterprise design, instrumentation and operations, to enable improved, systemic, real-time Enterprise Dynamic Control?

Indicating answer #2 - EE provides the means to rigorously assure the required and adequate observability of the Organization, using carbon and silicon based real-time sensors to gather the data needed for the degree of the desired controllability. At the core of the observability is the capability to know the state of each and every essential ontological transaction in progress.

Question #3 - How can we explicitly represent the enterprise in real-time?

Indicating answer #3 – research about the eighteen vectors of the enterprise space: the explicit representation of the state of the enterprise-self, at a given instant in time, requires an universal *"set of coordinates"* to span the enterprise space, and the ability to map in such space all the entities, the facts and the other essential primitives of the organization. Actually, several powerful mechanisms exists to do so, *e.g.*, EE offers the capability to *"compile"* all mapped partial representations of reality onto the *"One"* Space, so as to ensure global coherence, completeness and consistency.

4   Conclusion

This paper challenges the EE researchers and practitioners to frame the EE BoK within the GST. EE is of core importance because it supports design foundations principles that provides adequate observability and controllability can be made accountable before society, through it Human actors, and for its actions. It is our duty to *"engineer"* such organizations, so that the responsibility and the authority for their acts can always be traced back to specific human actors, in a provable and almost real-time way.

Society and Human responsibility: with the intense penetration of silicon servers everywhere, with active devices implanted in our individual and collective living spaces, Humanity faces a tremendous challenge! For a Human Centered Future: either we engineer our habitats and organizations to be under the ultimate control of Humans! Or the Machines will take control of the connected Humanity! The choice is ours.

References

1. Aveiro, D., Silva, A.R., Tribolet, J.: Extending the design and engineering methodology for organizations with the generation operationalization and discontinuation organization. In: Winter, R., Zhao, J.L., Aier, S. (eds.) DESRIST 2010. LNCS, vol. 6105, pp. 226–241. Springer, Heidelberg (2010). https://doi.org/10.1007/978-3-642-13335-0_16
2. von Bertalanffy, L.: General Systems Theory. George Braziller, New York (1968)
3. Caetano, A., et al.: Representation and analysis of enterprise models with semantic techniques: an application to ArchiMate, e3value and business model canvas. Knowl. Inf. Syst. **50**(1), 315–346 (2016). https://doi.org/10.1007/s10115-016-0933-0
4. Caetano, A., Silva, A.R., Tribolet, J.: Using roles and business objects to model and understand business processes. In: Proceedings of the 2005 ACM Symposium on Applied Computing, pp. 1308–1313 (2005)
5. Castela, N., Dias, P., Zacarias, M., Tribolet, J.M.: Collaborative maintenance of business process models. Int. J. Organ. Des. Eng. **2**(1), 61–84 (2012)
6. Dietz, J.L.G., et al.: The discipline of enterprise engineering. Int. J. Organ. Des. Eng. **3**(1), 86–114 (2013)
7. Dietz, J.L.G., Mulder, H.B.F.: Enterprise Ontology: A Human-Centric Approach to Understanding the Essence of Organisation. The Enterprise Engineering Series, 1st edn. Springer, Heidelberg (2020). https://doi.org/10.1007/978-3-030-38854-6
8. Guerreiro, S.: Conceptualizing on dynamically stable business processes operation: a literature review on existing concepts. Bus. Process Manag. J. **27**, 24–54 (2020)

9. Guerreiro, S., Tribolet, J.: Conceptualizing enterprise dynamic systems control for run-time business transactions. In: 2013 European Conference on Information Systems (ECIS), paper 5 (2013)
10. Marques, R.P., Santos, H., Santos, C.: An enterprise ontology-based database for continuous monitoring application. In: 2013 IEEE 15th Conference on Business Informatics, pp. 7–12 (2013). https://doi.org/10.1109/CBI.2013.10
11. Páscoa, C., Tribolet, J.: Organizational and design engineering of the operational and support components of an organization: the Portuguese air force case study. In: Harmsen, F., Proper, E., Schalkwijk, F., Barjis, J., Overbeek, S. (eds.) PRET 2010. LNBIP, vol. 69, pp. 47–77. Springer, Heidelberg (2010). https://doi.org/10.1007/978-3-642-16770-6_3
12. Vasconcelos, A., Sousa, P., Tribolet, J.: Information system architecture metrics: an enterprise engineering evaluation approach. Electron. J. Inf. Syst. Eval. **10**(1), 91–122 (2007)
13. Zacarias, M., Pinto, H.S., Magalhães, R., Tribolet, J.: A 'context-aware' and agent-centric perspective for the alignment between individuals and organizations. Inf. Syst. **35**(4), 441–466 (2010)

Formal Approaches and Modeling

On Domain Conceptualization

Henderik A. Proper[1,2](✉) [ID] and Giancarlo Guizzardi[3]

[1] Luxembourg Institute of Science and Technology (LIST), Belval, Luxembourg
e.proper@acm.org
[2] University of Luxembourg, Luxembourg, Luxembourg
[3] Free University of Bozen-Bolzano, Bozen-Bolzano, Italy
giancarlo.guizzardi@unibz.it

Abstract. The growing role of models across the life-cycle of enterprises, and their information and software systems, fuels the need for a
more fundamental reflection on the foundations of modeling. Two of the
core theories of the discipline of enterprise engineering (*Factual Information* (FI) theory and the *Model Universe* (MU) theory) aim at contributing to these foundations.

The latest versions of the FI- and MU-theories have recently been published. Offering an analysis and criticism to them enables us to continue
the important debate on the semiotic, ontological, and general philosophical foundations of domain modeling and enterprise modeling in particular.

A core concept in the field of domain modeling is the conceptualization
of the domain. In this paper, we specifically focus on the development
of a deeper understanding of domain conceptualizations, while reflecting
on the way this notion is positioned in the FI- and MU-theories.

1 Introduction

Models have come to play an important role in all stages of the life-cycle of enterprises, as well as their information and software systems. This life-cycle includes
their development, improvement, maintenance, operation, as well as their regula-
tion, while the models used cover amongst others enterprise (architecture) models, business process models, ontology models, organizational models, information
models, software models, etc. In this paper, we consider each of these kinds of models as being valued members of the larger family of *domain models*.

In our view, the increasing role of domain models fuels the need for more fundamental reflection on the foundations of domain modeling. These foundations
have certainly been studied by different scholars (see e.g. [1, 20, 35, 44, 51, 52, 65,
66, 69, 70]), as well as by ourselves (see e.g. [5–7, 13, 23, 25–30, 40, 41, 50, 59, 63, 76]).
At the same time, many challenges remain. Some of these challenges have been
discussed in e.g. [5, 27, 29, 63].

The *Factual Information* (FI) and *Model Universe* (MU) theories aim at contributing to these foundations, and are considered by the enterprise engineering
community to be among the core theories of the field [14]. The latest versions of
these theories have recently been published in [15].

© Springer Nature Switzerland AG 2021
D. Aveiro et al. (Eds.): EEWC 2020, LNBIP 411, pp. 49–69, 2021.
https://doi.org/10.1007/978-3-030-74196-9_4

In this paper, we offer a partial analysis and criticism of these two theories. We focus on the development of a deeper understanding of domain conceptualizations in particular, which we see as a core concept in the field of domain modeling. This allows us to continue the important debate on the semiotic, ontological, and general philosophical foundations of domain modeling. In doing so, we follow the philosophical approach of developing arguments based on logical reasoning, while also synthesizing and incorporating results from different scholars.

In line with this, the remainder of this paper is structured as follows. In Sect. 2, we start by visiting the semiotic roots of modeling. This enables us to then, in Sect. 3, investigate the notion of domain conceptualizations. Before concluding, Sect. 4 then discusses our understanding of models and modeling, based on this.

2   Semiotic Foundations

We view domain modeling primarily from a communicative stance. Models are created by/for actors (be it human or IT-based actors) to communicate about different aspects of a domain. As a result, the semiotic triangle by Ogden and Richard [56] is a foundational element in our thinking about modeling.

In line with this, the aim of this section is to briefly explore the semiotic roots of modeling. In doing so, we will discuss: (1) the semiotic triangle [56] itself, (2) the fact that communication generally involves multiple actors, (3) the exchange of information between the involved actors, and (4) compositionality of symbols.

2.1   The Semiotic Triangle

The semiotic triangle by Ogden and Richard's [56], depicted in Fig. 1, is often used as a base to theorize about meaning in the context of language [12, 53, 67, 73].

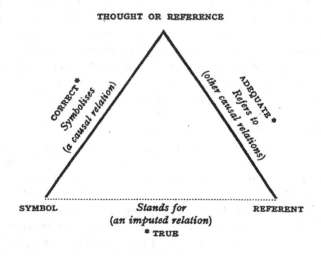

Fig. 1. Ogden and Richard's semiotic triangle [56]

Several authors, including ourselves, use it to reason about the foundations of (information) systems modeling (see e.g. [36,43,44,49]).

The semiotic triangle, as shown in Fig. 1, is concerned with the way we assign meaning to *symbols* (utterances in some language). The tenet of the semiotic triangle is that when we use *symbols* to speak about "something" (a *referent*), these symbols represent (*symbolise*) our thoughts (*thought or reference*) about that something (*referent*). The *thought or reference* is then the meaning we have assigned to the *symbols*. The *referent* can be anything, in an existing world, or in a desired/imagined world. It can involve physical phenomena (e.g., tree, car, bike, atom, document, picture, etc.), mental phenomena (e.g., thoughts, feelings, etc.), as well as social phenomena (e.g., marriage, mortgage, trust, value, etc.).

It is important to keep in mind that [56, pp. 11–12]: "*Symbol and Referent, that is to say, are not connected directly (and when, for grammatical reasons, we imply such a relation, it will merely be an imputed as opposed to a real, relation) but only indirectly round the two sides of the triangle.*"

In the context of modeling, the notion of "thought or reference" is sometimes replaced by the notion of *concept*. This, implies the assumption that a "thought or reference" pertaining to some referent that is to be modeled, takes the form of a *concept*. The latter assumption is certainly relevant in the context of modeling. At the same time, we should realize that, in the more general situation, symbols are also used to refer to things that may not correspond to clear concepts, such as tastes, smells, feelings, etc. Consider, for instance, the textual description of the taste of a good wine, where one uses terms such as a "fruity taste" or "hints of liquorice". While "taste" in the general sense can easily be regarded as a concept, the *actual* taste sometimes cannot. In communicating about the taste of wine, we use terms like "fruity taste" and "hints of liquorice" as placeholders (i.e. *symbols*) to symbolise the actual taste we think to experience when savouring a sip of wine[1]. Reading these terms, the symbols, in the description of a wine, then triggers our thoughts/memories of the taste. However, we prefer not to call these latter thoughts actual concepts.

A more fundamental change which some authors make, is to replace the "stands for" relationship with a solid line/arrow, seemingly ignoring its *imputed* status. Unless nuanced explicitly, such a replacement suggests there to be an objective binary relation between a referent and a symbol *only*, independent of a given conceptualization. Doing so would be a denial of the key message of the original semiotic triangle.

---

[1] These internal experiences such as particular perceptions of color or taste are termed *Qualia* in the philosophical literature [72]. For an interesting discussion on the non-conceptual content of perception, one is referred to [11]. Authors such as [21] provide a precise formulation for concepts in spaces such as color and taste, namely, as a convex region in those geometric space. So, we are not denying that things like taste can be associated with concepts. However, we would like to allow for the existence of experiences that can be (partially) symbolised but that are not conceptual. As an obvious example, think of a patient trying to communicate to their attending physician an experience of pain. Given the private nature of these experiences, communicating them with other agents is an obvious challenge.

The "*slightly adapted version*" [15, page 51] of the semiotic triangle as included in the latest version of the FI-theory actually makes three (implicit) changes to the original triangle. Firstly, "thought or reference" is replaced by "thought" only. Secondly, "symbol" is replaced by "sign"[2]. These could, indeed, be classified as "slight" changes. However, it also replaces the "stands for" dotted line with a solid arrow labelled (with the stronger) *denotes*. On the positive side, [15, page 52] does indeed state: "*... although the relationship between a sign and its referent is completely determined by their being connected through the thought, it is often also indicated separately: the sign is said to* denote *the referent.*", which provides some nuance regarding the "solidity" of the line. Nevertheless, the "*it is often also indicated separately*" does seem to indicate an intention to regard the original "stands for" relationship as an independent binary relationship, rather than an imputed one from the "symbolises" and "refers to" relations.

2.2　Communication Between Actors

Even though it was created from a communication oriented perspective, the semiotic triangle on its own is "single sided" in the sense that it only refers to one actor.

In the context of communication, it is important to acknowledge the fact that there are at least two actors involved[3]. Any language utterance (such as, in our discipline, models) has both a *writer* and a *reader* [67]. In terms of the

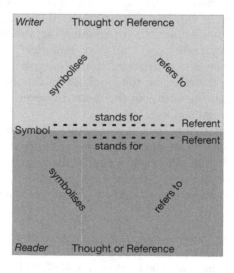

Fig. 2. Writer and Reader with their own semiotic triangles

----

[2] We actually agree on this replacement, as *sign* is a more generic way to refer to any form of "information carrying artifact" [60].

[3] Where writing a note to/for oneself could be seen as an extreme case, since the actor who reads the notes is not completely the same as the actor who wrote the note. The general mental state of the reader will still be different from the one of the writer.

semiotic triangle, this implies that both the author and writer have their own thoughts about the symbol, in the context of (possibly) the same referent.

This is illustrated in Fig. 2. Both reader and writer harbour their own thoughts, while using the same symbol to symbolise these. Even when both reader and writer think they are "talking" about the same referent, this may actually not be the case (hence the presence of two "Referents" in Fig. 2).

If the referent is a physical thing in the existing world, reader and writer have a chance of indeed looking at the same referent. When the referent is a physical thing in a possible/desired future world, it already becomes more challenging to ensure that they are considering the same referent. When the referent is not a physical thing, but rather a social thing, or even a mental thing, matters become even more challenging. The latter kind of situations might be mitigated by more meta-communication [39] between reader and writer, e.g., involving the description of their focus, paraphrasing, or using a domain-independent system of ontological categories to calculate the relations between their individual conceptualizations [31].

At a more general level, it is important to acknowledge that communication requires the actors to share their understanding using a broad *stream of symbols*. This stream of symbols may "meander" between the communication of the intended "message", as well as a clarification of the precise meaning of the symbols used (i.e. meta-communication [39]).

2.3 Information Exchange Between Actors

The strict separation between the *thoughts*, the *referents* these thoughts pertain to, and the *symbols* used to symbolise the thoughts, also enables us to make a clear distinction between the symbols we use to communicate and the actual "informational payload".

When a reader "reads" a symbol (including data, documents, models, etc.), then, assuming they understand the language used, they will form thoughts in their mind. If these thoughts are new, then the symbol has provided them with *information*[4]. Conversely, writers, in "writing" the symbol, presumably aim to convey their thoughts to others. These thoughts-to-be-conveyed are the intentional informational payload of the symbol. As such, the information that is (to be) carried by a symbol is in "the eye of the beholder". We experience this on a daily base, as we all know that a document may provide different information to different readers.

The latter view on information is in line with the perspective taken in e.g. the FRISCO report [17], cybernetics [37] as well as work in the context of information science and information discovery [3,60]. In this context, [37] also refers to the *"difference that makes the difference"*.

---

[4] For some authors such as, e.g., Floridi [19], *information* must be *truthful semantic content*, i.e., it is semantic content back up by the proper *truthmakers* in reality. For the sake of simplicity, we do not make this distinction here.

With regard to information, the FI-theory, [15, page 51] currently states: *Because minds cannot communicate directly, a vehicle is needed to accomplish it, and this vehicle is called information.* This seems to suggest that the vehicle *is* the information, whereas, as argued above, it seems more natural (and better aligned to the extended semiotic triangle as depicted in Fig. 2) to acknowledge the fact that the information that is actually *carried* by the vehicle is in the eye of the beholder.

Even more, when stating *"This makes information a dyadic notion: it has both content and form, inseparably connected"* [15, page 51], we immediately run the risk of turning a blind eye to the fact that communication involves multiple actors, each with their *own* thoughts about the symbol/vehicle used to communicate. As such, we would argue it to be a quadratic relation, involving: (1) form (the symbol), (2) meaning (the thought or reference) as harboured in the mind of (3) an actor, pertaining to some (4) referent as "seen" by the latter actor[5].

2.4   Compositionality of Symbols

A document, consisting of many sections, sentences, images, tables, etc., can be regarded as a "composed symbol". Models, as artifacts, can also be regarded as "composed symbols". Such composed symbols are likely to also relate to composed thoughts, while referring to a composed referent. In terms of the semiotic triangle, this triggers the question if the relations included in the triangle scale from basic symbols to increasingly composed symbols. Most authors (as well as ourselves) who apply the semiotic triangle in the context of modeling, essentially *implicitly* assume that these relations indeed scale in the above sense.

We are not arguing here that this would be a wrong assumption to make. However, we do consider it to be important to take note of this assumption, and reflect on its potential consequences. Especially since, in the context of domain modeling, we are usually dealing with *composed* referents, thoughts and symbols.

3   Domain Conceptualizations

In moving from the general discussion regarding the semiotic triangle towards modeling, we first need to further elaborate on the notion of *domain conceptualization*. To this end, this section will address: (1) distinction between perceptions and conceptions, (2) domain conceptions (such as enterprises), (3) the role of the purpose of a communicated artifact (such as a model), (4) the role of "normative frames" (such as philosophical stance, language definitions, design philosophies, etc.).

---

[5] Which is also aligned to the semiotic tetahedron as put forward in the IFIP 8.1 FRISCO report [17].

3.1   From Perception to Conception

In the context of modeling, we suggest to make a distinction between two kinds of (composed) thoughts: *conceptions* and *perceptions*. When an actor observes a (composed) referent, they will obtain (through their senses) a *perception* (indeed, including e.g. the taste of a good wine) of that referent. They may than be able to interpret, structure, and/or further abstract, this *perception* to form a *conception* in terms of concepts and their relations.

In *perceiving*, and *conceiving*, the many facets and nuances of the world around us, we will need to apply filters[6]; if only to deal with the complexities and richness of the world around us. When creating a conception, from our perception, we tend to filter even further, consciously leaving out details to be able to focus on what we think to be important (in particular when creating models). This is also where we apply our "hard-wired" ability to classify our observations and make generalizations [45, 46].

In the remainder of this section, we will come across three classes of such filters (that are relevant to domain modeling): *domain conceptualizations, purpose* and *normative frames*.

3.2   Domain Conceptualizations

In the context of domain modeling we assume a conception (of something to be modeled) to involve a set of *domain concepts* [26]. For example, the domain of genealogical relations (taken from [26]), includes the domain concepts: Person, Man, Woman, Father, Mother, Offspring, being the father of, being the mother of, etc. This part of a domain conception is what we prefer to call the *domain conceptualization* as it defines the fundamental concepts in which one creates one's conception of the world.

As also discussed in [26], a *domain conceptualization* then allows the actor to create *domain abstractions* of certain facts in an existing/imagined reality. The use of the word *abstraction* stresses the point that they are not the actual facts in the observed world, but rather abstractions thereof. An example would be the (representation of the domain abstraction of the) fact that a man named John is the father of another man named Paul. Domain abstractions are also (part of) domain conceptions, but rather at the instance level.

Needless to say that it is possible to take e.g. DEMO-modeling [15], ArchiMate-modeling[7] [47], or Fact-based modeling [34] as the domain of interest as well. In such a case, the *domain conceptualization* would pertain to the modeling constructs (Fact, Role, Actor, Process, realizes, etc.) where this would then enable enterprise engineers to create *domain abstractions* corresponding to the

---

[6] For an interesting paper on the role of goal-driven attention in perception and its relation to perception blindness, one can refer to [68].

[7] ArchiMate is a registered trademark of The Open Group (http://www.opengroup.org).

respective modeling languages. In this case, the *domain conceptualization* would actually be a *meta domain conceptualization*.

The MU-theory actually uses the term *conceptual schema* instead of *domain conceptualization*. We prefer to continue using the term *conceptualization*. Firstly, as it (see [26]) predates the use of the term *conceptual schema* to refer to the same. Secondly, the term *conceptual schema* may actually result in confusion with its use in the context of conceptual database design [42], where it refers to "*the*" description "*of the possible states of affairs of the universe of discourse including the classifications, rules, laws, etc., of the universe of discourse*" (stress added by us).

Given a domain conceptualization, an actor may imagine/observe different domain abstractions that are compatible with the conceptualization. This implies that the domain conceptualization essentially constitutes an (ontological) commitment when perceiving and conceiving of more specific situations/aspects of the observed referent. This commitment enables the actors to "carve out" different domain abstractions, where the domain conceptualization acts as a *filter* on how the actor can perceive and conceive a referent. Note that this also implies that when an actor would observe the same referent, using a different domain conceptualization, they will most likely arrive at different domain abstractions.

3.3   The Influence of Purpose

We argue that a symbol, in the sense of the semiotic triangle, is always selected/authored/uttered for a purpose. In the case of a model, this is even more obvious. As such, there will always be some communicative purpose involved, if only to communicate with oneself (e.g. note taking). This overarching communicative purpose may be (situationally) refined in terms of the underlying reasons for the communication [62]. This may be related to a desire to e.g., convey an understanding about the world, make changes in the world, analyze a potential problem, etc.

Consider for instance a situation in which an enterprise engineer needs to create a high level view of the transactions between the main actor roles regarding a the pizzeria "Perla del Nord" (taken from [57]). Imagine that the target audience of the model is not fluent in DEMO [15], but rather well versed in the use of ArchiMate [2]. Given this purpose, i.e. to communicate a high level view of the transactions between the main actor roles to an audience which is not fluent in DEMO but rather in ArchiMate, the enterprise engineer may decide to create the model as depicted in figure. For this purpose, the enterprise engineer has decided to not use ArchiMate as-is, but rather use DEMO's transaction symbol for the transactions.

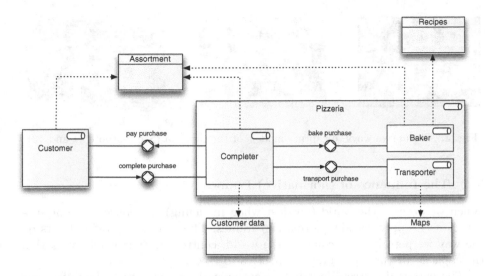

Fig. 3. High level construction model of pizzeria "Perla del Nord"

In the context of enterprise modeling, [58] suggest (at least) seven high-level purposes for the creation of enterprise models: *understand, assess, diagnose, design, realize, operate* and *regulate*.

The purpose may also be (situationally) refined in terms of e.g. properties of the target audience [62]. This includes, for instance, the interests/concerns, of the target audience, their background, cognitive abilities, etc.

The communicative purpose will influence the way an actor shapes their thoughts (i.e. their perception and conception) regarding a referent/domain, and their selection/creation of a (composition of) symbol(s) to symbolise these, and as such act as a filter.

In the example of Fig. 3, the enterprise engineer used a DEMO-based conceptualization to study the domain of pizzeria "Perla del Nord", to then produce a domain abstraction that resulted in the model shown in Fig. 3. In representing the domain abstraction in terms of a model, the enterprise engineer decided to use primarily to ArchiMate models to bridge to the background of the target audience. However, for another audience, the enterprise engineering may have decided to use drastically different artifacts in the role of models of the pizzeria, including animations or games [22]. As illustrated in Fig. 4, one may choose to use the "My Pizza Shop"[8] computer game (left illustration) to communicate the workings of the pizzeria, or even use a more *tangible* form using, e.g., Playmobil[9] (the right two images).

---

[8] By Tapps Games (http://tappsgames.com).

[9] Playmobil is a registered trademark of geobra Brandstätter Stiftung & Co. KG (http://company.playmobil.com).

Fig. 4. Alternative ways to capture models of the pizzeria (See footnote 11 and 12)

3.4 The Influence of (normative) Frames

When we observe the world (not just when modeling), we consciously, or subconsciously, apply certain (normative) frames. These frames provide filters on the way we perceive and conceive the world, controlling that what we (within the capacity of our senses) allow ourselves to "see".

The earlier discussed domain conceptualizations are a first class of examples of such frames. As such, the enterprise engineer who produced Fig. 3 used the DEMO-based conceptualization as a normative frame shaping their domain abstraction, while using ArchiMate as a normative frame in producing the representation. However, there are more frames that play a role when we observe domains, and thus influence the way we (are able to) model.

These frames may be the result of what we learned at an early stage in our lives [46], but may also be based on our cultural environment, the language(s) we use, our upbringing, our educational background [50], and our philosophical stance. Some of these frames may have an explicit normative character, e.g. reflecting societal, cultural and/or professional norms[10].

Quite often, we may not even be aware of the (normative) frames we use. An interesting quote in this regard, attributed to Poincaré, can be found in [56]: *"We have to make use of language, which is made up necessarily of preconceived ideas. Such ideas, unconsciously held, are the most dangerous of all."*

In [59] we already identified some of the normative frames that may influence us when creating domain models. Modeling frameworks, paradigms, metaphors, (foundational) ontologies, classification/typing mechanisms, taxonomies, dictionaries, domain conceptualizations, etc., can all be seen as (normative) frames.

(Normative) frames have possible advantages and disadvantages. They enable us to make sense of the world around us, manage its complexities, and focus the way we observe the world. That also empowers us to express/gather knowledge, while making communication easier as they can provide us with a common background. The communicative purpose (see above) also leads to the selection/use of a specific (normative) frame. At the same time, there are moments where such

---

[10] Nisbett [55] is an example of an author who discusses the influence of social and cultural norms in perception, conceptualization and reasoning. It is important to highlight that he talks about cultural *effect* (or *influence*) on thought without committing to *linguistic relativism* (and neither do we make such a commitment).

frames may actually act as a straitjacket, disabling us to innovate or see the real problems. A key challenge is, to be aware of the (normative) frames we use [59], and use them wisely.

One may also identify a certain hierarchy among the used frames. For instance, a domain conceptualization may be compliant to a specific modeling language, which in itself may be compliant to a foundational ontology. It is also interesting to not that the ArchiMate language was actually designed in terms of multiple layers of increasingly more specific modeling concepts [48] (mirroring the work on meta-model hierarchies as reported in [16]), potentially also enabling modellers to apply a process of step-wise selection of interpretation (in terms of an increasingly more specific meta-model) when modeling a domain [64].

In terms of the semiotic triangle, (normative) frames obviously have a (positive and/or negative) influence on the way an actor shapes their thoughts (i.e. their perception and conception) regarding a referent/domain, and their selection/creation of a (composition of) symbol(s) to symbolise these.

With regards to the current version of the FI-theory [15] it is relevant to observe that it bases itself strongly on the theory of Mario Bunge [9]. In particular concerning the things the world is composed of. As such, this implies the adoption of a specific view on the composition of the world; in other words, the adoption of a specific frame. By positioning the FI-theory as an explicit cornerstone of enterprise engineering, it (together with the TAO, PSI theories), becomes a normative frame towards enterprise engineering.

The goal of this paper is not to argue if that would be a good choice for enterprise engineering or not. We do, however, think it is important to make such a choice explicit[11].

4   Domain Models

In this section, we discuss the notion of model itself. In doing so, we will: (1) discuss our current understanding of model, (2) clarify that modeling involves the alignment of multiple conceptions, and (3) discuss the need to distinguish between conceptual models and computational design models.

4.1   Defining the Notion of Model

The MU-theory [15, page 73] bases its notion of model exclusively on the definition provided by Apostel in [1]: "*The foundations part starts with this definition of model: any subject using a system A to obtain knowledge of a system B is using A as a model of B.*" What is interesting to note is that in [1], Apostel provides this definition as a summary of the discussion provided in that paper. More specifically, immediately before providing the above definition, Apostel states [1]: "*This will be our final and most general hint towards the definition of model*".

---

[11] For example, one of us has argued at length elsewhere against the adequacy of Bunge's ontology as a foundation for conceptual modeling [24,25,33].

This definition should, therefore, not be seen as the final word of what a model is, but rather as an intermediate state in an ongoing debate. A debate to which other scholars [20,35,44,51,52,65,66,69,70], as well as ourselves [5,27,29,63], have, or endeavoured to, contribute to.

Based on these foundations, our current understanding of the definition of the notion of *domain model* is:

> A *social artifact* that is *acknowledged* by an *observer* to *represent* an *abstraction* of some *domain* for a particular *purpose*.

Each of the stressed words in this definition requires a further explanation, where *domain* and *purpose* have already been discussed in the earlier sections.

A model is seen as a *social artifact*. It is a social artifact in the sense that its role as model should be recognizable by a collective agent[12]. Moreover, for this reason, it should exist outside of our minds. In other words, in the view defended here, a model *generically depends* on some external medium in order to exist [71][13]. In "our" field of application, this artifact typically takes the *form* of some "boxes-and-lines" diagram (see e.g. Fig. 3). These diagrams, expressed (again, typically) in some form of concrete visual syntax, can have its grammar specified by a set of rules (e.g., a meta-model, a graph grammar [75]), and its semantics defined by a mapping to a mathematical structural (*formal semantics* [38]) or to an ontological theory (*ontological or real-world semantics* [13]).

More generally, however, domain models can, depending on the *purpose* at hand, take other forms as well, including text, mathematical specifications, games, animations, simulations, and physical objects (also see our earlier discussion regarding Fig. 4).

When the modeled *domain* pertains to a part/perspective/aspect of an enterprise, then we can indeed refer to the resulting domain model as an *enterprise model*.

In requiring a model to be an artifact, we deviate from the definition suggested in the MU-theory, where a model can be (in terminology of the MU-theory) a "symbolic complex", a "concrete complex" (in the tangible sense), or a "conceptual complex" (in one's mind). Of these, the "symbolic complex" and a "concrete complex" are artifacts. As such, in our definition, the "conceptual

---

[12] Notice that, unlike [8], we do not require the model *type* to be recognizable *a priori*. For example, the aforementioned Playmobil set is not a type of modeling grammar for modeling pizzerias. Nonetheless, a particular use of that set to model a specific pizzeria can be shared and recognized as such by a particular collective agent.

[13] In [54], John Mylopoulos also defends the view that models are social artifacts. His main argument is that models typically represent shared conceptualizations of collective agents, which have to be produced through a social dialectic process from the individual conceptualizations of the members of those collectives. Once more, in order for that to be possible, for all realistic conceptualizations, a concrete representation existing outside the mind of those members must exist.

complexes" are (consciously) left out[14]. The motivation for this lies in the observation that for models to be used in a context involving (often asynchronous) communication, and collective problem-solving between humans (including, e.g. enterprise engineering efforts), specially when dealing with complex abstractions, they must exist as concrete artifacts. In this way, we can point at them, we provide them explicit identities, speak about their authors/creators, preserve them, etc.

This does not mean, as we will discuss below, that the notion of "conceptual complex" does not play a role. We only suggest not to consider these to be (able to play the role of) *models*.

As it is ultimately the observer who needs to *acknowledge* the fact that an *artifact* is indeed a model of the domain, it actually makes sense to treat *their* conception of the domain (involving a domain conceptualization and compatible domain abstractions) as the de-facto "proxy" for the domain. It also, in line with [1], points at the fact that *being a model* (in the eyes of an observer) is a *role* of an artifact[15].

We should also realize that the *observer* observes the model (as artifact) as well, which therefore also creates a conception (in their mind) of the model. As a consequence, the observer needs to validate the alignment between their conception of the model and their conception of the domain, where the *purpose* of the model determines the alignment criteria. For instance, in creating the model shown in Fig. 3, or creating a computer-based game or game involving physical objects, to enable stakeholders to experience the "working" of the

---

[14] A potential counterexample is the case of *Blind Chess*, in which two players play the game without physical chess boards or pieces. In this case, we have individual conceptions, which are updated by a sequence of explicit and mutually acknowledged utterances. One could argue the sequence of these utterances *is* the model of the game, since the game could be completely reconstructed from the shared initial state plus that sequence (in a way that is analogous to the *event sourcing* (https://martinfowler.com/eaaDev/EventSourcing.html) notion of a domain representation). However, even the log of utterances in this case only exist in the players' minds. For the sake of this paper, we consider this as a case of a *shared conception* but not a model.

[15] Authors such as [8], defend that although artifacts must be created by acts of intention, preexisting entities that are not artifacts can become constituents of artifacts via intentional acts of creation. For example, if one decides to use a pebble as a paper weight, then a new entity is created (that paper weight), which is then constituted by the original pebble. According to this view, a "box-and-lines" drawing (or a Playmobil set) *constitutes* an artifact (model) due to an intentional act of creation - as opposed to saying that the diagram (Playmobil set) *plays the role* of a model. This view is also adopted in [74], in which, for example, a program is said to be constituted by a source code. We ignore this detail here and simply speak of an artifact playing the role of a model in a looser sense. However, according to the former view, we could also have non-artifactual entities playing the role of (or constituting) a model. Take for example the situation in which we use a grass field and a set of pebbles as a model of a football game. Again, for the sake of simplicity, we ignore this case here.

pizzeria "Perla del Nord" (as hinted at in Fig. 4), the modeler needs to align the creation/structuring of the model (the artifact) and the domain abstraction it needs to capture.

4.2   Alignment of Conceptions

A model is the representation of an *abstraction* of the domain [5,26,28,41]. This implies that, in line with the *purpose* of the model, some "details" of the domain are consciously left out. As a corollary to this definition, it implies that an observer (when acknowledging that that some artifact is indeed a model of the domain), must also be able to identify ("carve out") details in the domain that are *not* represented in the model.

In the context of domain modeling, four important flavors of abstraction are [4]: (1) *selection*, where we decide to only consider certain elements and/or aspects of the domain; (2) *classification*; (3) *generalization*; and (4) *aggregation*. In our field of application, selection typically leads to frameworks of aspects/layers by which to model an enterprise, but also to mechanisms for view extraction, as well as clustering and model summarization [18,32]. Classification, typically leads to some class-instance and/or type-instance relationships, including type-instance relationships between types and higher-order types, i.e., multi-level structures [10]; generalization leads to the formation of specialization/generalization *taxonomies*, in which sub-types specialize properties of super-types; aggregation leads to the formation of *partonomies* of various kinds in which entities, seen as integral wholes, can be decomposed into parts. Parts, on the other hand, hang together bound by some unity criterion that forms the whole [30].

As a consequence of the above, an observer actually needs to harbour (at least) four conceptions: (1) a "full" conception of the domain (as they "see" it), (2) a conception of the purpose for the model, (3) an abstracted conception of the domain, (4) a conception of the artifact that is (to be) the model representing the latter abstraction.

It is important to realize that each of these four conceptions involves its own domain conceptualization (and associated set of possible domain abstractions); each with different (yet connected) domains as their focus. In the case of the *conception of the domain* this involves the actual domain to be modeled. In the case of the *abstracted conception of the domain* this involves the domain of possible abstractions on the domain to be modeled. For the *conception of the artifact*, the domain pertains to the constructional properties of the artifact in relation to the domain to be modeled. For the *conception of the purpose for the model* the domain involves the possible purposes for modeling the domain to be modeled.

Figure 5 provides an overview of the involved conceptions, where the conception of the purpose modifies the abstraction(s) and the alignment between the conceptions of the model and the desired abstraction. We should also not forget that the (normative) frames as discussed in the previous section influence the formation of all four conceptions.

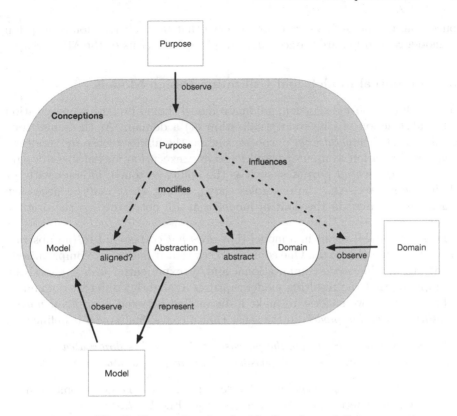

Fig. 5. Conceptions involved in domain modeling

When the model-conception corresponds to the abstraction-conception, then the observer would agree that the artifact is a model of the domain for the given purpose. As a consequence, different models (as artifacts) may indeed result in the same model-conception, in which case (for the observer) they are equivalent models of the same domain (for the same purpose).

If the observer is "the modeler", i.e. the person creating the model, they also need to "shape" the model in such a way that it best matches their *desired* model-conception.

What is not shown explicitly in Fig. 5 is the fact that the normative frames as discussed in the previous section, influence the way an observer creates (and aligns) the four conceptions shown in Fig. 5. This specifically also includes the modeling languages we use. Even more, when the observer has an explicit understanding of the normative frames they (consciously or unconsciously) use, these understandings lead to conceptualizations in themselves. For instance, a conceptualization of (their understanding of) the DEMO method or the ArchiMate modeling language.

Returning briefly to the discussion above, where we limited our understanding of models only, i.e., leaving out what the MU-theory suggests to refer to as "conceptual complexes", we can now observe that both abstraction-conception and model-conception are "conceptual complexes" in terms of the MU-theory.

4.3   Conceptual Models and Utilization Design Models

In line with the above discussion, a domain model should be (the representation of) the abstraction of (the conceptualization of) a domain. At the same time, for different (1) *computational* purposes, such as the ability to use the model as a base for simulation, computer-based reasoning, execution, or database design, and/or (2) *experiential* purposes, such as the ability to touch, interact with, or feel the model (see, e.g., the examples shown in Fig. 4), it may be necessary to include "features" in the domain model that are not "true" to the original domain.

These "features" result in a model that does *not* correspond to (an abstraction of) the original domain. One could even say that it has been "compromised" in order to provide some computational and/or experiential *utility*, effectively also implying that the resulting model captures a (slightly) different domain.

This is where we suggest to make a distinction between *conceptual models* and *utilization design models* in the sense that a *conceptual model* is defined as:

A model of a domain, where the purpose of the model is dominated by the ambition to remain as-true-as-possible to the original domain conception

while a *utilization design model* includes "compromises" to enable some computational and/or experiential (such as a game; see Fig. 4) *utility*[16].

Note the use of the word *ambition* in the definition of conceptual model. As discussed in [61], we are not suggesting there to be a crisp border between conceptual models and utilization design models. However, the word *ambition* also suggest that a modeler/observer, as their insight in a domain increases, should be driven to reflect on the conceptual purity of their conceptualization and of the resulting model.

Utilization design models certainly have an important role to play. However, it is important to be aware of the "compromises" that had to be "designed into" the original domain conceptualization, to obtain the desired computational/experiential utility of the model. As such, it is also possible that one conceptual model has different associated utilization design models, each meeting different purposes.

5   Conclusion

In this paper, we reflected on the semiotic roots of domain modeling (and enterprise modeling in particular), the important notion of domain conception, and

---

[16] An example is the case of the so-called *Operational Ontologies* in Description Logics, which trade *domain appropriateness* for certain computational properties (e.g., decidability) [26].

models themselves. We positioned domain conceptions (with their underlying domain conceptualization and associated domain abstractions) as a bridge from the semiotic roots to the world of domain models.

In our discussions we also reflected on the current versions of two of the core theories of the discipline of enterprise engineering (*Factual Information* (FI) theory and the *Model Universe* (MU) theory).

We regard this paper as part of an ongoing "journey", with the aim of deepening our insights into the foundations of domain modeling. We certainly do not claim this paper to be a fully finished work. It provides a snapshot of our current understanding, and we hope that debates with our colleagues will aid us in continuing our journey.

Acknowledgements. We would like to thank the anonymous reviewers. Their feedback has resulted in many improvements to the original paper. In addition, we would like to thank the participants of EEWC2020 who participated in the many on-line discussions, not only regarding our own paper. These discussions have provided us with additional inspirations for improvements to this paper, as well as our ongoing journey to better understand the foundations of domain modeling.

The first author would like to thank Marija Bjeković, Jan Dietz, and Stijn Hoppenbrouwers, for insightful discussions on the topics covered in this article. The second author would like to thank Nicola Guarino, John Mylopoulos, and João Paulo Almeida for fruitful discussions on the topics of this article.

References

1. Apostel, L.: Towards the formal study of models in the non-formal sciences. Synthese **12**, 125–161 (1960). https://doi.org/10.1007/BF00485092
2. Band, I., et al.: ArchiMate 3.0 specification. The Open Group (2016)
3. Barwise, J.: The Situation in Logic. CSLI Lecture Notes, CLSI, Stanford, California (1989)
4. Batini, C., Mylopoulos, J.: Abstraction in conceptual models, maps and graphs. In: Tutorial presented at the 37th International Conference on Conceptual Modeling, ER 2018, Xi'an, China (2018)
5. Bjeković, M., Proper, H.A., Sottet, J.-S.: Embracing pragmatics. In: Yu, E., Dobbie, G., Jarke, M., Purao, S. (eds.) ER 2014. LNCS, vol. 8824, pp. 431–444. Springer, Cham (2014). https://doi.org/10.1007/978-3-319-12206-9_37
6. Bjeković, M., Proper, H.A., Sottet, J.-S.: Enterprise modelling languages - just enough standardisation? In: Shishkov, B. (ed.) BMSD 2013. LNBIP, vol. 173, pp. 1–23. Springer, Cham (2014). https://doi.org/10.1007/978-3-319-06671-4_1
7. Bommel, P.V., Hoppenbrouwers, S.J.B.A., Proper, H.A., Roelofs, J.: Concepts and strategies for quality of modeling. In: Halpin, T.A., Krogstie, J., Proper, H.A. (eds.) Innovations in Information Systems Modeling, chap. 9. IGI Publishing, Hershey (2008)
8. Borgo, S., Vieu, L.: Artefacts in formal ontology. In: Philosophy of Technology and Engineering Sciences, pp. 273–307. Elsevier (2009)
9. Bunge, M.: The Furniture of the World, Treatise on Basic Philosophy, vol. 3. D. Reidel Publishing Company, Dordrecht (1977)

10. Carvalho, V.A., Almeida, J.P.A., Fonseca, C.M., Guizzardi, G.: Multi-level ontology-based conceptual modeling. Data Knowl. Eng. **109**, 3–24 (2017). https://doi.org/10.1016/j.datak.2017.03.002
11. Crane, T.: The nonconceptual content of experience. In: Crane, T. (ed.) The Contents of Experience - Essays on Perception. Cambridge University Press (1992). https://doi.org/10.1017/CBO9780511554582
12. Cruse, A.: Meaning in Language, An Introduction to Semantics and Pragmatics. Oxford University Press, Oxford (2000)
13. de Carvalho, V.A., Almeida, J.P.A., Guizzardi, G.: Using reference domain ontologies to define the real-world semantics of domain-specific languages. In: Jarke, M., et al. (eds.) CAiSE 2014. LNCS, vol. 8484, pp. 488–502. Springer, Cham (2014). https://doi.org/10.1007/978-3-319-07881-6_33
14. Dietz, J.L.G., et al.: The discipline of enterprise engineering. Int. J. Organ. Design Eng. **3**(1), 86–114 (2013)
15. Dietz, J.L.G., Mulder, J.B.F.: Enterprise Ontology - A Human-Centric Approach to Understanding the Essence of Organisation. The Enterprise Engineering Series. Springer, Heidelberg (2020). https://doi.org/10.1007/978-3-030-38854-6
16. Falkenberg, E.D., Oei, J.L.H.: Meta model hierarchies from an object-role modelling perspective. In: Halpin, T.A., Meersman, R. (eds.) Proceedings of the First International Conference on Object-Role Modelling, ORM-1, Magnetic Island, Australia, 4–6 July 1994. pp. 218–227. Key Centre for Software Technology, University of Queensland, Brisbane. Magnetic Island, Queensland (1994)
17. Falkenberg, E.D., et al. (eds.): A framework of information systems concepts. IFIP WG 8.1 Task Group FRISCO, IFIP, Laxenburg, Austria (1998)
18. Figueiredo, G., Duchardt, A., Hedblom, M.M., Guizzardi, G.: Breaking into pieces: an ontological approach to conceptual model complexity management. In: 2018 12th International Conference on Research Challenges in Information Science (RCIS), pp. 1–10. IEEE (2018)
19. Floridi, L.: Information: A Very Short Introduction. OUP, Oxford (2010)
20. Frank, U.: Multi-perspective enterprise modeling (MEMO) - conceptual framework and modeling languages. In: HICSS 2002: Proceedings of the 35th Annual Hawaii International Conference on System Sciences (HICSS'02), vol. 3, p. 72. IEEE Computer Society Press, Los Alamitos (2002)
21. Gärdenfors, P.: Conceptual Spaces: The Geometry of Thought. MIT Press, London (2004)
22. Groenewegen, J., Hoppenbrouwers, S., Proper, E.: Playing archimate models. In: Bider, I., et al. (eds.) BPMDS/EMMSAD -2010. LNBIP, vol. 50, pp. 182–194. Springer, Heidelberg (2010). https://doi.org/10.1007/978-3-642-13051-9_16
23. Guarino, B., Guizzardi, G., Mylopoulos, J.: On the philosophical foundations of conceptual models. Inf. Model. Knowl. Bases XXXI **321**, 1 (2020)
24. Guarino, N., Guizzardi, G.: In the defense of ontological foundations for conceptual modeling. Scand. J. Inf. Syst. **18**(1), 1 (2006)
25. Guizzardi, G.: Ontological foundations for structural conceptual models. Ph.D. thesis, University of Twente, Enschede, The Netherlands (2005)
26. Guizzardi, G.: On Ontology, ontologies, conceptualizations, modeling languages, and (meta)models. In: Vasilecas, O., Eder, J., Caplinskas, A. (eds.) Databases and Information Systems IV - Selected Papers from the Seventh International Baltic Conference, DB&IS 2006, Vilnius, Lithuania, 3–6 July 2006. Frontiers in Artificial Intelligence and Applications, vol. 155, pp. 18–39. IOS Press (2006)
27. Guizzardi, G.: Theoretical foundations and engineering tools for building ontologies as reference conceptual models. Semant. Web **1**(1–2), 3–10 (2010)

28. Guizzardi, G.: Ontology-based evaluation and design of visual conceptual modeling languages. In: Reinhartz-Berger, I., Sturm, A., Clark, T., Cohen, S., Bettin, J. (eds.) Domain Engineering, pp. 317–347. Springer, Heidelberg (2013). https://doi.org/10.1007/978-3-642-36654-3_13

29. Guizzardi, G.: Ontological patterns, anti-patterns and pattern languages for next-generation conceptual modeling. In: Yu, E., Dobbie, G., Jarke, M., Purao, S. (eds.) ER 2014. LNCS, vol. 8824, pp. 13–27. Springer, Cham (2014). https://doi.org/10.1007/978-3-319-12206-9_2

30. Guizzardi, G., Ferreira Pires, L., van Sinderen, M.: An ontology-based approach for evaluating the *domain appropriateness* and *comprehensibility appropriateness* of modeling languages. In: Briand, L., Williams, C. (eds.) MODELS 2005. LNCS, vol. 3713, pp. 691–705. Springer, Heidelberg (2005). https://doi.org/10.1007/11557432_51

31. Guizzardi, G.: Ontology, ontologies and the "i" of fair. Data Intell. **2**(1–2), 181–191 (2020)

32. Guizzardi, G., Figueiredo, G., Hedblom, M.M., Poels, G.: Ontology-based model abstraction. In: 2019 13th International Conference on Research Challenges in Information Science (RCIS), pp. 1–13. IEEE (2019)

33. Guizzardi, G., Masolo, C., Borgo, S.: In defense of a trope-based ontology for conceptual modeling: an example with the foundations of attributes, weak entities and datatypes. In: Embley, D.W., Olivé, A., Ram, S. (eds.) ER 2006. LNCS, vol. 4215, pp. 112–125. Springer, Heidelberg (2006). https://doi.org/10.1007/11901181_10

34. Halpin, T.A., Morgan, T.: Information Modeling and Relational Databases. Data Management Systems, 2nd edn. Morgan Kaufman, Burlington (2008)

35. Harel, D., Rumpe, B.: Meaningful modeling: what's the semantics of "semantics"? IEEE Comput. **37**(10), 64–72 (2004). https://doi.org/10.1109/MC.2004.172

36. Henderson-Sellers, B., Gonzalez-Perez, C., Walkerden, G.: An application of philosophy in software modelling and future information systems development. In: Franch, X., Soffer, P. (eds.) CAiSE 2013. LNBIP, vol. 148, pp. 329–340. Springer, Heidelberg (2013). https://doi.org/10.1007/978-3-642-38490-5_31

37. Hillis, W.D.: The first machine intelligences. In: Brockman, J. (ed.) Possible Minds: Twenty-Five Ways of Looking at AI, pp. 170–180. Penguin Publishing Group, New York (2019)

38. ter Hofstede, A.H.M., Proper, H.A.: How to formalize it?: Formalization principles for information system development methods. Inf. Softw. Technol. **40**(10), 519–540 (1998)

39. Hoppenbrouwers, S.J.B.A.: Freezing Language; Conceptualisation processes in ICT supported organisations. Ph.D. thesis, University of Nijmegen, Nijmegen, The Netherlands (2003)

40. Hoppenbrouwers, S., Proper, H.A., Nijssen, M.: Towards key principles of fact based thinking. In: Debruyne, C., Panetto, H., Guédria, W., Bollen, P., Ciuciu, I., Meersman, R. (eds.) OTM 2018. LNCS, vol. 11231, pp. 77–86. Springer, Cham (2019). https://doi.org/10.1007/978-3-030-11683-5_8

41. Hoppenbrouwers, S.J.B.A., Proper, H.A.E., van der Weide, T.P.: A fundamental view on the process of conceptual modeling. In: Delcambre, L., Kop, C., Mayr, H.C., Mylopoulos, J., Pastor, O. (eds.) ER 2005. LNCS, vol. 3716, pp. 128–143. Springer, Heidelberg (2005). https://doi.org/10.1007/11568322_9

42. ISO/IEC JTC 1/SC 32 Technical Committee on Data management and interchange: Information processing systems - Concepts and Terminology for the Conceptual Schema and the Information Base. Technical report, ISO/TR 9007:1987, ISO (1987)

43. Kecheng, L., Clarke, R.J., Andersen, P.B., Stamper, R.K., Abou-Zeid, E.S. (eds.): IFIP TC8/WG8.1 Working Conference on Organizational Semiotics - Evolving a Science of Information Systems. Kluwer, Deventer, The Netherlands (2002)
44. Krogstie, J.: A semiotic approach to quality in requirements specifications. In: Kecheng, L., Clarke, R.J., Andersen, P.B., Stamper, R.K., Abou-Zeid, E.S. (eds.) Proceedings of the IFIP TC8/WG8.1 Working Conference on Organizational Semiotics: Evolving a Science of Information Systems, pp. 231–250. Kluwer, Deventer, The Netherlands (2002)
45. Lakoff, G.: Women, Fire, and Dangerous Things: What Categories Reveal About the Mind. University of Chicago Press, Chicago (1997)
46. Lakoff, G., Johnson, M.: Metaphors We Live By. University of Chicago Press, Chicago (2003)
47. Lankhorst, M.M., et al.: Enterprise Architecture at Work - Modelling, Communication and Analysis. The Enterprise Engineering Series, 4th edn. Springer, Heidelberg (2017). https://doi.org/10.1007/978-3-662-53933-0
48. Lankhorst, M.M., Proper, H.A., Jonkers, H.: The anatomy of the ArchiMate language. Int. J. Inf. Syst. Model. Design 1(1), 1–32 (2010)
49. Lankhorst, M.M., Torre, L.v.d., Proper, H.A., Arbab, F., Boer, F.S.d., Bonsangue, M.: Foundations. In: Enterprise Architecture at Work - Modelling, Communication and Analysis [47], pp. 41–58
50. van der Linden, D., Proper, H.A., Hoppenbrouwers, S.J.B.A.: Conceptual understanding of conceptual modeling concepts: a longitudinal study among students learning to model. In: Iliadis, L., Papazoglou, M., Pohl, K. (eds.) CAiSE 2014. LNBIP, vol. 178, pp. 213–218. Springer, Cham (2014). https://doi.org/10.1007/978-3-319-07869-4_19
51. Mahr, B.: On the epistemology of models. In: Abel, G., Conant, J. (eds.) Rethinking Epistemology, pp. 1–301. De Gruyter, Berlin (2011)
52. Moody, D.L.: The "Physics" of notations: toward a scientific basis for constructing visual notations in software engineering. IEEE Trans. Softw. Eng. 35(6), 756–779 (2009)
53. Morris, C.: Signs, Language and Behaviour. Prentice Hall, Englewood Cliffs (1946)
54. Mylopoulos, J.: Philosophical foundations of conceptual modeling: what is a conceptual model? In: Guizzardi, G., Franconi, E. (ed.) EROSS - ER Online Summer Seminars (2020). https://eross2020.inf.unibz.it/wp-content/uploads/2020/07/UniBZ-John.pdf. Accessed 3 Aug 2020
55. Nisbett, R.: The Geography of Thought: How Asians and Westerners Think Differently... and Why. Simon and Schuster, New York (2004)
56. Ogden, C.K., Richards, I.A.: The Meaning of Meaning - A Study of the Influence of Language upon Thought and of the Science of Symbolism. University of Cambridge, Oxford, United Kingdom, Magdalene College (1923)
57. Op't Land, M., Proper, H.A., Waage, M., Cloo, J., Steghuis, C.: Enterprise Architecture - Creating Value by Informed Governance. The Enterprise Engineering Series. Springer, Heidelberg (2008). https://doi.org/10.1007/978-3-540-85232-2
58. Proper, H.A.: Digital Enterprise Modelling - Opportunities and Challenges. In: Roelens, B., Laurier, W., Poels, G., Weigand, H. (eds.) Proceedings of 14th International Workshop on Value Modelling and Business Ontologies, Brussels, Belgium, 16–17 January 2020. CEUR Workshop Proceedings, vol. 2574, pp. 33–40. CEUR-WS.org (2020). http://ceur-ws.org/Vol-2574/short3.pdf
59. Proper, H.A., Bjeković, M.: Fundamental challenges in systems modelling. In: Mayr, H.C., Rinderle-Ma, S., Strecker, S. (eds.) 40 Years EMISA 2019, pp. 13–28. Gesellschaft für Informatik e.V, Bonn (2020)

60. Proper, H.A., Bruza, P.D.: What is information discovery about? J. Am. Soc. Inf. Sci. **50**(9), 737–750 (1999)
61. Proper, H.A., Guizzardi, G.: On domain modelling and requisite variety - current state of an ongoing journey. In: Grabis, J., Bork, D. (eds.) PoEM 2020. LNBIP, vol. 400, pp. 186–196. Springer, Cham (2020). https://doi.org/10.1007/978-3-030-63479-7_13
62. Proper, H.A., Hoppenbrouwers, S.J.B.A., Veldhuijzen van Zanten, G.E.: Communication of enterprise architectures. In: Enterprise Architecture at Work - Modelling, Communication and Analysis [47], pp. 59–72
63. Proper, H.A., Verrijn-Stuart, A.A., Hoppenbrouwers, S.J.B.A.: On utility-based selection of architecture-modelling concepts. In: Hartmann, S., Stumptner, M. (eds.) Conceptual Modelling 2005, Second Asia-Pacific Conference on Conceptual Modelling (APCCM2005), Newcastle, NSW, Australia, January/February 2005. Conferences in Research and Practice in Information Technology Series, vol. 43, pp. 25–34. Australian Computer Society, Sydney (2005)
64. Proper, H.A., Weide, T.P.V.D.: Modelling as selection of interpretation. In: Mayr, H.C., Breu, H. (eds.) Modellierung 2006, 22.-24. März 2006, Innsbruck, Tirol, Austria, Proceedings. Lecture Notes in Informatics, vol. P82, pp. 223–232. Gesellschaft für Informatik, Bonn, Germany (2006)
65. Rothenberg, J.: The nature of modeling. Artificial Intelligence, Simulation & Modeling, pp. 75–92. Wiley, New York (1989)
66. Sandkuhl, K., et al.: From expert discipline to common practice: a vision and research agenda for extending the reach of enterprise modeling. Bus. Inf. Syst. Eng. **60**(1), 69–80 (2018). https://doi.org/10.1007/s12599-017-0516-y
67. Searle, J.R.: A taxonomy of illocutionary acts. In: Expression and Meaning: Studies in the Theory of Speech Acts. Cambridge University Press, Cambridge (1979)
68. Simons, D.J., Chabris, C.F.: Gorillas in our midst: sustained inattentional blindness for dynamic events. Perception **28**(9), 1059–1074 (1999)
69. Stachowiak, H.: Allgemeine Modelltheorie. Springer, Heidelberg (1973)
70. Thalheim, B.: The theory of conceptual models, the theory of conceptual modelling and foundations of conceptual modelling. In: Embley, D., Thalheim, B. (eds.) Handbook of Conceptual Modeling, pp. 543–577. Springer, Heidelberg (2011). https://doi.org/10.1007/978-3-642-15865-0_17
71. Thomasson, A.L., et al.: Fiction and Metaphysics. Cambridge University Press, Cambridge (1999)
72. Tye, M.: Qualia. In: Stanford Encyclopedia of Philosophy. Stanford University (1997). https://plato.stanford.edu/entries/qualia/
73. Ullmann, S.: Semantics: An Introduction to the Science of Meaning. Basil Blackwell, Oxford (1967)
74. Wang, X., Guarino, N., Guizzardi, G., Mylopoulos, J.: Software as a social artifact: a management and evolution perspective. In: Yu, E., Dobbie, G., Jarke, M., Purao, S. (eds.) ER 2014. LNCS, vol. 8824, pp. 321–334. Springer, Cham (2014). https://doi.org/10.1007/978-3-319-12206-9_27
75. Zambon, E., Guizzardi, G.: Formal definition of a general ontology pattern language using a graph grammar. In: 2017 Federated Conference on Computer Science and Information Systems (FedCSIS), pp. 1–10. IEEE (2017)
76. Zarwin, Z., Bjeković, M., Favre, J.M., Sottet, J.S., Proper, H.A.: Natural modelling. J. Object Technol. **13**(3), 4:1–4:36 (2014)

Modeling the Emergence of Value and Risk in Game Theoretical Approaches

Glenda Amaral[1]([✉])[iD], Daniele Porello[2][iD], Tiago Prince Sales[1][iD], and Giancarlo Guizzardi[1][iD]

[1] Conceptual and Cognitive Modeling Research Group (CORE), Free University of Bozen-Bolzano, Bolzano, Italy
{gmouraamaral,tiago.princesales,giancarlo.guizzardi}@unibz.it
[2] ISTC-CNR Laboratory for Applied Ontology, Trento, Italy
daniele.porello@loa.istc.cnr.it

Abstract. Game theory is largely about interactions of agents whose decisions affect each other. The combination of agents' actions corresponds to outcomes, which may impact agents' goals, either positively or negatively. The analysis of the probable consequences and expected utilities of all possible outcomes is fundamental to support agents when deciding whether to engage in a certain strategy. In this paper, we move in this direction by initiating the investigation of the ontological foundation of the emergence of value and risk from outcomes in game theoretical approaches. In order to understand the influence of these forces over outcomes, a precise and rigorous conceptualization, based on foundational ontologies, is needed. To this aim, we present and discuss here a preliminary ontological modeling of basic concepts of game theory, as well as the relation to value, risk and outcomes.

Keywords: Game theory · Value · Risk · Unified Foundational Ontology (UFO) · Enterprise Architecture · Archimate

1 Introduction

Game theory has become an important field of study and has been employed by practitioners of different disciplines, including economics, management, political science, biology, law, among others. In general, "game theory is concerned with situations in which decision-makers interact with one another, and in which the satisfaction of each participant with the outcome depends not just or her own decisions but on the decisions made by everyone" [6]. Game-theoretic analysis include the modeling of the possible results of each strategy chosen by the players, taking into account uncertainties that neither player directly controls but that may influence outcomes, and assessing the expected utilities of these possible results. If we take the notion of risk presented in the ISO 3100:2018 [18,19] standard, which defines risk as the "effect of uncertainty on objective", we can conclude that an important part of choosing a strategy is understanding the risks involved in this decision.

© Springer Nature Switzerland AG 2021
D. Aveiro et al. (Eds.): EEWC 2020, LNBIP 411, pp. 70–91, 2021.
https://doi.org/10.1007/978-3-030-74196-9_5

Game outcomes may have either a positive or a negative effect on players' welfare, which are traditionally modeled in game theory by means of the Expected Utility Theory, cf [24].

As we shall see, in our account the positive and negative results shall be construed by means of the concepts of 'value' and 'risk', respectively; this move is motivated by the intent to provide a semantically transparent and interoperable qualitative account of the abstract quantitative theory of utilities. Thus, players must weight value and risks against each other when deciding whether to engage in a certain strategy. From this perspective, traditional risk analysis may help to advance the current state of the art of practical applications of game theory by modeling and assessing probable consequences for each outcome, thus allowing for understanding how value and risk emerge from combinations of actions of players.

Research into the foundations and the proper applications of game theory to real world scenarios has evolved at a vigorous pace throughout the past century, cf. [24] and nowadays the theoretical analysis provided by game theory is nicely complemented by advanced sets of computational tools, cf. [23, 36]. Over the past years "mathematicians and economists enriched the foundation, gradually building one of the most powerful and influential toolboxes of modern social science" [41].

Although the formalization of game components is quite well established, a detailed ontological understanding of the fundamental notions of game theory is missing. In particular, a clear ontological foundation of the objectives, or goals, of the interacting agents and of the emergence of value and risk from the outcomes of interaction is still to be developed. Without a precise conceptualization and rigorous definition of fundamental game theory notions, modeling and communication problems may arise. For example, when various modelers share a model without a clear semantics, different modelers come to different interpretations of the same model and are not aware of the conflict, running into a False Agreement problem [9]. As a result, practitioners have to make their own interpretations about the key concepts proposed in such models, which may lead to incorrect usage, and subsequently, them not obtaining the expected results [20]. This problem can manifest itself, for example, in the modeling of Enterprise Architectures. A main challenge of incorporating the fundamental notions of game theory in enterprise architecture lies in identifying a precise conceptualization for these notions. Without such a precise conceptualization, different modelers may come to different interpretations of the same model, thus resulting in enterprise architecture models that cannot serve their purpose as tools for communication between stakeholders, decreasing the value of enterprise architecture models in the pursuit of informed decision-making.

In this paper, we intend to contribute to filling these gaps by initiating the investigation of the ontological foundation of the emergence of value and risk in game theoretical approaches. We believe that a proper ontological understanding and modeling of the basic notions of game theory is mandatory to apply this rich body of knowledge and computational tools in designing information systems and supporting strategic decision making.

The contribution of this paper is threefold. Firstly, we make use of the concepts and relations defined in the Common Ontology of ValuE and Risk (COVER) [33] (Sect. 3.2) - a novel well-founded reference ontology that explains value and risk as dual and intrinsically connected notions –to analyse the payoffs of a game in terms of value and risk, as well as how they emerge from outcomes in game theory. Secondly, we propose a precise representation of our analysis by means of an ontologically well-founded model, specified in OntoUML [12] and thus, compliant with the meta-ontological commitments of the Unified Foundational Ontology (UFO) [12]. Finally, we apply our ontological account for game theory concepts to model game outcomes in the context of Enterprise Architectures.

The remainder of this paper is organized as follows. In Sect. 2, we provide an overview of some basic concepts of game theory and a discussion on the emergence of value and risk from outcomes. In Sect. 3, we briefly introduce the Unified Foundational Ontology (UFO), as well as the Common Ontology of ValuE and Risk (COVER) [33], which serve as conceptual foundation for the analysis conducted in this paper. In this section, we also present a number of modeling patterns based on COVER that support the modeling of value and risk in the standard enterprise architecture language Archimate. In Sect. 4, we represent the results of our analysis in a concise OntoUML model. In Sect. 5, we instantiate the model using a Bank Run game example. To demonstrate the contribution of our proposal to the modeling practice, in Sect. 6, we apply these results to represent the emergence of value and risk from game outcomes in enterprise architecture models in Archimate. We conclude with some final remarks in Sect. 7.

2   On Game Theory

2.1   Strategic Games

"Game Theory studies decisions in which the outcome depends partly on what other people do, and in which this is known to be the case by each decision maker" [27]. Shoam and Leyton-Brown [37] define game theory as "the mathematical study of interaction among independent, self-interested agents."

In game theory, a game is intended to refer to any social situation involving two or more agents, named players. A player may be interpreted as an individual or as a group of individuals making a decision. Two basic assumptions about players are that: (i) they are rational [24], meaning that they make decisions consistently in pursuit of their own objectives and aiming at maximizing the expected value of their payoff; and (ii) they take into account their knowledge or expectations of other decision-makers' behavior [37]. According to Shoam and Leyton-Brown [37], each player "has his own description of which states of the world he likes" and "acts in an attempt to bring about these states of the world".

The dominant approach to modeling an agent's interests is Utility Theory, which aims at quantifying an agent's degree of preference across a set of available alternatives [37]. Under a wide range of circumstances, the preference relation of a player in a strategic game can be represented by a utility function (also called a payoff function) [25]. A utility function is a mapping from states of the world to real numbers. These numbers are interpreted as measures of an agent's level of happiness in the given states.

A strategic game is a model of interactive decision-making in which players (agents) simultaneously choose their plan of action to perform in the environment. The combination of each agent action (the *action profile*, in the game-theoretical jargon) brings about a possible outcome o in a set of outcomes O, that depends on the actions performed by the agents, cf. [42]. We can represent an agent utility function as a function from O to the real numbers $\mathbb{R}$ ($u : O \to \mathbb{R}$) that assigns to each outcome o in O a measure of how good o is for the considered agent. The greater the number, the better o is for that agent.

Based on the above-mentioned definitions, a (strategic) game includes (cf. [42]): a finite set N of n agents, indexed by i; for each agent $i \in N$, a nonempty set A_i of actions (or strategies) available to agent i; a set of outcomes O; the preferences or utilities u_i of the agents over the combinations of actions (outcomes). In Game Theory, to simplify the model, the set of outcomes is usually identified with the set of all possible combinations of agents' actions; however, we prefer to keep the two sets distinct, as in [42], to facilitate our subsequent ontological analysis.

Let us take as example a set of agents $N = \{x, y\}$ and a set of actions $A = \{C, D\}$ available to both agents x and y. Assume that each combination of agents' actions brings about a distinct outcome, i.e. we have the following set $O = \{o_1, o_2, o_3, o_4\}$, where $o_1 = (C, C)$, $o_2 = (C, D)$, $o_3 = (D, C)$ and $o_4 = (D, D)$. In addition, for each agent, we can define the preferences or utilities directly on the combinations of actions (or outcomes). For instance:

$$u_x(C, C) = 2, u_x(D, C) = 1, u_x(C, D) = 2, u_x(D, D) = 3$$
$$u_y(C, C) = 2, u_y(D, C) = 3, u_y(C, D) = 1, u_y(D, D) = 2$$

A natural way to represent games is via an n-dimensional matrix, also known as *payoff matrix*. For example, in a two-dimensional matrix, in general, each row corresponds to a possible action for player x, each column corresponds to a possible action for player y, and each cell is a combination of actions that corresponds to one possible outcome. Each player's utility for an outcome is written in the cell corresponding to that outcome, with player x's utility listed first. Table 1 illustrates the payoff matrix for the example just mentioned.

Table 1. Payoff matrix example

		Player y	
		C	D
Player x	C	2,2	2,1
	D	1,3	3,2

A fundamental concept in game theory is that of Nash equilibrium. A Nash equilibrium is a set of actions (an action profile), one for each player (agent), such that no player could improve their payoff by unilaterally deviating from their assigned action. For example, considering two agents x and y, two actions a_1 and a_2 are in Nash equilibrium if: (i) assuming that agent x plays a_1, y can do no better than playing a_2; and (ii) assuming that agent y plays a_2, x can do no better than playing a_1. The game presented in Table 1 has a unique Nash equilibrium, namely (C, C).

2.2   Example: Bank Run

The game theoretical literature on bank runs is largely built on the seminal paper by Diamond and Dybvig [5].

A bank holds only a fraction of its deposits as cash reserves. It lends out as much of its deposits as it can (subject to a banking regulator's capital-adequacy requirements), making a profit from the interest it charges. A bank run occurs when a large number of customers of a bank or another financial institution withdraw their deposits simultaneously due to concerns about the bank's solvency, which is common in times of crisis. If the depositors do not withdraw and give bank enough time to tide over crisis, then payoff is highest and they can get their money with interest. However, if there is panic among depositors and all of them rush to withdraw their money, then due to insolvency each will end up getting a lesser amount. Finally, if few withdraws and the others do not, then the one who withdraws gets more than the one who do not withdraw.

To simplify, let us consider the example of a bank with just two depositors. Each depositor makes a deposit of 1000 euros in the bank. The bank invests these deposits in a long term project. If the bank is forced to liquidate its investments before the project matures, a total of 1600 euros can be recovered. However, if the bank allows the investment to reach maturity, the project will pay out a total of 2400 euros. Therefore, if both depositors make withdrawals before the project matures, each agent will receive 800 euros. If only one depositor withdrawal her money before the project matures, she receives 1000 euros and the other one, 600 euros. Finally, if both depositors retain the payment until the project matures, the bank returns 1200 euros for each one. Table 2 presents the payoff-matrix for this example, considering that the depositors may only choose between withdrawing their deposits before the project matures or retaining their deposits until it matures. Note that although in this example the payoffs are related to the value returned to depositors by the bank, payoffs are not necessarily the same as monetary worth. This is because payoffs or utilities identify the players' preferences, which are not necessarily measured in terms of profit or money, cf. [27].

This game has two Nash equilibria: (i) both depositors withdraw; and (ii) both depositors retain. The first of these two outcomes (i) can be interpreted as a run on the bank. If depositor A believes that depositor B will withdraw before the project matures, then her best response is to withdraw as well, even though both depositors would be better off if they waited until the project matures.

Table 2. Bank Run example

		Depositor B	
		Withdraw	Retain
Depositor A	Withdraw	800,800	1000,600
	Retain	600,1000	1200,1200

Recently, some authors have compared the shortage of toilet paper, associated to the spread of coronavirus, to a bank run [26]. They state that "this panic buying is the result of the fear of missing out and is a phenomenon of consumer behaviour similar to what happens when there is a run on banks" [26]. According to Payolo [26], "both banking and the toilet-paper market can be thought of as a coordination game with two players (one individual and everyone else) and two strategies (panic buy or act normally). Each strategy has an associated pay-off. If everyone acts normally, we have an equilibrium: there will be toilet paper on the shop shelves, and people can relax and buy it as they need it. But if others panic buy, the optimal strategy for the individual is to do the same, otherwise she'll be left without toilet paper. The result is another equilibrium, which is everyone panic buys".

2.3   Value, Risk and Outcomes

According to Sun and Sun [38], "game theory is mainly about choosing the most advantageous plan of action given the effect the opponent has on us". Agents perform actions motivated by intentions, which are related to their goals. In game theory, an outcome corresponds to a combination of actions performed by agents. Payoffs are related to outcomes results, which can contribute to the achievement of agents' goals. Sun and Sun [38] state that payoff "refers to the reward received after the player has chosen a certain strategy or action".

As extensively discussed in the literature [21,22,33], value is directly connected to the achievement of goals. Things and experiences have value to people because they allow them to achieve their goals. For example, an object has value to an agent because it has properties (e.g., capacities, "affordances", i.e., ultimately, *dispositions*) that can be leveraged to enact events that, in turn, bring about situations that contribute to satisfy that agent's goals [2,16]. In summary, the more an event makes progress towards achieving an agent's goals (i.e., the more the situation it brings about contributes to satisfying those goals), the more valuable it is to that agent. In other words, the results of outcomes, represented by payoffs, may create value for agents as they can positively impact their goals. But, as value is not an *intrinsic property*, the same object or experience may have different values to different agents, or even according to different goals adopted by the same agent. Thus, since the players have different goals and under different circumstances, they may feel differently w.r.t. the same reward. For example, a mask has a higher value during the COVID-19 pandemic because by wearing it, one is better protected from getting infected.

Interestingly, at the same time that outcome results can generate value, they also entails some risk, as they can negatively impact an agent's goal. The relation between value and risk is pointed out by several works in the literature. According to Sales et al. [33], "the notion of risk is irreducibly intertwined with the notion of value" and one of the differences between them rely on "the expected impact on goals: negative for risks and positive for value".

Having a clear understanding of the influence of these forces over outcomes is fundamental to the agent's decision making. For example, "in an uncertain game, a rational agent would not always play the strategy that gives the highest expected payoff if the risk is too high. For a risk-averse agent, the strategy that takes the least risk has the highest dominance. For a risk-seeking agent, the strategy that may give the highest payoff has the highest dominance regardless of the risk and the expected payoff. For a risk-neutral agent, the dominant strategy is the one that gives the highest expected payoff" [8]. Risk analysis, including probabilistic risk assessment of how events may unfold, can be very useful (perhaps even essential) for realistically complex problems, in populating the cells in payoff matrices. Therefore, as stated by Cox [4], "risk analysis and game theory are also deeply complementary". Game-theoretic analyses require modeling the probable consequences of each choice of strategies by the players and assessing the expected utilities of these probable consequences. Decision and risk analysis methods are well suited to accomplish these tasks.

3   Ontology-Based Foundations

Our aim is to provide a first ontological analysis of the emergence of value and risk from game outcomes. Our analysis is grounded in the Unified Foundational Ontology (UFO) [12], which was created with the specific purpose of providing foundations for conceptual modeling. UFO is formally connected to a set of engineering tools including a modeling language (OntoUML), as well as a number of methodological (e.g., patterns, anti-patterns) and computational tools [15]. Research shows that UFO is among the most used foundational ontologies in conceptual modeling and the one with the fastest adoption rate [40]. In particular, we rely on the concepts and relations defined in the Common Ontology of ValuE and Risk (COVER) [33], a novel well-founded reference ontology grounded on UFO that explains value and risk as dual and intrinsically connected notions. In this section we briefly discuss these ontological foundations.

3.1   The Unified Foundational Ontology

The Unified Foundational Ontology (UFO) is an axiomatic, domain independent, formal theory, developed based on a number of theories from Formal Ontology, Philosophical Logics, Philosophy of Language, Linguistics and Cognitive Psychology. UFO is divided into three incrementally layered compliance sets: UFO-A, an ontology of endurants (objects) [12], UFO-B, an ontology of events (perdurants) [16], and UFO-C, an ontology of social entities built on the top of UFO-A and UFO-B, which addresses terms related to the spheres of intentional and social things [13,17]. For an in-depth discussion and formalization, one should refer to, for example, [2,7,12,14].

UFO is the theoretical basis of OntoUML, a language for Ontology-driven Conceptual Modeling that has been successfully employed in a number of academic and industrial projects in several domains, such as services, value, petroleum and gas, media asset management, telecommunications, and government [15]. Models created in OntoUML have a clear formal semantics, and a comprehensive support for model verification, validation and code generation, including versions in languages such as OWL [15]. In the sequel, we briefly explain a selected subset of ontological distinctions put forth by the Unified Foundational Ontology, which are relevant to our discussion.

UFO makes a fundamental distinction between individuals (particulars), and types (or universals), i.e., patterns of features that are repeatable across individuals. Individuals can be endurants (roughly, things or object-like entities) and perdurants (roughly, events, occurrences, processes). Within the category of endurants, UFO distinguishes substantials and aspects (or moments). Substantials are existentially independent objects, such as Mick Jagger, the Moon, the United Nations organization. Moments, in contrast, are existentially dependent individuals, such as (a) Mary's capacity to speak italian (which depends on her) and (b) the marriage between John and Mary (which depends on both John and Mary). Moments of type (a) are termed modes; those of type (b) are termed relators. Relators are individuals with the power of connecting entities. For example, an "enrollment" relator connects an individual playing the "student" role with an "educational institution". Furthermore, there is a third sort of moments termed qualities. Qualities are individual moments that can be mapped to some quality space, e.g., a flower's color which may change from red to brown while maintaining its identity and a person's weight, which can be mapped to a one-dimensional structure of positive real numbers.

The metamodel of the OntoUML language was designed to reflect the ontological distinctions put forth by UFO. For this reason, the distinctions of the latter are reflected as modeling primitives (mostly stereotyped classes and relations) of the former. In OntoUML, the stereotypes «phase», «role» and «roleMixin» represent the respective ontological types of anti-rigid universals (which contingently instantiate their instances): phases are anti-rigid universals with an associated intrinsic contingent instantiation condition (e.g., being a child is being a person who contingently is in a certain age range); roles are anti-rigid universals with an associated relation contingent instantiation condition (e.g., being a student is being a person who contingently participates in a enrollment relation with an educational institution); rolemixins are anti-rigid and relationally dependent universals that aggregate properties that are common to different roles (e.g., the type customer that aggregates properties of individual customers and corporate customers). Furthermore, the stereotype «mixin» is used to represent semi-rigid universals (which are necessarily instantiated by some of its instances and contingently instantiated by others). Finally, the stereotype «category» is used to represent rigid universals (which necessarily instantiate their instances such as physical object, which aggregates essential properties of tables, cars, books). The reader interested in more details on the modeling primitives of OntoUML is referred to [1,7,14].

3.2 The Common Ontology of ValuE and Risk (COVER)

In this section, we briefly present the Common Ontology of ValuE and Risk (COVER) [33], a well-founded ontology that makes the deep connections between the concepts of value and risk explicit. COVER is grounded on several theories from marketing, service science, strategy and risk management. It is specified in OntoUML in [12].

COVER proposes an ontological analysis of notions such as Value, Risk, Risk Event (Threat Event, Loss Event) and Vulnerability, among others. This ontology characterizes and integrates different perspectives of value and risk.

COVER makes the following ontological commitments on the nature of value:

– Value emerges from impacts on goals. Value emerges from events that affect the degree of satisfaction of one or more goals of an agent.
– Value is relative. The same object or experience may be valuable to a person and of no value to another.
– Value is experiential. Even though value can be ascribed to objects, it is ultimately grounded on experiences. For instance, in order to explain the value of a smartphone, one must refer to the experiences enabled by it.
– Value is contextual. The value of an object can vary depending on the context in which it is used.

As for risk, COVER makes the following ontological commitments:

– Risk is relative. This means that an event might be simultaneously considered as a risk by one agent and not as a risk by another (it may even be considered as an opportunity by such an agent).
– A risk is perceived according to its impact on goals, i.e. in order to talk about risk, one needs to account for which goals are "at stake".
– Risk is experiential. This means that we ultimately ascribe risk to events, not objects.
– Risk is contextual. Thus, the risk an object is exposed to may vary even if all its intrinsic properties (e.g. its vulnerabilities) are the same.
– Risk is grounded on uncertainty about events and their outcomes.

Given the objectives of this paper, we focus here on the perspective of value and risk as a chain of events that impacts an agent's goals, which the authors named Value Experience and Risk Experience, respectively.

COVER breaks down Value Experiences into "smaller" events, dubbed Value Events. These are classified into Impact and Trigger Events. The former are those that directly impact a goal or bring about a situation (named Impactful

Outcome) that impacts a goal. On contrast, Trigger Events are simply parts of an experience that are identified as causing Impact Events, directly or indirectly. To formalize goals, COVER reuses the concept of Intention from UFO [12], as a type of mental state that describes a class of state-of-affairs that an agent is committed to bring about. Note that, since agents in UFO's view include both physical and social agents, COVER is able to represent value being ascribed from the perspective of a customer and an employee, but also from that of a business unit or even a whole enterprise.

Risk Experiences focus on unwanted events that have the potential of causing losses and are composed by events of two types, namely threat and loss events. A Threat Event is the one with the potential of causing a loss, which might be intentional or unintentional. A Threat Event might be the manifestation of: (i) a Vulnerability (a special type of disposition whose manifestation constitutes a loss or can potentially cause a loss from the perspective of a stakeholder); or (ii) a Threatening Capability (capabilities are usually perceived as beneficial, as they enable the manifestation of events desired by an agent. However, when the manifestation of a capability enables undesired events that threaten agent's abilities to achieve a goal, it can be seen as a threatening capability). The second mandatory component of a Risk Experience is a Loss Event, which necessarily impact intentions in a negative way (captured by a Hurts relation between Loss Event and Intention).

Figures 1 and 2 depicts two COVER diagrams in OntoUML, which captures part of the aforementioned ontological notions.

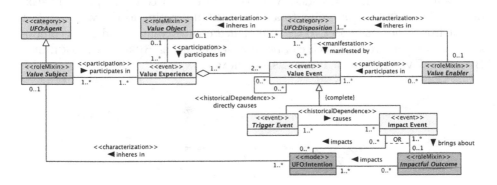

Fig. 1. A fragment of COVER depicting value experiences [33]

3.3   Value and Risk Experience Modeling in Archimate

Archimate is a modeling standard that defines a layered structure by means of which the architecture of enterprises can be described [39]. Based on the Common Ontology of Value and Risk, Sales et al. [35] propose a pattern language for value modeling in Archimate that allows the representation of Value Experiences

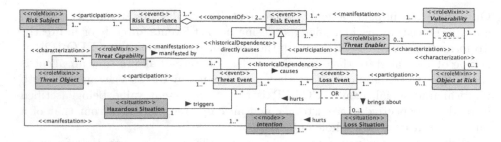

Fig. 2. A fragment of COVER depicting risk experiences [33]

as well as Experience Valuations, among others. Similarly, in [32] Sales et al. conduct an ontological analysis of risk modeling in Archimate in the light of COVER, in which they propose a pattern to represent Risk Experiences. By deriving patterns from COVER, they provide clear real-world semantics for its constituting elements, thus reducing the ambiguity and conceptual complexity found in previous approaches to model value and risk in the literature.

In the sequel we briefly describe three patterns that are relevant in the context of our paper, namely the Value Experience Pattern, the Experience Valuation Pattern and the Risk Experience Pattern. For a more detailed discussion on value and risk modeling patterns, one should refer to [35] and [32], respectively.

Value Experience. This pattern allows modelers to detail experiences that creates value for a given stakeholder. As shown in Fig. 3, it consists of a «ValueExperience» GROUPING connected to a STAKEHOLDER acting as the value subject (agent from whose perspective the experience creates value), and its decomposition into value events, which can be represented using BUSINESS PROCESSES, BUSINESS EVENTS and/or BUSINESS INTERACTIONS.

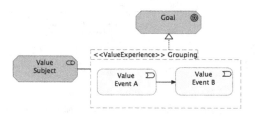

Fig. 3. The Value Experience Pattern

Experience Valuation. This pattern allows modelers to describe value judgments made towards experiences. As shown in Fig. 4, it consists of a «Valuation» ASSESSMENT made by a STAKEHOLDER (Value Assessor) that a «ValueExperience» creates VALUE for another STAKEHOLDER (Value Subject). The VALUE element corresponds to an entry in a scale chosen by the modeler.

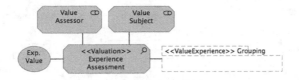

Fig. 4. The Experience Valuation Pattern

Risk Experience. According to Sales et al. [32] risk experiences focus on unwanted events that have the potential of causing losses and are composed by events of two types, namely threat and loss events. A threat event is the one with the potential of causing a loss. As described in [32], it might be the manifestation of a vulnerability or a threatening capability. The second mandatory component of a risk experience is a loss event, which necessarily impact intentions in a negative way.

In [32] the authors map risk experience as a GROUPING stereotyped as a «RiskExperience», which aggregates the elements and the relations in the experience. They associate the «RiskExperience» GROUPING with risks, which are mapped as «Risk» DRIVERS, as drivers represent "conditions that motivate an organization to define its goals and implement the changes necessary to achieve them" [39]. For the sake of simplicity, we represent here a simplified version of the Risk Experience pattern (Fig. 5), containing only the experience elements and relations that are relevant to our proposal.

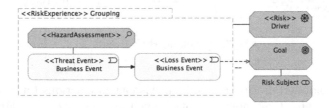

Fig. 5. The Risk Experience Pattern

4 Modeling the Emergence of Value and Risk from Outcomes in the Unified Foundational Ontology (UFO)

In this section, we use the aforementioned theories to present a preliminary model of the emergence of value and risk from games outcomes. Our analysis relies on the concepts of value and risk defined in COVER, the Common Ontology of ValuE and Risk [33].

Note that, as argued in [34], value can be ascribed to past, actual or envisioned experiences. Risk, however, is only ascribed to envisioned experiences that

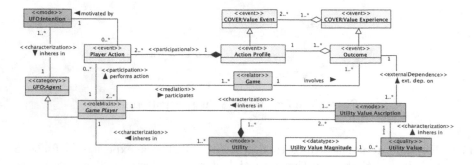

Fig. 6. Modeling the emergence of Value Risk from Outcomes in OntoUML

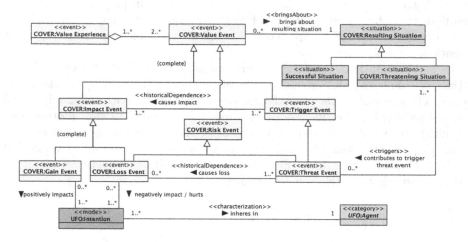

Fig. 7. Value and Risk Events

may (but are not certain to) happen [33]. Also agents' actions (or strategies) in a game may be about envisioned events (which may never occur). For instance, if a depositor decides to withdraw her money instead of retaining it in the bank, then the action of retaining the money will not happen. This means that we need to refer to future or envisioned events – whose expected temporal properties are not completely fixed – in our domain of discourse. Therefore, we shall talk of expected events as regular entities of our domain, not differently from, say, a planned air trip in a flight reservation system. In order to use this non-classical notion of events in our analysis while maintaining its ontological rigour, we employ the formulation of events as proposed in [10], which was already successfully employed in [33] and [34].[1]

Our model is specified in OntoUML [12] and thus, compliant with the meta-ontological commitments of the Unified Foundational Ontology (UFO) [12]. In

---

[1] A different strategy that avoids introducing future or possible events is to rephrase the model using *types* of actions and events, cf. [29].

the diagram depicted in Figs. 6 and 7, we represent events in yellow, relators in green, objects in pink, qualities and modes in blue, situations in orange and datatypes in white.

We use the notion of *agent* defined in UFO-C to model a participant of a game as an AGENT that plays the *role* of GAME PLAYER in a GAME (Fig. 6). In UFO-C, agents are individuals that can perform actions, perceive events and bear mental aspects. A relevant type of mental aspect for our proposal is the *intention*. Intentions are desired state of affairs for which the agent commits to pursuing (e.g., the intention of going to a beach resort for the next summer break) [3]. For this reason, intentions cause the agent to perform *actions*. In the ontology, INTENTIONS are represented as modes that inhere in AGENTS.

The ACTIONS performed by GAME PLAYERS are modeled as intentional events, in the sense that they have the specific purpose of satisfying some INTENTION. As events, actions can be atomic or complex. A complex action is composed of several actions. ACTION PROFILES are complex events composed of ACTIONS performed by the players in a GAME.

In the ontology, the ACTION PROFILE is modeled as a type of Value Event [33] (as defined in COVER [33]) and can be classified into IMPACT and TRIGGER EVENT (Fig. 7). The former is the one that directly impact an INTENTION of reaching a goal. By contrast, a TRIGGER EVENT is simply the one that causes an IMPACT EVENT. Within the category of IMPACT EVENTS we can further distinguish into GAIN EVENT and LOSS EVENT. The difference between them rely on the nature of the impact caused on goals (positive for GAIN EVENTs and negative for LOSS EVENTs).

A GAME involves a set of OUTCOMES. OUTCOMEs are modeled as a type of Value Experience [33] (as defined in COVER [33]) and thus are composed of Value Events. Among the Value Events that compose an OUTCOME there is exactly one ACTION PROFILE. Figure 7 presents a fragment of COVER depicting the different types of Value Events that can compose a Value Experience.

OUTCOMEs have impact on GAME PLAYERS' INTENTIONS, which may affect her goals either positively or negatively. We analyze the emergence of risks from OUTCOMEs, based on COVER [33]. An ACTION PROFILE is a complex event that brings about a RESULTING SITUATION (Fig. 7). The RESULTING SITUATION may satisfy the GAME PLAYER's goals (and in this case it is considered a SUCCESSFUL SITUATION) or, in the worst case, it may not have the desired result and the GAME PLAYER will not be able to achieve her goal. In this case, the RESULTING SITUATION stands for a THREATENING SITUATION that may trigger a THREAT EVENT, which may cause a loss. The LOSS EVENT is a RISK EVENT that impacts intentions in a negative way, as it hurts the GAME PLAYER's INTENTIONs of reaching a specific goal.

As we have previously discussed, value emerges from achieving goals. Thus, the more an event contributes to the achievement of a goal, the more valuable it is. OUTCOMEs that positively impact GAME PLAYERS' INTENTIONS can create value. However, whether or not value is produced in the realization of an OUTCOME is, in fact, a subjective notion, which depends on how the GAME PLAYERs assess their participation, i.e., whether they ascribe to the experience a positive assessment [33, 34].

The entity UTILITY VALUE ASCRIPTION represents this assessment. The UTILITY VALUE ASCRIPTION is an example of a mode that inheres in the AGENT and is externally dependent on the OUTCOME. As aforementioned, a mode is an existentially dependent entity that, as such, can only exist by inhering in some other individual. In particular, the UTILITY VALUE ASCRIPTION is a relationally dependent mode (or an externally dependent mode), i.e., a mode that inheres in an individual but which is also externally dependent on a different individual. The UTILITY VALUE ASCRIPTION mode takes a value in at least one (but possibly several) UTILITY VALUE MAGNITUDE SPACEs, via the quality UTILITY VALUE. These spaces have, in OntoUML, the semantics of abstract conceptual spaces, delimiting the possible values an intrinsic property can be projected into, cf. [12].

Finally, the UTILITY is composed of the UTILITY VALUE ASCRIPTIONS of the possible OUTCOMES, under the perspective of a particular GAME PLAYER. In the model, UTILITY is represented as a complex externally dependent mode that inheres in the GAME PLAYER and is composed of the mereological sum of UTILITY VALUE ASCRIPTION modes[2].

5   Use Case Illustration: Bank Run

In this section, we instantiate our model with two outcomes of the Bank Run example, described in Sect. 2.2, which are Nash Equilibria.

Firstly, in Fig. 8, we illustrate the instantiation of the OUTCOME in which both DEPOSITOR A and DEPOSITOR B retain the invested amount until the project matures. In this case both GAME PLAYERs have the INTENTION of 'making profit from the investment'. The ACTION PROFILE is composed of the ACTION of DEPOSITOR A, who decides to retain her money and the ACTION of DEPOSITOR B, who also decides to retain her deposit. Note that this is a case of Nash Equilibrium as once DEPOSITOR A has retained her deposit, DEPOSITOR B can do no better than retaining her deposit too. This ACTION PROFILE brings about a situation in which 'the bank does not need cash before the project completion', which stands for a SUCCESSFUL SITUATION. Consequently, the bank sells the project to another bank at price of 2400 euros, which is considered a TRIGGER EVENT that triggers two GAIN EVENTS, namely 'Bank pays out more than the amount invested by Depositor A' and 'Bank pays out more than the amount invested by Depositor B'. These two GAIN EVENTS positively impact the INTENTIONs of DEPOSITORs A and B of 'making profit from their investments', as they will receive 1200 euros, which is more than the invested value (1000 euros).

Secondly, in Fig. 9, we illustrate the instantiation of the OUTCOME in which both DEPOSITOR A and DEPOSITOR B withdraw the invested amount before

---

[2] This is compatible with the modeling of preferences according to UFO in [28].

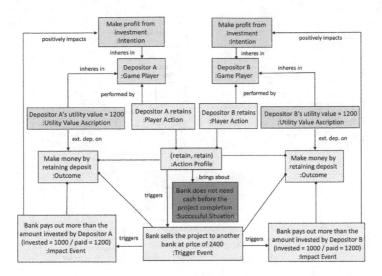

Fig. 8. The emergence of Value from Outcomes

the project matures. Also in this case, both GAME PLAYERs have the Intention of 'making profit from the investment'. The ACTION PROFILE is composed of the ACTION of DEPOSITOR A, who decides to withdraw her money and the ACTION of DEPOSITOR B, who also decides to withdraw her deposit. Note that here we also have a case of Nash Equilibrium. Although this outcome is not the one with the best payoff for both players, it can be seen as "a steady state, in which each player holds the correct expectation about the other players' behavior and acts rationally" [25]: if DEPOSITOR A believes that DEPOSITOR B will withdraw before the project matures, then her best response is to withdraw as well.

In the sequel, this ACTION PROFILE brings about a situation in which 'the bank needs cash to repay the deposits before the project completion' that can be considered a THREATENING SITUATION. This situation may trigger a THREAT EVENT if, for example, 'the bank is forced to liquidate its investments before the project matures, and recovers only 1600 euros'. This THREAT EVENT causes two LOSS EVENTs, which are 'the bank paying out less than the amount invested by Depositor A and Depositor B, respectively'. These LOSS EVENTs, in turn, hurt the DEPOSITORS' INTENTIONS of 'making profit from their investments'.

We focused on the Nash Equilibria of the game; clearly our approach can be used also for modelling non-equilibrium states. It is interesting to notice that our models illustrate *why* in a Nash equilibrium players have no incentives to deviate from the current course of action. The chosen action (e.g. "retain" for both players *A* and *B* in Fig. 8) is the action that positively impacts the intention of each player more than any other action, given the other players' move (by definition). Thus, assuming that rational players are pursuing actions that better impact their intentions, players have indeed no reason to deviate from that choice in that context. By contrast, in a non-Nash Equilibrium outcome, players would have

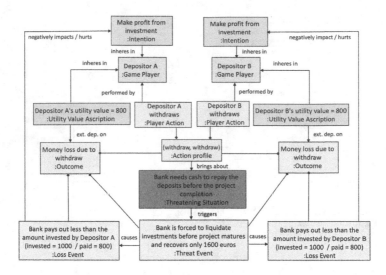

Fig. 9. The emergence of Risk from Outcomes

actions at their disposal that promote their intentions better, thus providing an incentive to deviate to the action that better impact their intention. Therefore, the ontological analysis provides a rich semantic understanding of equilibrium outcomes, associating the stability of the outcome with the satisfaction of the intentions of the players.

6 Modeling Game Outcomes in Enterprise Architecture: The Bank Run Example in Archimate

In order to provide enterprise architects with a common ground to apply game theory notions in coherent enterprise architecture descriptions, we apply the results of the analysis conducted in the previous section to represent the emergence of value and risk from game outcomes in Enterprise Architecture.

In particular, we employ the Archimate modeling patterns based on COVER and presented in Sect. 3.3. We use these patterns to represent the emergence of value and risk from outcomes in the context of the Bank Run example (Sect. 2.2), under the perspective of DEPOSITOR A.

To illustrate the emergence of value, we represent the situation in which both DEPOSITOR A and DEPOSITOR B retain their deposits until the project matures. We start with the application of the Value Experience pattern. The value subject identifies the perspective from which the judgment is made and whose goals are considered, which in this case corresponds to DEPOSITOR A. We represent DEPOSITOR A's goal of "Making profit from investment" as the goal the experience realizes. The experience corresponds to the OUTCOME and is composed of the ACTION PROFILE RETAIN-RETAIN (a complex event composed of the actions DEPOSITOR A RETAINS and DEPOSITOR B RETAINS) that triggers the event "Bank sells the project to another bank after it matures", which in turn triggers the gain event "Bank pays out more than the amount invested". This gain event positively impacts DEPOSITOR A's goal of "Making profit from investment".

In order to represent how DEPOSITOR A ascribes value to the experience, we apply the Experience Valuation pattern. We connect a VALUATION ASSESSMENT to the value experience named "Outcome Make profit by retaining deposit" (which corresponds to the OUTCOME) and to DEPOSITOR A, who plays the roles of value assessor and value subject simultaneously. The value ascribed corresponds to DEPOSITOR A's UTILITY VALUE for this OUTCOME. Figure 10 depicts the application of the patterns just described.

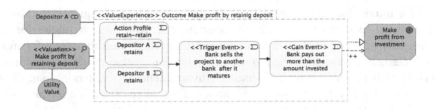

Fig. 10. Application of the Value Experience and Experience Valuation Patterns

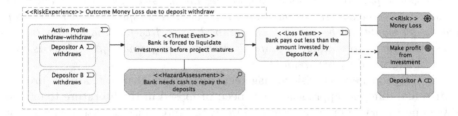

Fig. 11. Application of the Risk Experience Pattern

We illustrate the emergence of risk, by representing the situation in which both DEPOSITOR A and DEPOSITOR B withdraw their deposits before the project matures.

Using the Risk Experience pattern we represent, in Fig. 11, the emergence of the risk of "Money loss", under the perspective of DEPOSITOR A, who is the risk subject. The risk experience of "Outcome Money loss due to deposit withdraw" represents the OUTCOME and is composed of the ACTION PROFILE WITHDRAW-WITHDRAW (a complex event composed of the actions DEPOSITOR A WITHDRAWS and DEPOSITOR B WITHDRAWS) that brings about a situation in which the "Bank needs cash to repay the deposits". As a result, the "Bank is forced to liquidate investments before project matures", which stands for a threat event that triggers the loss event "Bank pays out less than the amount invested by Depositor A". This loss event hurts DEPOSITOR A's goal of "Making profit from investment".

7   Final Remarks

We presented an ontological analysis characterizing some basic concepts in game theory, which make clear the emergence of value and risks from game outcomes. We formalized it in OntoUML, aiming at providing an accessible and shareable conceptual model, which may be applied across domains to foster the interoperability and the mutual understanding among modelers.

The model proposed here illustrates a process of *conceptual clarification* that allows for unpacking the relevant domain notions that are frequently hidden in mathematical formulations of domain phenomena. Moreover, it allows for the *ontological grounding* of the variables constituting these mathematical formulations. These are in line with the requirements for conceptual models as discussed in [11]. In that paper, the authors discuss why a mathematical model (e.g., Newton's Second Law) is not a conceptual model. They argue that in a formula such as F = M * A *"the modeling constructs are operators and variables. The latter do not denote concepts, but rather actual values of physical quantities. Of course we need a mental model to make sense of such relationship, but such mental model is just presupposed, and not made explicit. In contrast, a conceptual model of the phenomenon described by Newton's second law would not represent the values of such physical quantities without representing the physical quantities themselves, which would be considered as qualities...But just having qualities in the conceptual model would not be enough: we cannot have a free-floating quality (say, a mass) without representing its bearer, which is a physical object...This is what we call the grounding requirement"*.

The relation between risk management and game theory has been broadly studied and different approaches have been proposed in the literature to explain how game theory approaches can be integrated into classical risk management [4,8,30,31]. Differently from other approaches, our proposal explores the deep connections between the concepts of value and risk to analyse the impact (either positive or negative) of game outcomes on player's welfare.

As future work, we plan to validate our ontology by means of systematic comparisons with other theories and formalizations of risk and value in the context of game theoretical approaches. We also plan to introduce a mechanism to help rational agents weight value and risks against each other to find an equilibrium when deciding whether to engage in a certain strategy.

Acknowledgments. CAPES (PhD grant 88881.173022/2018-01) and NeXON project (UNIBZ).

References

1. Almeida, J.P.A., Falbo, R.A., Guizzardi, G.: Events as entities in ontology-driven conceptual modeling. In: Laender, A.H.F., Pernici, B., Lim, E.-P., de Oliveira, J.P.M. (eds.) ER 2019. LNCS, vol. 11788, pp. 469–483. Springer, Cham (2019). https://doi.org/10.1007/978-3-030-33223-5_39
2. Botti Benevides, A., Bourguet, J.R., Guizzardi, G., Peñaloza, R., Almeida, J.P.A.: Representing a reference foundational ontology of events in SROIQ. Appl. Ontol. **14**(3), 293–334 (2019)
3. Castelfranchi, C.: Commitments: from individual intentions to groups and organizations. In: 1st International Conference on Multi-Agent Systems (ICMAS), vol. 95, pp. 41–48 (1995)
4. Cox Jr., L.A.: Game theory and risk analysis. Risk Anal. Int. J. **29**(8), 1062–1068 (2009)
5. Diamond, D.W., Dybvig, P.H.: Bank runs, deposit insurance, and liquidity. J. Polit. Econ. **91**(3), 401–419 (1983)
6. Easley, D., Kleinberg, J., et al.: Networks, crowds, and markets: reasoning about a highly connected world. Significance **9**, 43–44 (2012)
7. Fonseca, C.M., Porello, D., Guizzardi, G., Almeida, J.P.A., Guarino, N.: Relations in ontology-driven conceptual modeling. In: Laender, A.H.F., Pernici, B., Lim, E.-P., de Oliveira, J.P.M. (eds.) ER 2019. LNCS, vol. 11788, pp. 28–42. Springer, Cham (2019). https://doi.org/10.1007/978-3-030-33223-5_4
8. GhavamiFar, F., Taghiyareh, F., Razavi, M.: Game theory as a tool for converting risk to opportunity (2007)
9. Guarino, N.: Formal ontology in information systems. In: Proceedings of the First International Conference (FOIS 1998), Trento, Italy, 6–8 June, vol. 46. IOS Press (1998)
10. Guarino, N.: On the semantics of ongoing and future occurrence identifiers. In: Mayr, H.C., Guizzardi, G., Ma, H., Pastor, O. (eds.) ER 2017. LNCS, vol. 10650, pp. 477–490. Springer, Cham (2017). https://doi.org/10.1007/978-3-319-69904-2_36
11. Guarino, N., Guizzardi, G., Mylopoulos, J.: On the philosophical foundations of conceptual models. Inf. Model. Knowl. Bases **XXXI**(321), 1 (2020)
12. Guizzardi, G.: Ontological foundations for structural conceptual models. Telematica Instituut/CTIT (2005)
13. Guizzardi, G., Falbo, R.A., Guizzardi, R.S.S.: Grounding software domain ontologies in the Unified Foundational Ontology (UFO). In: 11th Ibero-American Conference on Software Engineering (CIbSE), pp. 127–140 (2008)
14. Guizzardi, G., Fonseca, C.M., Benevides, A.B., Almeida, J.P.A., Porello, D., Sales, T.P.: Endurant types in ontology-driven conceptual modeling: towards OntoUML 2.0. In: Trujillo, J.C., et al. (eds.) ER 2018. LNCS, vol. 11157, pp. 136–150. Springer, Cham (2018). https://doi.org/10.1007/978-3-030-00847-5_12
15. Guizzardi, G., Wagner, G., Almeida, J.P.A., Guizzardi, R.S.S.: Towards ontological foundations for conceptual modeling: the Unified Foundational Ontology (UFO) story. Appl. Ontol. **10**(3–4), 259–271 (2015)
16. Guizzardi, G., Wagner, G., de Almeida Falbo, R., Guizzardi, R.S.S., Almeida, J.P.A.: Towards ontological foundations for the conceptual modeling of events. In: Ng, W., Storey, V.C., Trujillo, J.C. (eds.) ER 2013. LNCS, vol. 8217, pp. 327–341. Springer, Heidelberg (2013). https://doi.org/10.1007/978-3-642-41924-9_27

17. Guizzardi, R.S.S., Guizzardi, G.: Ontology-based transformation framework from TROPOS to AORML. In: Social Modeling for Requirements Engineering, pp. 547–570. The MIT Press (2010)
18. ISO: Risk Management - Vocabulary. Standard, International Organization for Standardization (2018)
19. ISO: Risk Management - Guidelines. Standard, International Organization for Standardization (2009)
20. Jarzabkowski, P., Wilson, D.C.: Actionable strategy knowledge: a practice perspective. Eur. Manag. J. **24**(5), 348–367 (2006)
21. Kambil, A., Ginsberg, A., Bloch, M.: Re-inventing value propositions. Information Systems Working Papers Series (1996)
22. Lanning, M.J., Michaels, E.G.: A business is a value delivery system. McKinsey Staff Paper **41**(July) (1988)
23. McKelvey, R.D., McLennan, A.M., Turocy, T.L.: Gambit: software tools for game theory (2006)
24. Myerson, R.: Game Theory: Analysis of Conflict. Press, Cambridge (1991)
25. Osborne, M.J., Rubinstein, A.: A Course in Game Theory. MIT Press, Cambridge (1994)
26. Payolo, A.R.: A toilet paper run is like a bank run. The economic fixes are about the same. The Conversation, March 2020. https://theconversation.com/a-toilet-paper-run-is-like-a-bank-run-the-economic-fixes-are-about-the-same-133065
27. Peterson, M.: An Introduction to Decision Theory. Cambridge University Press, Cambridge (2017)
28. Porello, D., Guizzardi, G.: Towards an ontological modelling of preference relations. In: Ghidini, C., Magnini, B., Passerini, A., Traverso, P. (eds.) AI*IA 2018. LNCS (LNAI), vol. 11298, pp. 152–165. Springer, Cham (2018). https://doi.org/10.1007/978-3-030-03840-3_12
29. Porello, D., Guizzardi, G., Sales, T.P., Amaral, G.: A core ontology for economic exchanges. In: Dobbie, G., Frank, U., Kappel, G., Liddle, S.W., Mayr, H.C. (eds.) ER 2020. LNCS, vol. 12400, pp. 364–374. Springer, Cham (2020). https://doi.org/10.1007/978-3-030-62522-1_27
30. Rajbhandari, L., Snekkenes, E.A.: Mapping between classical risk management and game theoretical approaches. In: De Decker, B., Lapon, J., Naessens, V., Uhl, A. (eds.) CMS 2011. LNCS, vol. 7025, pp. 147–154. Springer, Heidelberg (2011). https://doi.org/10.1007/978-3-642-24712-5_12
31. Rass, S.: On game-theoretic risk management (part three)-modeling and applications. arXiv preprint arXiv:1711.00708 (2017)
32. Sales, T.P., Almeida, J.P.A., Santini, S., Baião, F., Guizzardi, G.: Ontological analysis and redesign of risk modeling in ArchiMate. In: 2018 IEEE 22nd International Enterprise Distributed Object Computing Conference (EDOC), pp. 154–163. IEEE (2018)
33. Sales, T.P., Baião, F., Guizzardi, G., Almeida, J.P.A., Guarino, N., Mylopoulos, J.: The common ontology of value and risk. In: Trujillo, J.C., et al. (eds.) ER 2018. LNCS, vol. 11157, pp. 121–135. Springer, Cham (2018). https://doi.org/10.1007/978-3-030-00847-5_11
34. Sales, T.P., Guarino, N., Guizzardi, G., Mylopoulos, J.: An ontological analysis of value propositions. In: 21st IEEE International Enterprise Distributed Object Computing Conference (EDOC), pp. 184–193. IEEE (2017)

35. Sales, T.P., Roelens, B., Poels, G., Guizzardi, G., Guarino, N., Mylopoulos, J.: A pattern language for value modeling in ArchiMate. In: Giorgini, P., Weber, B. (eds.) CAiSE 2019. LNCS, vol. 11483, pp. 230–245. Springer, Cham (2019). https://doi. org/10.1007/978-3-030-21290-2_15
36. Savani, R., von Stengel, B.: Game theory explorer: software for the applied game theorist. Comput. Manag. Sci. **12**(1), 5–33 (2015)
37. Shoham, Y., Leyton-Brown, K.: Multiagent Systems: Algorithmic, Game-Theoretic, and Logical Foundations. Cambridge University Press, Cambridge (2008)
38. Sun, S., Sun, N.: The fundamentals of non-cooperative games. In: Sun, S., Sun, N. (eds.) Management Game Theory, pp. 1–21. Springer, Singapore (2018). https:// doi.org/10.1007/978-981-13-1062-1_1
39. The Open Group: ArchiMate 3.0.1 Specification. Standard C179 (2017)
40. Verdonck, M., Gailly, F.: Insights on the use and application of ontology and conceptual modeling languages in ontology-driven conceptual modeling. In: Comyn-Wattiau, I., Tanaka, K., Song, I.-Y., Yamamoto, S., Saeki, M. (eds.) ER 2016. LNCS, vol. 9974, pp. 83–97. Springer, Cham (2016). https://doi.org/10.1007/978-3-319-46397-1_7
41. Watson, J.: Strategy: an Introduction to Game Theory, vol. 139. WW Norton New York (2002)
42. Wooldridge, M.: An Introduction to Multiagent Systems. Wiley, Hoboken (2009)

Identifying Scenarios to Guide Transformations from DEMO to BPMN

Marné De Vries[1]([✉]) [iD] and Dominik Bork[2] [iD]

[1] Department of Industrial and Systems Engineering,
University of Pretoria, Pretoria, South Africa
Marne.DeVries@up.ac.za
[2] Business Informatics Group, TU Wien, Vienna, Austria
dominik.bork@tuwien.ac.at

Abstract. The heterogeneity in enterprise design stakeholders and models generally demands for consistent and efficient transformations of enterprise design knowledge between different conceptual modelling languages. A systematic process and precise model transformation specifications are a prerequisite for realizing such transformations. The Design and Engineering Methodology for Organizations (DEMO) approach represents the organization design of an enterprise in four linguistically based, semantically sound aspect models. The Business Process Model and Notation (BPMN) on the other hand enables more flexibility in creating models and benefits from wide adoption in industry, the execution of processes e.g., by simulations, and the availability of proper tooling. A transformation of DEMO models into BPMN models is thus desirable to avail of both, the semantic sound foundation of DEMO and the wide adoption and execution possibilities of BPMN. Previous research already developed some principles and practices for transforming DEMO models into BPMN models, based on DEMOSL 3.7. This study focuses on the latest DEMO language specification, DEMOSL 4.5, since we believe that more clarity is required to specify consistent, well-motivated transformation specifications. We present a list of main requirements for developing transformation specifications to transform concepts represented in a Coordination Structure Diagram and Process Structure Diagram of DEMO into corresponding concepts in a BPMN collaboration diagram. The article makes three contributions: (1) Generic requirements for developing DEMO-to-BPMN transformation specifications; (2) Nine transformation scenarios that are validated by multiple demonstration cases; and (3) A comprehensive college case that demonstrates all transformation scenarios.

Keywords: DEMO · BPMN · Model transformation · Organization design

1 Introduction

We live in an era where enterprises increasingly depend on digital technologies to enhance the speed of product development/service provision as well as communication with customers and collaboration within ecosystems. Within this context, agile

© Springer Nature Switzerland AG 2021
D. Aveiro et al. (Eds.): EEWC 2020, LNBIP 411, pp. 92–110, 2021.
https://doi.org/10.1007/978-3-030-74196-9_6

(re-)engineering of an enterprise, involving heterogeneous stakeholders, there is a need to represent an enterprise using different modelling languages. The problem is that these representations (i.e., conceptual models) are often based on different meta-models that need to be kept consistent [1]. Horizontal consistency refers to consistency between models at the same development phase, such as the analysis phase, whereas vertical consistency refers to consistency between models across different phases [2]. A recent systematic literature review (SLR) highlighted that the majority of studies focus on vertical integration and raised the need to also develop approaches that address horizontal consistency amongst models [3]. Another SLR [4] on existing tools that support horizontal transformations, indicate that only 7 out of 40 prominent modelling approaches support multi-view artefact creation, whereas only 6 of these 7, provide semi-automated support with for instance "wizards in the modelling environment".

Enterprises are organized complexities, i.e., too organized for applying statistics to understand their behavior and too complex to being studied by analytical methods [5]. Different stakeholders use different cognitive perspectives to understand and represent the enterprise [6]. Some stakeholders prefer structural thinking (demonstrated in DEMO's Coordination Structure Diagram (CSD) [5]), whereas others prefer flow thinking (demonstrated in BPMN [7]). Table 1 compares DEMO models to BPMN models in terms of their focus, strengths and weaknesses.

Table 1. Comparing focus, strenghs and weaknesses of DEMO versus BPMN

DEMO focus	BPMN focus
Often used *top-down* to represent the ideal design of a new enterprise [8]	Often used for *bottom-up* analysis of implemented processes as a starting point for re-design [7]
Represent *no implementation* [5]	Represent *implementation* [7]
Used to *reduce complexity*, extracting the essence of enterprise operation [5]	Used to *elucidate complexity*, since the models represent implementation
DEMO strengths	**BPMN weaknesses**
Comprehensive representation of human collaboration during enterprise operation, since collaboration is based on the PSI theory, i.e., acknowledging a *complete* transaction pattern that exists between two actor roles [5]	The style and practice associated with BPMN modelling do not acknowledge the existence of the PSI theory [9] and hence models may be *incomplete* in representing the complete transaction pattern
Provides a means for *clear scoping*, since CSDs use composite transactors to indicate where further elaboration of the model is needed [5]	Scope of a BPMN diagram is *unclear*, unless specified in a narrative that is associated with the diagram [7]
DEMO weaknesses	**BPMN strengths**
Although management appreciates the compact representation of enterprise operations, shown in the CSD, experienced modelers are needed. *Additional methods* are required to facilitate collaborative developments with relevant stakeholders [10]	Due to their descriptive and expressive abilities, BPMN models are *widely adopted* [11]

Based on their different foci, strengths and weaknesses we believe that enterprises will benefit by using both modelling languages, but also ensure horizontal consistency between the DEMO and BPMN models. DEMO models focus on intellectual manageability and reduction of complexity, representing business processes in a compact manner by focusing on a company's operations [5]. BPMN, on the other hand, allows for detailed descriptions of business processes, adding implementation logic that facilitates process execution [7]. The ontological model of the enterprise, as provided by DEMO, is needed, since it exhibits four qualities: *comprehensiveness, coherency, consistency* and *conciseness* [5]. Yet, conceptual models that encounter for technological issues are also needed, since they allow for processing, such as simulation and workflow execution, as demonstrated by BPMN-based industrial tools. Due to their descriptive and expressive abilities, BPMN models are widely adopted [11]. Although BPMN models allow for flexibility to express knowledge about a process, modelers who are not properly guided are likely to produce ambiguous, inconsistent and incomplete models [12].

Researchers have already identified the need for transforming DEMO models into other models for various reasons, e.g.,: (1) transforming concepts from DEMO to concepts contained within the ArchiMate business layer meta-model for the purpose of modelling the essential aspects of an enterprise first in DEMO, followed by a transformation into technological realization and implementation models [12]; (2) transforming the DEMO process models into Petri net models to facilitate simulation [12, 13]; (3) transforming DEMO action models into BPMN models [14, 15]; and (4) transforming DEMO organization construction diagrams into BPMN collaboration diagrams to semi-automate DEMO-to-BPMN transformations [16]. As indicated in Fig. 1, the ADOxx-based tool, called DMT [17] (downloadable from: https://austria.omilab.org/psm/con tent/demo) already facilitates transformation from an existing organization structure diagram (OCD) to a BPMN collaboration diagram. When a modeler selects a transaction kind (in this example T01) for transformation, the transformation script identifies the *student* as the initiating actor role and the *supervisor allocator* as the executing actor role. The transformed BPMN diagram, thus includes a *student pool* and a *supervisor allocator pool.*

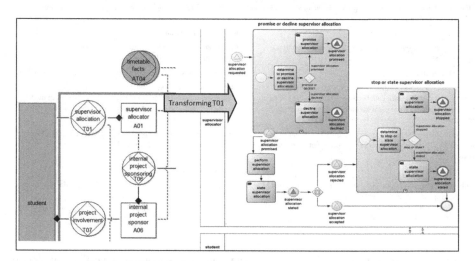

Fig. 1. DEMO-to-BPMN transformation, adapted from [16]

The transformation specifications that were used to generate the BPMN diagram shown in Fig. 1, were based on the *standard transaction pattern*, ensuring that the model explicitly incorporates coordination acts/facts that form part of the standard pattern, i.e. including: request, promise, decline, state, accept, and reject acts/facts. Without proper guidance in terms of the standard pattern, BPMN models tend to be incomplete [18]. As an example, an unguided modeler may omit some of the acts (that form part of the standard pattern) when designing enterprise operations, e.g. omitting the *promise* and *decline* acts. An essential part of coordination will not be supported when the model is further refined for implementation. With no explicit *promise* or *decline* built into the design of the process, an instance of this process implies that a student, requesting supervisor allocation, receives no feedback in terms of the status. Was the request valid? Was the request declined?

This paper extends the DEMO model transformation research stream with the objective of using a DEMO Coordination Structure Diagram (CSD), validated with a Transactor Product Table (TPT), and the transaction-interaction logic between transaction kinds, represented on the Process Structure Diagram (PSD) to derive consistent BPMN collaboration diagrams. Using Design Science Research (DSR), we indicate in Sect. 3, that a set of requirements need to be identified prior to the development of valid transformation specifications. Previous work already demonstrated the possibility of using a tool to transform some DEMOSL 3.7 concepts to BPMN 2.0 concepts [19]. The previous transformations were based on incomplete transformation specifications, including only four transformation scenarios. The objective of this article is thus to elicit *main requirements for a comprehensive model transformation specification*, and, consequently, to define a *comprehensive set of nine DEMO to BPMN transformation scenarios*. We present these transformation scenarios and validate them in multiple demonstration cases.

The article is structured as follows. In Sect. 2, we provide background on the DEMO aspect models, motivating the need to develop a comprehensive set of TK-BPMN transformation scenarios. Section 3 presents Design Science Research (DSR) as an appropriate research method, suggesting that a comprehensive demonstration case is developed (presented in Sect. 4) as well as *main requirements* for transformation (presented in Sect. 5). We present our main contribution, *nine transformation scenarios* and their validation in Sect. 6, concluding with suggestions for future research in Sect. 7.

2 Background Theory

Modelling an enterprise, is not a trivial task. The emerging discipline of enterprise engineering (EE), acknowledges the existence of several enterprise design domains [20]. De Vries [21] suggests that four main enterprise design domains exist: (1) Organization; (2) ICT; (3) Infrastructure (including facilities); and (4) Human skills & know-how. The organization design domain is a social system that includes human beings as system elements. The human beings form relationships due to their interactions and communications when they perform production acts [5]. In this article we focus primarily on the organization design domain and its representation using DEMO aspect models and BPMN models.

In representing the organization design domain, the ontological model of an enterprise is based on the *performance in social interaction* (PSI) theory that provides a universal building block of enterprise organization [5]. The PSI theory identified transaction patterns, each involving two actor roles, a production act (and fact), and multiple coordination acts (and facts) that are performed in a particular sequence. In terms of the identified pattern, Dietz and Mulder [5] indicated that a *complete* transaction pattern exists to represent the possible coordination acts (and facts) that describe interactions between two actor roles for a particular transaction. Most of the transactions follow the *basic* transaction pattern (i.e., the happy flow), where two actor roles (i.e., *initiator* and *executor*) are in consent to each other's intentions when following four coordination acts in sequence, namely *request*, *promise*, *declare*, and *accept*. Yet, when the actor roles do not comply with each other's intentions, they follow a *standard* transaction pattern, which allows for a *decline act* (instead of a promise act) and a *reject act* (instead of an accept act). It is possible that actor roles need to revoke some of the coordination acts that were already performed. Once a *request act* was performed, the initiator may have second thoughts, requesting to revoke the initial *request act*. Likewise, the *promise* act, *declare* act and *accept* act may be revoked. The *complete* transaction pattern extends the *standard* pattern with four revocation patterns [5].

Even though every transaction follows a path through a *complete* transaction pattern, transactions differ in the kind of product they produce. A transaction is thus an instance of a transaction kind (TK) executed by an actor role (AR), to produce a product kind (PK). The three concepts represent two different facets of the organization domain. Whereas TKs and ARs represent the coordination world, the PKs represent the production world.

Since our main objective is to transform DEMO concepts into BPMN concepts we need to relate the conceptual schema and its corresponding symbolic formalism of DEMO to that of BPMN. The conceptual schema of DEMO indicates that any enterprise can be represented by four aspect models that include a Process Model (PM), Action Model (AM), Cooperation Model (CM), and Fact Model (FM). Each model is represented by different diagram types and tables.

Since a BPMN collaboration diagram (CD) focuses on coordinating activities performed by actors or departments [7], it should be possible to relate the concepts included in the CD to concepts and logic included in aspect models that focus on coordination. As illustrated in Fig. 2 (left-hand side), the CM, PM and AM focus on coordination. According to [5], the AM is the most detailed model of the four aspect models. If the main objective is to perform a comprehensive transformation of coordination logic from DEMO to BPMN, we need to use the AM to generate a BPMN CD. Yet, from a management perspective the CM is more useful, since it provides bird's-eye view of coordination structures [5, 22]. Thus, from a pragmatic viewpoint, we want to extract coordination logic from appropriate aspect models that are already used in industry. We envision a tool that would enable semi-automatic transformation from transaction kinds that feature on a validated CM to a BPMN CD. Starting with the well-validated CM, and a means to indicate how events in one TK restrict transaction progress for other TKs (usually depicted on the PM), a modeler should select a single TK that needs to be transformed into a corresponding BPMN CD. The diagrams/tables that represent the CM and PM are therefore the most relevant for the envisioned transformations. In this article we demonstrate how we intend to transform knowledge from the CM, represented by the Coordination Structure Diagram (CSD) and the Transactor Product Table (TPT), as well as the PM, represented by the Process Structure Diagram (PSD).

We exclude the action model (AM) from our transformation scope, conceding that the transformed BPMN CD's will exclude detailed action rules that guide the actor roles.

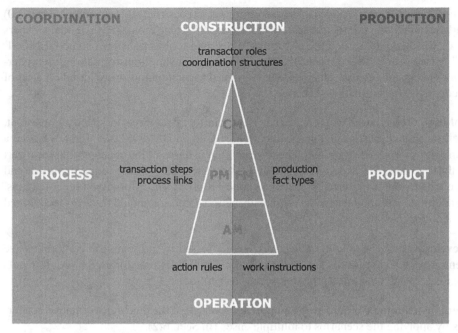

Fig. 2. Aspect models from [5]

Again, from a pragmatic viewpoint, the detail of the AM may simply not be available. Yet, in Sect. 7 we also suggest that our transformation specifications need to allow for extensions points to incorporate detailed action rules. We also exclude the fact model (FM) from our transformation, since it represents the state space and the transition space of an organization's *production world* [5]. Instead, this article focuses primarily on the transformation space of the *coordination world*.

Unlike most common modelling languages, DEMO comes with a built-in quality of completeness with respect to the applied *patterns*. DEMO thereby guides the modeler toward the creation of complete models that cover all coordination acts and facts. Even though DEMO comes with a Process Model (discussed in Sect. 4.1), the DEMO Process Model is not as widely used as the Cooperation Model [22]. In our approach, we aim at amplifying the respective and complementary strengths of both modelling languages, DEMO and BPMN, i.e., the completeness and sound foundation of DEMO models with the wide-adoption and execution possibilities of BPMN process models.

3   Research Method

This study applies the *five phases* of the Design Science Research Methodology [23] as follows:

Problem: Although BPMN is a well-adopted modelling standard applied by industry to model business processes, additional guidance is required to create consistent and executable BPMN models [24]. Mraz *et al.* [25] and Rodrigues [15] have already developed some principles and practices for transforming OCD constructs (based on DEMOSL 3.0) and the underlying transaction patterns for *transaction kinds* into BPMN models. Others [19] already demonstrated the possibility of using a tool to transform some DEMOSL 3.7 concepts to BPMN 2.0 concepts, but a sub-set of invalid transformations are generated when using the tool, since the transformation specifications were based on a set of incomplete transformation scenarios.

Solution Objectives: We believe that more clarity is required to specify consistent, well-motivated transformation specifications, based on DEMOSL 4.5. First, we need a demonstration case that is comprehensive enough in terms of the concepts that form part of the CSD and PSD, as defined in DEMOSL 4.5. Then, a set of main requirements should be elicited, prior to the development of detailed TK-BPMN transformation specifications. In addition, a comprehensive set of transformation scenarios should be developed, based on a comprehensive case.

Development: The solution objectives are addressed by presenting a comprehensive demonstration case (in Sect. 4), a list of main TK-BPMN transformation requirements (in Sect. 5) and nine transformation scenarios (in Sect. 6.1).

Demonstration: We validate the comprehensiveness of the nine transformation scenarios by applying the scenarios to multiple cases (in Sect. 6.2).

4   College Demonstration Case

In order to explain the DEMO language, we start with the instance level, i.e., a model of a fictitious enterprise where the scope-of-interest is *some operations at a college*. We introduce two of DEMO's four aspect models (PM and CM) and the symbolic formalism that is used to express the essence of *some operations at a college*. Our objective is to highlight concepts that will be used to distinguish between nine transformation scenarios that are presented later in Sect. 6.1.

4.1   The Process Model

The Process Model is the ontological model of the state space and the transition space of its coordination world and is depicted by two diagrams: (1) the Transaction Pattern Diagram (TPD), based on the *complete* transaction pattern, and (2) the Process Structure Diagram (PSD) [5]. The same pattern may apply to different *kinds of transactions*. Each *transaction* is thus an instance of a particular *transaction kind (TK)*, and the transaction produces a *product* that is an instance of a *product kind (PK)*. As an example from Fig. 3, the TK 06 (named *internal project sponsoring*) may produce PK06 of which the name is indicated in Table 2 (i.e. *the internal sponsorship of [project] is done*). The PK incorporates variables (indicated in square brackets) as placeholders for entities. Thus, for PK06, [project] is a placeholder that is used to differentiate between projects that are created from different instances of TK06.

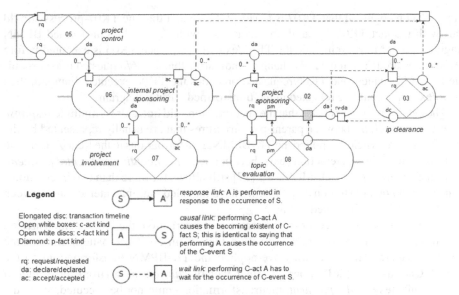

Fig. 3. The PSD indicates parent-part structures

When we consider an enterprise, e.g., our *fictitious college* that offers a project-based course to students, the enterprise may be responsible for various different TKs associated with this project-based course offering. For each of the TKs, it is possible to identify the *initiator* and *executor* that are coordinating their actions to realize a particular PK for the particular TK. Yet, the TKs are not detached from one another. The *process structure diagram* (PSD) is useful to delineate transitions in the coordination world, e.g., indicating how TK06 (e.g., *internal project sponsoring* is *declared*) has a response (indicated with a *response link*) on the transition of TK07 (i.e., zero-to-many instances of *project involvement* is *requested*). Also, the *accept* act of T06 (i.e., of *internal project sponsoring*) has to wait (indicated with a *wait link*) for the occurrence of zero-to-many *accept facts* from T07 (i.e. from *project involvement*).

Figure 3 indicates that a hierarchy exists between TKs, implying that TK07 (i.e. *project involvement*) is a part of the parent TK06 (i.e. *internal project sponsoring*). The PSD *only* includes those coordination acts/facts from the interacting TKs that control progress of the two TKs. Thus, the *promise* act/fact of TK06 (in Fig. 3) is *not shown*, since the *promise* act/fact does not have a transitional effect on TK07.

4.2 Problems Identified in Previous TK-Based Transformations to BPMN

Having discussed the purpose of a PSD, we highlight four problems with previous TK-BPMN transformations and the scenarios that were used in [19]. We have also adapted our demonstration (already reflected in Fig. 3) to explicate these problems.

The *first problem* reflects that the transformation specifications failed to represent the relevant parts of the transaction pattern when the initiating fact from the parent TK changes. With reference to Fig. 3, when a modeler selected TK07 for transformation, the

BPMN CD recognized that TK07 is a part of TK06 and that the TK07-process should start with the fact TK06/declared. In accordance with Fig. 3, the transformed BPMN diagram did not have to include the TK06/execute act, since TK06 is executed before TK06 is declared. Yet, if the PSD changed, indicating that TK06/requested is a prerequisite for TK07/request and TK06/requested precedes the TK06/executed diamond, then TK06/execute should be reflected in the transformed BPMN diagram.

The *second problem* reflects that the specifications did not address multiple *response links* and *causal links* between parent-part structures that are usually represented by the PSD. Therefore, when we applied the TK-BPMN transformations to the Rent-A-Car case (of [26]), where three interactions exist between *rental concluding* and *rental payment*, the transformation failed. DEMOSL 4.5 [27] still allows for more than two interactions. Hence, for our demonstration case PSD, we have included multiple interactions between TK02 and TK08, as indicated in Fig. 3.

The *third problem* reflects that for parent-part interaction, the initial demonstration case in [19] only incorporated coordination facts from the *basic* pattern and not the *standard* pattern. Therefore, when we applied the TK-BPMN transformations to the Rent-A-Car case (of [26]), where a *reject* fact of *car returning* (from the *standard* pattern) initiates *penalty payment*, the transformation could not be executed, since the modeler could not select a *reject* fact from the list of interaction acts/facts. Our PSD (see Fig. 3) now includes a *decline* fact (from the *standard* pattern) for TK03.

The *fourth problem* reflects that for parent-part interaction, the initial demonstration case in [19] did not include interaction (interimpediment structures) between TKs, since interimpediment structures were only included in a more recent DEMO specification [5].

4.3   The Cooperation Model

The *cooperation model* (CM) provides a concise representation of enterprise operations and consists of three representations: (1) a Coordination Structure Diagram (CSD), (2) a Transactor Product Table (TPT), and (3) a Bank Contents Table (BCT). The TPT indicates that every transaction kind (TK) produces a product kind (PK) via an executing actor role (AR). The BCT indicates that every TK produces/uses several independent/dependent facts during the execution of the TK. The CSD also represents TKs, but in a different format. Since every elementary TK can only be executed by one AR, the TK and AR are consolidated into a transactor role (TAR). As an example, a TAR named *supervisor allocator* implies that AR named *supervisor allocator* is the executor of the TK named *supervisor allocation*.

We explain the constructs of the TPT and CSD using a fictitious college as a demonstration case, presented in Table 2 and Fig. 4 respectively.

We now discuss the main constructs of DEMOSL 4.5 [27], as represented in Fig. 4, using **bold** style to indicate the type of construct from DEMOSL 4.5 and *italics* when referring to an instance of the construct.

Since it may not be possible to analyze all the operations at an enterprise, Dietz and Mulder [5] suggest that a Scope of Interest (SoI) is explicitly stated. The SoI for our college demonstration case, is *some operations at a college*, e.g., operations where students register for a course and industry partners become sponsors of projects.

Table 2. TPT for the SoI defined for the college

Transaction kind	Product kind	Executor role
TK01 supervisor allocation	PK01 [supervisor allocation] **is** done	AR01 supervisor allocator
TK02 project sponsoring	PK02 **the** sponsorship **of** [project] **is** done	AR02 project sponsor
TK03 ip clearance	PK03 **the** ip-clearance **for** [project] **is** done	AR03 ip clearer
TK04 module revision	PK04 module revision **for** [year] **is** done	AR04 module revisor
TK05 project control	PK05 project control **for** [year] **is** done	AR05 project controller
TK06 internal project sponsoring	PK06 **the** internal sponsorship **of** [project] **is** done	AR06 internal project sponsor
TK07 project involvement	PK07 [project involvement] **is** done	AR07 project involver
TK08 topic evaluation	PK08 the topic evaluation of [project] **is** done	AR08 topic evaluator
TK09 course registration	PK09 [course registration] **is** done	AR09 course registrar
TK10 course payment	PK10 [course registration] **is** paid	AR10 course payer
TK11 course admission	PK11 [course admission] **is** done	AR11 course admitter
TK12 bursary allocation	PK12 [bursary allocation] **is** done	AR12 bursary allocator
TK13 study-pack sale completion	PK13 [study-pack sale] **is** completed	AR13 study-pack sale completer
TK14 study-pack sale preparation	PK14 [study-pack sale] **is** prepared	AR13 study-pack sale preparer
TK15 study-pack sale payment	PK15 [study-pack sale] **is** paid	AR15 study-pack sale payer
TK16 study-pack sale selection	PK16 [study-pack sale] **is** selected	AR16 study-pack sale selector
TK17 study item buying	PK17 [study item] **is** bought	AR17 study item buyer
TK18 course design	PK18 [course] **is** designed	AR18 course designer
TK19 candidate evaluation	PK19 [candidate evaluation] **is** done	AR19 candidate evaluator
TK20 academic progress evaluation	PK20 [academic progress evaluation] **is** done	AR20 academic progress evaluator
TK21 diploma control	PK21 diploma control **for** [offering period] **is** done	AR21 diploma controller
TK22 diploma allocation	PK22 **the** diploma allocation **of** [student course registration] **is** done	AR22 diploma allocator

One of the key concepts of the CSD is the **elementary transactor role** that resembles a white diamond-disc, combined with a quadrilateral. Three variations of an **elementary transactor role** exist: (1) elementary, (2) self-initiating elementary, and (3) environmental elementary. For each **elementary transactor role**, the TPT (Table 2) displays an associated **transaction kind, product kind** and **executor role.**

The TPT indicates that the **transactor role** *supervisor allocator (TAR01)* consists of an **executor role** *supervisor allocator (AR01)* and **transaction kind** *supervisor allocation (TK01)* to produce a **product kind** *[supervisor allocation] is done (PK01).* Given the SoI, Fig. 4 indicates that one **environmental or external composite transactor role** exists, i.e., the grey-shaded thick-bordered construct, *student (CTAR02).* Multiple **transactor roles** are linked via **initiator links**. As an example, *supervisor allocator (TAR01)* is initiated (via an **initiator link**) by the **environmental or external composite transactor role** *student (CTAR02).* The default cardinality range for an initiation link is one (1..1), as indicated by Dietz and Mulder [5]. It is also possible that a **transactor role** may initiate multiple instances of a **transaction kind**. As an example, in Fig. 4 the *project controller (TAR05)* initiates zero-to-many (0..*) instances of *project sponsoring (TK02).*

The SoI determines whether a **transactor role** is represented as white or gray-shaded. The white **elementary transactor role** *supervisor allocator (TAR01)* indicates that the *supervisor allocator* is inside the SoI. Yet, the grey-shaded **environmental or external**

elementary transactor role *project sponsor (TAR02)* indicates that the project sponsor is outside the SoI. The **self-activating transactor role** *module revisor (TAR04)* indicates that module revision is initiated and executed by the same transactor role, i.e., the *module revisor (TAR04)*.

Since **transactor roles** need to use facts created and stored in transaction banks, an **access link** is used to indicate access to facts. As an example, Fig. 4 indicates that the **transactor role** named *project controller (TAR05)* has reading access via an **access link** to coordination facts and production facts of **transaction kind** *module revision (TK04)*. It is also possible that **transactor roles** within the SoI need to use facts that are created via transaction kinds that are outside the SoI. As an example, Fig. 4 indicates that **transactor roles** within the SoI (with the SoI defined as *some operations at a college*) need to use facts that are created outside the SoI by two **external multiple original transaction kinds**, namely *MTK01* (with *college facts*) and *MTK02* (with *person facts*).

Facts created as a result of one **transaction kind** may delay (impede) actions of another **transactor role**. The **impediment link** is used to indicate this delaying behavior. As an example, Fig. 4 includes an **impediment link** (a dotted arrow-line) indicating that acts/facts produced via the **transaction kind** *project sponsoring (TK02)* impedes the **transactor role** *ip clearer (TAR03)*. The Process Model, discussed in Sect. 4.1 (Fig. 3) could be used to explain the impediment further, i.e. indicating that an instance of *project sponsoring (TK02)* has to reach the *declare* state before an instance if *ip clearance (TK03)* can be requested.

DEMOSL 4.5 [27] allows to consolidate some **elementary actor roles** within a **composite actor role**. As an example, Fig. 4 indicates that the *course owner (CTAR01)* is represented as a **composite actor role**, since the course owner is within the defined SoI, but may be performing multiple TKs that are not shown explicitly in the diagram. Another construct that is new in DEMOSL 4.5 [27] is the **multiple original transaction kind**, shown as a white double-disc-diamond shape, exemplified by MTK05, named *assessment facts*. MTK05 indicates that multiple *assessment facts* are created as original facts within the SoI.

5   Main Requirements for Transformation Specifications

Evaluating previous TK-BPMN transformations, based on DEMOSL 3.7 [19], we abstracted key requirements to guide the TK-BPMN transformation specifications based on DEMOSL 4.5. The transformation specifications should:

1. Ensure that *appropriate* concepts from BPMN are identified that are conceptually closely related to the DEMO counterpart.
2. Render BPMN CDs to *hide complexity* related to the transaction pattern in a *consistent way*.
3. Render BPMN CDs to ensure easy distinction between *parent-part structures*, as is the case with the PSD.
4. Ensure that the transformed models enable efficient/smooth extension toward execution on dedicated simulation platforms/tools.
5. Ensure that the BPMN CDs are comprehensible for a human being, i.e., it should be possible to generate BPMN CDs with reduced clutter/noise.

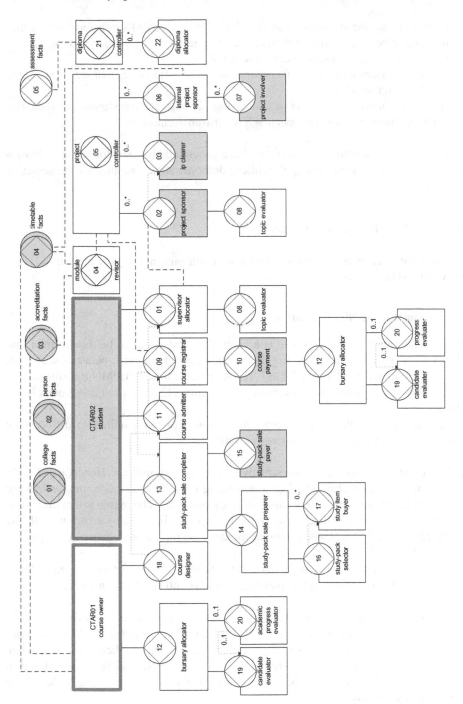

Fig. 4. The CSD for the college case

6. Accommodate the *standard* pattern for the default TK-BPMN transformation. Since interaction between parent-part structures may initiate a revocation pattern, all four revocation patterns should be accommodated.
7. Allow for extension points to incorporate detailed action rules that are stipulated in DEMO's Action Model.
8. Be comprehensive by means of addressing all possible transformation scenarios when an end-user selects a particular TK for transformation.

In terms of the eighth requirement, we have generated nine transformation scenarios that we present and validate using the college demonstration case that was presented in Sect. 4.

6   Transformation Scenarios

The nine transformation scenarios as our main contribution, are presented in Sect. 6.1 and validated in Sect. 6.2.

6.1 Proposition of Nine Scenarios

For each scenario, an end user selects a single TK that needs to be transformed into BPMN CDs. We identified three key differentiators to distinguish between scenarios, indicated as shaded headings in Table 3. A TK selected for TK-BPMN transformation: (1) is initiated by an actor role that is *not a self-initiating*, (2) *is self-initiating*, and (3) *has part(s)*.

In accordance with Table 3, some distinctions are not required to differentiate between scenarios due to the following reasons:

1. TK-BPMN transformations are sensitive for the type of initiator. Hence, we classify the examples extracted from Fig. 4 according to CTAR (includes *composite* actor role and environmental *composite* actor role), and TAR. The reason is that the CTAR will be modelled as a black box. Yet, when a TK is initiated by a parent TAR, the transformed BPMN should represent the detailed interactions between the parent-part TKs.
2. Nested scenarios are possible during a TK-BPMN transformation, e.g., TK10 conforms to Scenario 2, but its part (i.e., TK12) conforms to Scenario 6.

The nine scenarios in Table 3 highlight another interesting fact, namely that TK12 is classified as an instance of *Scenario 6*, but the TK is initiated by different types of initiators, CTAR-initiated, as well as TAR-initiated. The implication is that when a modeler selects TK12 for transformation, both initiators should be modelled, but in different ways. The CTAR will be modelled as a black box, whereas the TAR will be modelled as a white box.

In Fig. 5 we highlight the nine scenarios that are demonstrated in the college case. For simplicity, we have only indicated one or two examples per scenario on Fig. 5,

Table 3. TK-to-BPMN transformation scenarios.

TK init. by 1 vs * ARs	TK is self-init.	TK has part(s) (0, 1 vs *)	Example from Fig. 4 CTAR-initiated	Example from Fig. 4 TAR-initiated
Scenario 1: TK is initiated by 1 AR *AND* has 0 parts				
1	-	0	TK18	TK03, TK07, TK11, TK15, TK16, TK17, TK19, TK20, TK22
Scenario 2: TK is initiated by 1 AR *AND* has 1 part				
1	-	1	TK01, TK9	TK02, TK06, TK10
Scenario 3: TK is initiated by 1 AR *AND* has * parts				
1	-	*	TK13	TK14
Scenario 4: TK is initiated by * ARs *AND* has 0 parts				
*	-	0		TK08
Scenario 5: TK is initiated by * ARs *AND* has 1 part				
*		1		TK12 (when TK20 is removed)
Scenario 6: TK is initiated by * ARs *AND* has * parts				
*	-	*	TK12	TK12
Scenario 7: TK is self-initiating *AND* has 0 parts				
	x	0		TK04
Scenario 8: TK is self-initiating *AND* has 1 part				
	x	1		TK21
Scenario 9: TK is self-initiating *AND* has * parts				
	x	*		TK05

differentiating between CTAR-initiated and TAR-initiated. Table 3 indicates that the college case offers multiple examples for some of the scenarios.

Addressing the four problems discussed in Sect. 4.2, the new transformation specifications should:

1. Determine, based on the modeler's selection of parent-part interactions, the valid *acts* and *facts* that need to be included in the BPMN CD, allowing for different initiation scenarios for the parent TK.
2. Provide for multiple *response links* and *wait links* between parent-part structures, incorporating the sequence of acts and facts as indicated in the *complete* transaction pattern.
3. Provide *interimpediment relationships* that exist between TKs, even if the TKs do not form part of parent-part structures.

6.2 Scenario Validation

We have already created a fictitious college case to demonstrate the comprehensive set of nine transformation scenarios (see Fig. 4) and the sub-scenarios within the main scenarios

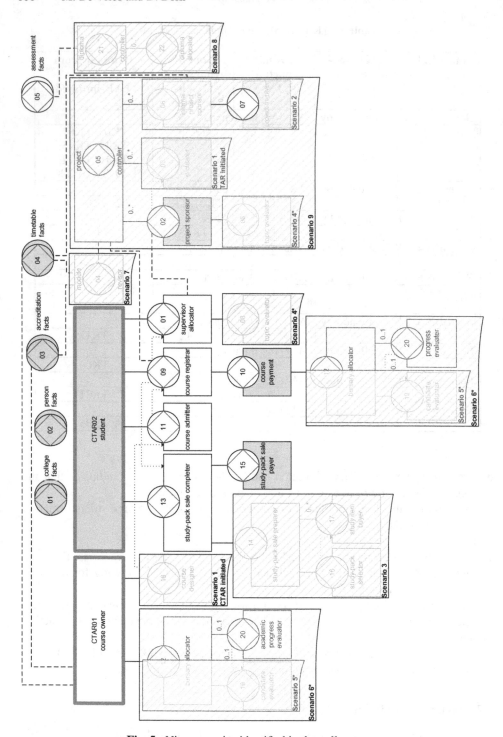

Fig. 5. Nine scenarios identified in the college case

(demonstrated in Fig. 3). For further validation, we used the five cases presented in [5] to validate the nine main transformation scenarios, as indicated in Table 4.

Table 4. Validating the nine scenarios using cases from [5].

Scenario	TK init. by 1 vs * ARs	TK is self-init.	TK has part(s) (0, 1 vs *)	Case Pizzeria	Case RAC	Case Library	Case PoliGon	Case GloLog
1	1	-	0	TK02, TK03, TK04	TK04, TK02, TK03, TK04	-	TK02, TK03, TK04	TK10, TK03, TK17, TK07, TK04, TK05, TK06, TK16, TK08, TK09
2	1	-	1	-	-	TK01, TK03	TK01	TK01
3	1	-	*	TK01	TK01		-	TK02, TK14, TK15
4	*	-	0	-	-	TK02, TK04	-	-
5	*		1	-	-	-	-	-
6	*	-	*	-	-	-	-	-
7		x	0	-	-	-	-	-
8		x	1	-	TK07	TK05	-	TK11, TK12, TK13
9		x	*	-	-	-	-	-

Our validation results in Table 4 indicate that the nine transformation scenarios are comprehensive to address all five cases presented in [5]. In addition, we highlighted four transformation scenarios that are currently under-represented by existing cases, namely scenario's 5, 6, 7 and 9. Since the fictitious college case addresses all nine scenarios, as indicated in Table 3, we believe that the college case could also be used as a valid case for developing the TK-BPMN transformation specifications that should be based on DEMOSL 4.5.

7 Conclusion and Future Research

The DEMO approach represents the organization design of an enterprise in four linguistically based, semantically sound aspect models. The Business Process Model and Notation (BPMN) on the other hand enables more flexibility during modelling and benefits from wide adoption in industry, the execution of processes and the availability of proper tooling. A transformation of DEMO models into BPMN models is thus desirable to enable both, the semantic sound foundation of the DEMO models and the wide adoption and execution possibilities of the de-facto industry standard BPMN.

Using Design Science Research, this paper presented a list of main requirements for developing model transformation specifications to transform concepts represented on the coordination structure diagram (CSD), associated transactor product table (TPT) and the process structure diagram (PSD) of DEMO to concepts of the BPMN Collaboration Diagrams (CDs). The main contribution of this article is the identification and presentation of nine generic transformation scenarios that we validated by applying them to multiple demonstration cases that already exist in literature. We thereby showed not only the comprehensiveness of the transformation scenarios but also the underrepresentation of four scenarios in current DEMO cases.

Since the fictitious college case addresses all nine scenarios, we believe that the college case could be used as a valid case for developing detailed TK-BPMN transformation specifications that are also based on DEMOSL 4.5. With this paper we thus, secondly, contribute a comprehensive DEMO case that the enterprise engineering community can further refine, validate, and use. We believe that the nine scenarios would not only by useful for TK-BPMN transformations, but also for transformations from DEMO coordination-related models to other coordination-related languages.

The eight requirements for TK-BPMN transformation specifications, combined with the nine transformation scenarios, as well as three additional parent-part-interaction requirements, will guide our future work.

References

1. Bork, D., Buchmann, R., Karagiannis, D.: Preserving multi-view consistency in diagrammatic knowledge representation. In: Zhang, S., Wirsing, M., Zhang, Z. (eds.) KSEM. LNCS, vol. 9403, pp. 177–182. Springer, Cham (2015). https://doi.org/10.1007/978-3-319-25159-2_16
2. Broy, M., Freilkas, M., Hermannsdoerfer, M., Merenda, S., Ratiu, D.: Seamless model-based development: from isolated tools to integrated model engineering environments. Proc. IEEE **98**(4), 526–545 (2010)
3. Awadid, A., Nurcan, S.: Consistency requirements in business process modeling: a thorough overview. Softw. Syst. Model. **18**(2), 1097–1115 (2017). https://doi.org/10.1007/s10270-017-0629-2
4. Cicchetti, A., Ciccozzi, F., Pierantonio, A.: Multi-view approaches for software and system modelling: a systematic literature review. Softw. Syst. Model. **18**(6), 3207–3233 (2019). https://doi.org/10.1007/s10270-018-00713-w
5. Dietz, J.L.G., Mulder, H.B.F.: Enterprise Ontology: A Human-Centric Approach to Understanding the Essence of Organisation. Springer, Heidelberg (2020). https://doi.org/10.1007/978-3-030-38854-6
6. Graumann, C.F., Kallmeyer, W.: Perspective and Perspectivation in Discourse. John Benjamins Publishing Company, Amsterdam (2002)
7. Dumas, M., La Rosa, M., Mendling, J., Reijers, H.A.: Fundamentals of Business Process Management, 2nd edn. Springer, Germany (2018)
8. Dietz, J.L.G.: Enterprise Ontology. Springer, Berlin (2006). https://doi.org/10.1007/3-540-33149-2
9. Silver, B.: BPMN Method and Style, Second Edition, with BPMN Implementer's Guide. Cody-Cassidy Press, Aptos (2011)

10. De Vries, M.: DEMO and the story-card method: requirements elicitation for agile software development at scale. In: Buchmann, R.A., Karagiannis, D., Kirikova, M. (eds.) PoEM 2018. LNBIP, vol. 335, pp. 138–153. Springer, Cham (2018). https://doi.org/10.1007/978-3-030-02302-7_9

11. Grigorova, K., Mironov, K.: Comparison of business process modeling standards. Int. J. Eng. Sci. Manag. Res. 1(3), 1–8 (2014). https://doi.org/10.1109/SOLI.2006.328910

12. Van Nuffel, D., Mulder, H., Van Kervel, S.: Enhancing the formal foundations of BPMN by enterprise ontology. In: Albani, A., Barjis, J., Dietz, J.L.G. (eds.) CIAO! 2009, EOMAS 2009. LNBIP, vol. 34, pp. 115–129. Springer, Heidelberg (2009). https://doi.org/10.1007/978-3-642-01915-9_9

13. Barjis, J.: Enterprise modeling and simulation within enterprise engineering. J. Enterp. Transf. 1(3), 185–207 (2011). https://doi.org/10.1080/19488289.2011.601399

14. Figueira, C., Aveiro, D.: A new action rule syntax for DEmo MOdels based automatic workflow procEss geneRation (DEMOBAKER). In: Aveiro, D., Tribolet, J., Gouveia, D. (eds.) EEWC. LNBIP, vol. 174, pp. 46–60. Springer, Cham (2014). https://doi.org/10.1007/978-3-319-06505-2_4

15. Rodrigues, D.P.: Modelling business processes in BPMN inspired by the DEMO principles. Técnico Lisboa (2017)

16. Gray, T., Bork, D., De Vries, M.: A new DEMO modelling tool that facilitates model transformations. In: Nurcan, S., Reinhartz-Berger, I., Soffer, P., Zdravkovic, J. (eds.) BPMDS/EMMSAD -2020. LNBIP, vol. 387, pp. 359–374. Springer, Cham (2020). https://doi.org/10.1007/978-3-030-49418-6_25

17. Bork, D., Buchmann, R.A., Karagiannis, D., Lee, M., Miron, E.-T.: An open platform for modeling method conceptualisation: the OMiLAB digital ecosystem. Commun. AIS 44(32), 673–697 (2019). https://doi.org/10.17705/1CAIS.04432

18. Caetano, A., Assis, A., Tribolet, J.: Using DEMO to analyse the consistency of business process models. In: Moller, C., Chaudhry, S. (eds.) Advances in Enterprise Information Systems II, pp. 133–146. Taylor & Francis Group, London (2012). https://doi.org/10.1201/b12295-17

19. Gray, T., De Vries, M.: Empirical evaluation of a new DEMO modelling tool that facilitates model transformations. In: Dobbie, G., Frank, U., Kappel, G., Liddle, S.W., Mayr, H.C. (eds.) 39th International Conference on Conceptual Modeling (2020, In press)

20. Hoogervorst, J.A.P.: Practicing Enterprise Governance and Enterprise Engineering - Applying the Employee-Centric Theory of Organization. Springer, Heidelberg (2018). https://doi.org/10.1007/978-3-319-73658-7

21. De Vries, M.: Towards consistent demarcation of enterprise design domains. In: de Cesare, S., Frank, U. (eds.) ER 2017. LNCS, vol. 10651, pp. 91–100. Springer, Cham (2017). https://doi.org/10.1007/978-3-319-70625-2_9

22. Décosse, C., Molnar, W.A., Proper, H.A.: What does DEMO do? a qualitative analysis about demo in practice: founders, modellers and beneficiaries. In: Aveiro, D., Tribolet, J., Gouveia, D. (eds.) EEWC. LNBIP, vol. 174, pp. 16–30. Springer, Cham (2014). https://doi.org/10.1007/978-3-319-06505-2_2

23. Peffers, K., Tuunanen, T., Rothenberger, M., Chatterjee, S.: A design science research methodology for information systems research. J. MIS 24(3), 45–77 (2008). https://doi.org/10.2753/MIS0742-1222240302

24. Guizzardi, G., Wagner, G.: Can BPMN be used for making simulation models? In: Barjis, J., Eldabi, T., Gupta, A. (eds.) EOMAS. LNBIP, vol. 88, pp. 100–115. Springer, Heidelberg (2011). https://doi.org/10.1007/978-3-642-24175-8_8

25. Mráz, O., Náplava, P., Pergl, R., Skotnica, M.: Converting DEMO PSI transaction pattern into BPMN: a complete method. In: Aveiro, D., Pergl, R., Guizzardi, G., Almeida, J.P., Magalhães, R., Lekkerkerk, H. (eds.) EEWC. LNBIP, vol. 284, pp. 85–98. Springer, Cham (2017). https://doi.org/10.1007/978-3-319-57955-9_7
26. Perinforma, A.P.C.: The Essence of Organisation. 3rd edn. Sapio (2017). www.sapio.nl
27. Dietz, J.L.G.: The DEMO specification language version 4.5 (2020)

Personal Space and Territorial Behavior – Sharing a Tabletop in Collaborative Enterprise Modeling

Anne Gutschmidt[✉][iD] and Henning D. Richter

Computer Science Department, University of Rostock, Rostock, Germany
{anne.gutschmidt,henning.richter}@uni-rostock.de

Abstract. Tabletops represent a convenient digital workspace that serves the purpose of collaborative enterprise modeling well. The participants of a modeling session must, however, share this workspace. In this paper, we will present a study on personal space and territorial behavior in collaborative modeling sessions of six different teams. We found that areas on the tabletop can be identified that are predominantly occupied by certain individuals. This, however, does not automatically imply the existence of personal territories. In fact, we state that personal territories were less represented than a general territory that seemed to belong to the whole team. The absence of an etiquette, e.g., participants usually did not ask for permission before taking away an item situated near a team colleague, underlines this finding and supports our assumption that the participants feel a collective ownership towards the model.

Keywords: Enterprise modeling · Collaborative modeling · Participatory modeling · Territorial behavior · Personal space · Psychological ownership · Tabletop · Empirical study

1 Introduction

Enterprise Modeling (EM) helps in capturing important information about a company, such as structures, processes and responsibilities. It serves depicting both a company's current state and planned changes [1]. Originally, enterprise models were supposed to be created for companies by (external) modeling experts based on interviews, documents etc. Approaches such as participatory enterprise modeling suggest a creation process where a team of stakeholders from the company is gathered who jointly and actively take part in modeling sessions. The main reasons for directly involving the stakeholders in that way is that model quality and acceptance of the models within the companies would be increased [1–3].

Different tools may be used for collaboratively drawing enterprise models, such as a plastic wall, a whiteboard or a tabletop. Tabletops, also known as multi-touch tables, represent a digital tool where users can work in parallel on

© Springer Nature Switzerland AG 2021
D. Aveiro et al. (Eds.): EEWC 2020, LNBIP 411, pp. 111–130, 2021.
https://doi.org/10.1007/978-3-030-74196-9_7

a shared workspace. In a previous study, tabletops were shown to be equally suited as whiteboards for small enterprise modeling tasks [4,5].

Like other tools, the tabletop must be shared. However, space on the tabletop is particularly limited. Consequently, it might be difficult to ensure that each participant has the same chance of contributing to the overall result. Users might establish personal territories where others must not enter. They might hesitate to let go of items on the tabletop that they have created and convey them to others to continue on working with these items [6–8].

In this paper, we will present a study where we observed six teams of three persons taking part in a collaborative enterprise modeling session. For our investigation, we dealt with the following research questions: 1) Can we identify personal spaces predominantly used by particular individuals, and a group space used by all team members as described in former studies? 2) Do participants develop a feeling of ownership towards the model? 3) Are the ownership feelings connected with an etiquette for the collaboration at the tabletop? The last two questions will give more insight on whether a personal space can eventually be considered as personal territory indicated by feelings of ownership and respecting/guarding objects within that space.

First, we will present the state of research and theoretical background concerning collaborative and participatory enterprise modeling, territorial behavior, personal space, and psychological ownership, especially with regard to tabletops. In Sect. 3, we will describe our research method. Section 4 contains the results of our study, followed by a discussion in Sect. 5.

2 State of Research and Theoretical Background

2.1 Collaborative and Participatory Enterprise Modeling

Enterprise Modeling can be implemented in different ways. One may, for example, scan documents, observe working procedures and interview stakeholders to collect information. This information may then be used by modeling experts to draw the models [1].

Models may also be created in collaborative and participatory modeling sessions. Collaborative modeling is usually considered to be carried out by method experts alone. Its goal is to create complete models in a fast and accurate way [9].

Participatory enterprise modeling (PEM) is an approach where several stakeholder representatives are gathered to jointly create models. This makes it a method that may also be used for knowledge acquisition [9]. In a participatory modeling session, the stakeholders act as domain experts contributing their knowledge and experience. They are usually supported by method experts who help the domain experts with their knowledge about modeling [1,2]. With PEM, one expects the quality of the models and the participants' commitment to the models to be higher because the whole process is characterized by discussion and coming to a joint understanding [2,3]. By letting the stakeholders actively create the models themselves, a feeling of ownership may arise, leading to commitment to the models and possibly planned future changes documented in the models. This connection has already been stated in other application fields, e.g. feelings of ownership and resulting commitment to organizations [10], or higher commitment to products where the consumer was involved in the production process [11].

In enterprise modeling, different interconnected models represent different perspectives on a company. A goal model, which is part of the 4EM method [1], particularly requires a joint view of the goals and problems of a company and their interrelations. 4EM provides a notation that is very easy to understand and use by domain experts, quickly enabling them to independently develop models. So, goal modeling can, for example, be carried out in a collaborative way even without the support of method experts from outside the company.

Besides non-digital tools such as a whiteboard or a plastic wall, one may use a digital tool such as a tabletop. A tabletop is a large touch screen embedded in or placed on top of a table [4]. In case the modeling software allows parallel input, the participants should be able to collaboratively create models without any restrictions [12].

According to [2], modeling sessions should include 4–8 participants, who would be standing around the tabletop. In a participatory approach, the participants may come from different parts of the company and work at different levels of the company's hierarchy. During the modeling session, they have to share the tabletop as a working space, and they have to share the space around the table. Thus, it is important to consider personal space and the possible emergence of territories during collaborative and participatory modeling sessions.

2.2 Personal Space and Territories

Hall (1966) described four major distances in human encounters [13]: 1) We allow intimate distance only to persons who are close to us. The physical closeness can be overwhelming (e.g. smell), sometimes even distort perceptions (e.g. vision). 2) Personal distance is characterized as a protective bubble between the person and their surroundings. You can see the other one very clearly, but you keep a safe distance, at least an arm's length. 3) Social distance is more common in professional interaction. The farther away a person is located, the less information is conveyed, e.g. smell, heat, or intimate details of the face. 4) In a threatening situation, at a public distance of 12 to 25 feet, one decides whether to flee or to attack. At larger distances, the voice is usually used more loudly.

In collaborative and participatory modeling sessions, intruding others' personal space is inevitable when jointly and physically using the same modeling tool, such as a tabletop. People have to stand close to each other to have equal access to the medium. Too much closeness may however induce stress [13]. In that case, we try to evade the situation or at least to move as little as possible [14]. According to Altman (1975), this effect may however be mitigated by furniture such as a table situated between persons, or when people stand or sit side by side. This is usually the case in collaborative modeling.

There has also been research on personal space on tabletops [6,7,15]. Personal space may be seen as a private workspace on the tabletop where individual work is possible. Usually, this space is located close to its owner, contained objects are oriented towards its owner, and the objects are often smaller, probably to increase privacy by making them less visible to other team members [15,16]. Some authors speak of a personal territory [6,17,18] when referring to personal space on a tabletop. Territoriality would however imply a feeling of ownership towards the space [8]. This would be in accordance with [6] who state that others would usually respect personal territories and not take away or manipulate objects without asking the owner for permission.

Consequently, we define personal space as an area on the tabletop that is predominantly used by one individual. It is a prerequisite for a territory which additionally implies a feeling of ownership to what is contained by this area.

As the opposite to personal space, group space is used by all members of a team working with the tabletop [6,15]. It is often located in the center of the screen and objects are typically oriented in a way which allows a comfortable view by all team members. Although group space seems to belong to all team members, the coordination of activities is mostly determined by proximity, i.e. nearness to an area or objects usually implies a responsibility for it. This results in areas that may be dominated by individuals but that still belong to the whole group [6,19]. Following our argumentation from above, group territory would be linked to feeling ownership, only that it would be a collective feeling [20].

As a first step, we want to investigate whether personal space and group space also emerge in collaborative modelling sessions. Consequently our first research question is:

RQ1: Can we identify personal spaces and a group space on the table-top during collaborative modeling?

2.3   Ownership and Etiquette

As mentioned above, personal space is not automatically the same as a personal territory. Perceiving a certain area as personal territory would imply a feeling of ownership. People try to preserve and protect what they see as their own from others [8]. Psychological ownership is defined as a feeling that something or somebody is "MINE" without the necessity to legally possess the target. The target may also be intangible such as an idea [10]. The most desired consequence of psychological ownership is a stronger affective commitment to the model [10, 21,22] which is particularly intended by participatory modeling.

The feeling of ownership emerges when we control the target, when we are particularly familiar with it, and when we invest a part of our selves into the target such as knowledge, ideas, time, labor etc. [10,23]. PEM should make the fulfilment of these three prerequisites possible: By modeling themselves, the participants take control. By discussing, they learn to know others' perspectives and get a more detailed knowledge about the model and its contents. Moreover, the participants invest time, effort and contribute their knowledge during the modeling sessions. When participants work on a part of the tabletop screen, they will probably consider this as their territory. Others will usually respect such a personal territory and ask before taking away or manipulating objects contained in that territory [7,15]. Psychological ownership may emerge on an individual level, but also on a collective level when the three above-mentioned prerequisites are also perceived at a collective level [20]. Thus, participants of a modeling session may develop a collective feeling of ownership towards a model and perceive the area on the tabletop where they work collaboratively as a group territory. Objects may be passed from personal to group territory where the new position and orientation signal the release of the objects for all team members [15].

To sum up, psychological ownership should give hint on personal and group territories. While it is difficult to assess ownership feelings towards the workspace or parts of it, we are able to capture psychological ownership towards the overall model which usually takes a significant part of the workspace. Eventually, the model is the target we are mainly interested in. That is why our second research question is:

RQ2:Do the participants of a collaborative modeling session develop feelings of individual and collective ownership towards the model?

Based on feelings of ownership, it should be possible to observe an etiquette among the participants of a collaborative modeling session. An etiquette would further confirm the presence of real territories. Consequently, our third research question is:

RQ3: Do the participants of a modeling session show an etiquette during their collaboration at the tabletop, e.g. by asking for objects?

3   Method

3.1   Procedure and Setting of the Study

In our study, six teams of three persons had the task of collaboratively creating a goal model for a fictitious company, a pizza delivery service, within thirty minutes. They had to use a tabletop that was equipped with a self-developed modeling software. The editor could be used by several users in parallel. It allows creating rectangles representing goals, problems etc., connecting the components with arrows and adding text descriptions to components and relations. Several instances of touch keyboards and menus could be opened at every location on the screen (a detailed description of the editor is to be found in [12]). The tabletop was a 3M Multi-Touch Display C5567PW (size: 1210×680 mm) embedded in a wooden frame. The three team members stood around the table (see Fig. 1) and were able to move freely as long as they did not cover the view of the camera

 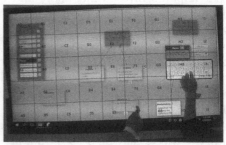

Fig. 1. Re-enacted scene: three persons modeling at the tabletop.

Fig. 2. Ceiling perspective with an over-layed grid (photos from own source).

filming the participants from the front. Another camera recorded the session from the ceiling.

A facilitator was present who helped the participants when questions about modeling and notation emerged. As goal modeling with the 4EM method is very easy and intuitive, participants are usually able to work almost without the support of method exports. In fact, due to the simplicity of the modeling notation, the participants quickly became method experts themselves which is why the setting can be considered as collaborative modeling. However, we were guided by the idea of participatory enterprise modeling in choosing participants who had not modeled before and had a very different domain background. We decided to not let the facilitator give further guidance to ensure that every modeling team was exposed to the same conditions.

3.2   Sample

On the whole, the sample comprised 18 persons, among them eleven women and seven men, who were between 20 and 45 years old ($\mu = 26.9, \sigma = 5.4$). Eleven of the participants were students, where psychology students represented the largest group with seven persons. The other participants worked or studied in various fields such as physics, biology or pedagogy. Except for one participant who had experience in process modeling, the participants did not have any modeling experience. Only in two of the three-person-groups had the participants met before. With the heterogeneous sample of participants who were generally not experienced in modelling, we intended to re-enact a participatory setting.

3.3   Identifying Personal and Group Space

It has to be underlined that space that is frequently used by a person is not necessarily a territory claimed for possession. To identify territories, we have, however, first to observe whether certain areas of the tabletop are used predominantly by individuals or by the whole team. We followed a research method suggested by [6]. We watched the videos of the ceiling camera and positioned a transparent grid over the recorded screen as can be seen in Fig. 2. The grid contained five rows (numbered 1–5) and nine columns (numbered A-I).

Using the software ELAN [24], an observer annotated all time segments where the different team members interacted with the software in each single segment of the grid. When deciding on a grid format, we had to weigh up costs and benefits. On the one hand, the more fine-grained the segmentation of the workspace would be the more detailed but also the more laborious would the annotation of activity be. On the other hand, bigger segments could be connected with information loss. Possibly, we would not be able to sufficiently reconstruct where the individuals' interactions with the tabletop were concentrated and how personal spaces evolved and changed over time.

We finally decided on a 5×9 format, closely corresponding to the screen format of 16:9, where a segment has approximately the size of a component of a goal model. The second question was how to document interaction, as users may work on components that overlap several grid segments at a time. This was especially the case when a component was edited and a touch keyboard was attached to the component enlarging it. We let all segments count that were occupied by a significant part of a component including possible keyboard or context menu. If only an edge or a corner of the component edited was contained, the segment did not count.

For each segment we registered the overall duration of the interaction of each user with the software. We created activity maps for each person following the approach of [6]. Each participant was represented by a color. A segment was completely filled with a certain participant's color when the segment held the global maximum working time for all screen segments.

The other segments were filled with color to an extent that was calculated by working time in that segment in proportion to the maximum working time in a segment among all participants.

In the original method suggested by [6], the maximum working time of an individual was taken as the basis, thus, the whole picture was constructed using independent activity maps of the individuals. Since this may in some cases lead to a distorted view, because it relates only to an individual's activities, we created the activity maps based on the global maximum working time in a segment, taking into consideration all participants.

According to [6,15], both group space and personal space do not remain at a fixed location. Klinkhammer et al. (2018) state, that this territorial flow is caused, amongst other factors, by alternating forth and back between individual and collaborative working mode. That is why we investigated the activity maps in time intervals to observe possible changes over time. Again, we had to weigh up costs and benefits, i.e. the time intervals had to be small enough to still notice interesting development while keeping the effort of evaluation reasonable. Eventually we decided to divide the working time of approximately 30 min into quarters. We additionally created an accumulated activity map showing the extent of interactions for the whole duration.

3.4   Investigating Psychological Ownership and Etiquette

Psychological ownership was assessed with a questionnaire using a scale by [25] where statements had to be rated on a 5-point-scale. We used a German translation that was validated by [26] and adapted the original formulations to the context of a modeling session. A former investigation using the same scale [27] showed a separation of the used items into those measuring individual psychological ownership, and those measuring collective psychological ownership. Example items can be found in Table 1. Thus, for the evaluations in this paper we also considered both kinds of psychological ownership separately. We calculated the respective values by forming the average values of the ratings of the items corresponding to the respective construct. To test whether there exists a significant difference between individual and collective psychological ownership for the 18 participants we conducted a Wilcoxon test which is preferred to a t-test for related samples in the case of absence of normal distribution and small sample sizes.

Table 1. Items that had to be rated in the questionnaire on a 5-point scale to measure individual and collective psychological ownership towards the model, based on the scale by [25].

	Example items
Individual PO	*This is MY model*
	I feel a very high degree of personal ownership for this model
Collective PO	*This is OUR model*
	Most of the team members feel as though they own the model

To get hints on etiquette, an observer analyzed the videos and annotated those points in time where objects changed their "authors" by either being asked for by another person, by being just taken by someone else, or by being handed over by its original author. A second observer re-checked the annotations. In two of the six videos, the transfer of objects was so hard to follow, e.g. through repeated renaming, that we eventually had to exclude these videos to keep the effort of our analysis reasonable. Thus, we analyzed four videos with respect to etiquette.

4   Results

4.1   Analysis of Activity Maps

Due to limitations of space we cannot present all of the activity maps created from the data set. Figure 3, 4 , 5 and 6 show the activity maps of team A of the four time quarters of the session to document the development of personal and group space over time. For each segment in the grid, we have depicted a participant's level of activity with a colored bar. Each participant had a color code, either "Red", "Green" or "White". The size of each bar is calculated by the time the participant was active in that segment in proportion to the maximum duration one of the participants had been active in one of all the segments.

On the whole, we could discover areas that were dominated by single users. These did, however, often show activity from other users, too. Areas showing interactions by the whole team were predominant in our analyses. There is in fact a tendency that segments with interactions of several users become more over time.

One can easily deduce from the activity maps where the persons stood, e.g. in team A, White stood left, Green in the middle and Red at the right while Red sometimes changed position by moving to the short right side or even to the opposite side of the table which can bee seen in the Figs. 3, 4 , 5 and 6. In the middle of the session, person Green and White changed sides, i.e. Green went from the middle position to the left hand side and White changed from the left hand side to the middle position.

We found the teams to work very differently. Some teams remained in fixed positions resulting in more cleanly separated areas as can be seen in Fig. 7 showing the accumulated activity map of team B. In other teams, e.g. team F, the members changed their positions during the session which resulted in extremely mixed segments in the accumulated activity map (see Fig. 8).

The person in the middle often seemed to have easier access to all parts of the tabletop which is probably why activity signs of the middle person spread over the whole table such as to be seen in Fig. 8, with mostly Red in the middle. We observed that a person's size and arm length also played a role. Consequently, it seems that the area dominated by a person is determined by reachability, and that is why we often see that a person mostly works on the space in front of them. Areas less reachable show more balanced activities.

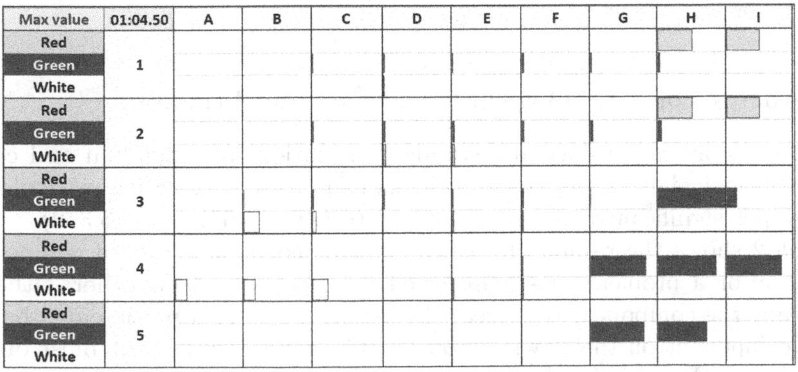

Fig. 3. Activity map for Team A for time interval 1. (Color figure online)

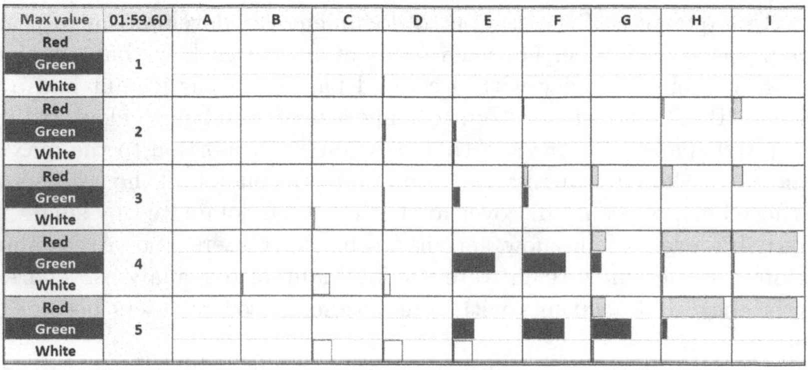

Fig. 4. Activity map for Team A for time interval 2. (Color figure online)

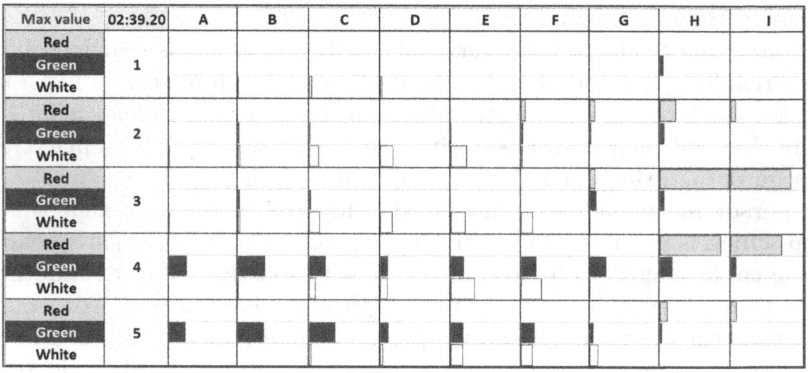

Fig. 5. Activity map for Team A for time interval 3. (Color figure online)

4.2   Analysis of Psychological Ownership and Etiquette

In Fig. 9, the average values and standard deviations of individual and collective psychological ownership are shown. As can be seen, collective psychological ownership is significantly higher (Wilcoxon test: $p < 0.001; z = -3.312$).

Table 2 shows the results of our evaluations concerning how a component, e.g. a goal or a problem, was transferred from one user to another: either by just taking the component (unasked), by asking for it, or if participants handed over a component on their own initiative. The table reveals that most objects were taken without asking beforehand. Almost never did the participants ask for permission.

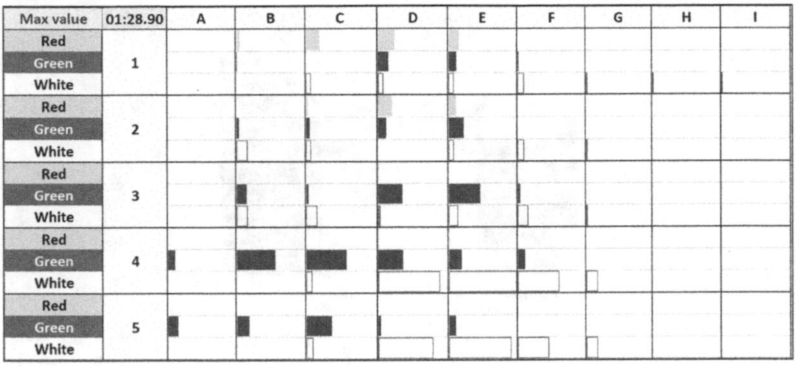

Fig. 6. Activity map for Team A for time interval 4. (Color figure online)

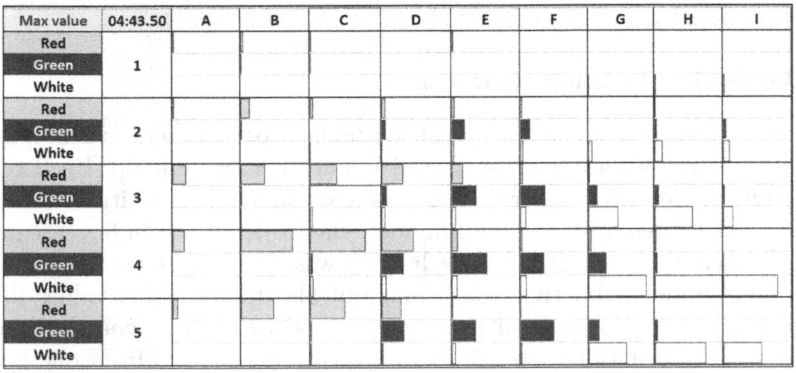

Fig. 7. Accumulated activity map for Team B.

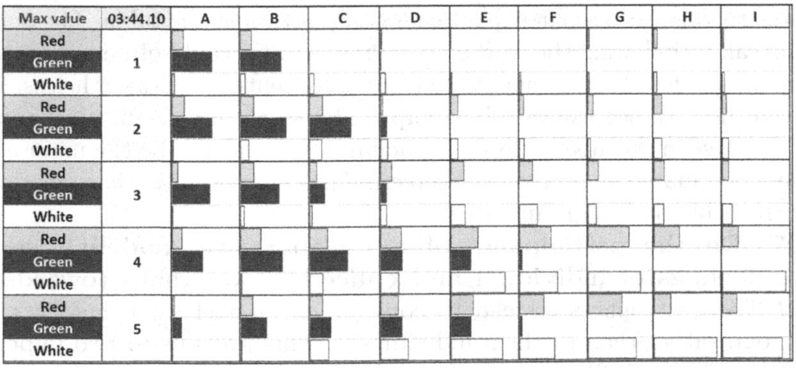

Fig. 8. Accumulated activity map for Team F.

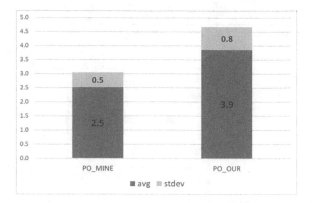

Fig. 9. Individual and collective psychological ownership, average values and standard deviations

5   Discussion

5.1   Answering Research Questions

We analysed six modeling sessions each with three participants, with regard to personal and group space, and territorial behavior on a tabletop. Each session took 30 min where each team created a joint goal model for a fictitious company. To analyze the video recordings, we divided the work surface in 5 × 9 segments and documented how much time each user was active in each segment. We considered accumulated activity duration, but also the duration values in four time intervals. We also assessed the participants' feeling of ownership for the model and their behavior with regard to transferring objects from one user to another. Our analyses were to help us answer the following research questions:

RQ1: Can we identify personal spaces and a group space on the tabletop during collaborative modeling? In fact, we found areas that were dominated by single persons. We could recognize from the activity maps depicting time intervals when a participant changed position at the table. The activity maps also allow following the working progress, i.e. we could often see on which parts of the model the participants were just concentrated. Nevertheless, these areas were usually not exclusively occupied by single users, often other users were also active in the areas. Physical reachability seemed to be the main reason why users dominated an area on the screen. Thus, we conclude that most of the area of the tabletop is a group space.

RQ2: Do the participants of a collaborative modeling session develop feelings of individual and collective ownership towards the model? The participants seemed to consider the model as belonging to the whole group rather than to them individually. This leads us to two important conclusions. First, this finding supports the assumption that the participants did not establish personal territories. Instead they considered the whole workspace as a (common) group territory. Second, this way of working, i.e. working purely

Table 2. Component transfers

Team	Way of transfer	Number
A	Unasked	19
	Asked for	1
	Handed over	5
	Σ	25
B	Unasked	34
	Asked for	0
	Handed over	5
	Σ	39
E	Unasked	41
	Asked for	0
	Handed over	3
	Σ	44
F	Unasked	61
	Asked for	0
	Handed over	8
	Σ	69

collaboratively during the whole time without establishing personal territories, possibly strengthens a feeling of owning the model as a group and might reduce individual claims. Depending on the goal of a modeling project, this should be taken into consideration. Probably, the more participants work as a team, the more the result will be considered as coming from the whole team.

RQ3: Do the participants of a modeling session show an etiquette during their collaboration at the tabletop, e.g. by asking for objects? The findings with regard to an etiquette provide further support for our assumption that there was usually one group territory and no personal territory. It was common to just take an object that was previously edited by someone else without asking. Consequently, we conclude that those objects were not considered to be belonging to another user but to the whole team.

The question is now why we did not find any personal territories. In the following paragraphs, we will provide some possible explanations and draw conclusions for the implementation of PEM sessions.

5.2   Space as a Scarce Resource

One reason why we did not discover personal territories may be a lack of space. Some participants in fact complained that the tabletop was too small to accommodate all their ideas, and that the model would become too big for the screen. Probably, the participants just did not have enough space to establish a private space of their own. According to [6,19] the problem will become even more severe with growing team size. One remedy could be to use a bigger table. However, Ryall et al. (2004) [7] found that bigger tables did not increase productivity. Furthermore, with a bigger tabletop, more parts of the screen become unreachable such that group territories or parts of it cannot be accessed by all team members, and there would be more areas no one would feel responsible for. The second remedy would be to decrease the size of user interface objects [17]. However, making the objects too small would result in some participants being unable to recognize all details of an object from their position.

A third remedy would be to use tangible interface elements. In the modeling editor we used, multiple instances of a menu can be opened to create new components. The menu is approximately three times the size of a component, e.g. a goal. Thus, it takes a lot of space. This space could be saved by offering tangible objects serving for the creation of the different components. Examining territorial behavior of children working with tabletops, Olson et al. (2010) found that tangible interface elements even helped resolving conflicts [28]. It has, however, to be considered that tangible objects cannot be used for every tabletop depending on the technology used.

Klinkhammer et al. (2018) suggest to use additional devices such as tablets which give users additional space to establish their own personal territory [17]. However, a study comparing the use of tabletops combined with personal tablets versus tabletops alone showed that collaboration was closer and awareness of what the partners were doing was higher when working on the tabletop alone [29]. Consequently, when preparing a PEM session we have to think about the effects personal devices might have on collaboration. The degree of collaboration might again have an influence on collective and individual ownership feelings.

5.3   The Task Determines Behavior

The emergence of personal and group territories may also be influenced by the task and its execution as suggested by Klinkhammer et al. (2018) [17]. From the beginning, the teams worked in a collaborative way which could be assigned to the following three collaboration modes as defined by [30]: 1) Participants work on the same problem in the same area, 2) one participant is working and the others are watching in engaged manner, and 3) participants are working on the same problem, but in different areas.

During the modeling session, a facilitator was present but did not actively steer the discussion and modeling activity. In the case of goal modeling, continuously close collaboration is important because all the participants have to agree on the goals of the company. Nevertheless, a stronger separation of collecting ideas and subsequently integrating them in a model as suggested by Stirna and Persson (2018) [2] could be applied. This might, however, change the way of working. A systematic way of planning and designing the collaboration process would be to construct this process from so-called thinkLets. A thinkLet is defined as *"the smallest unit of intellectual capital required to create one repeatable, predictable pattern of thinking among people working toward a goal"* [31, p. 2].

Thus, they are reusable building blocks for collaboration patterns. Example thinkLets would be Free Brainstorming or MoodRing (continously track the level of consensus concerning a certain issue) [31,32]. For each thinkLet, it is described when to use it, which thinkLet can be predecessor and successor, and how to use it including a script for the facilitator and the tools that have to be provided. Certain thinkLets will automatically require personal space and maybe even lead to the emergence of territories.

The development of personal space and territories may also depend on the kind of model that should be created. While goal models might spread in all directions, process models often show a horizontal alignment. This will have an influence on how persons are positioned and possibly restrict access to particular places in the model. As mentioned above, goal models usually require close collaboration. In process modeling, not every participant is an expert for the whole process but maybe only for a part of it. In that case a division into sub-tasks executed by sub-teams might make sense [33]. For large-scale models, this would lead to a need for additional devices and result in separate territories.

5.4   Consequences for PEM

The study has shown that for collaborative goal modeling that is connected to the continuous search for consensus, the participants of the modeling sessions developed a feeling of collective ownership towards the model. The lack of personal territories seems to be connected with this collective psychological ownership. Just like the model, the participants seem to consider the common workspace as belonging to all of them as also indicated by the mixed activity maps and the lack of etiquette. We claim that in the context of PEM, it is intended that the participants consider the overall model as belonging to all of them. Only then will they develop a joint commitment to the model which will be crucial if the model is to be implemented in the company.

In some cases, it might make sense to divide the group of participants to work on sub-tasks, e.g. due to different expertise, or to use phases of individual work to collect a multitude of different ideas. The particular challenge for both facilitation methods, including the choice of tools, and the design of user interfaces is to allow such diverse ways of working and also make it possible to join all perspectives at intermediate stages as well as at the end of a modeling session in order to guarantee the emergence of collective ownership. Thus, we believe that temporary personal territories, especially on additional devices, could be very beneficial, but everything must eventually lead back to a joint workspace without personal territories such as the tabletop. The latter would only cost valuable space and might distract from the collective result.

Lastly, the study has shown that most participants did not seem to be bothered by physical closeness although most of them had not met before. A reason for this might be that the persons were standing side by side most of the time. Altman (1975) claims that this position mitigates the negative effects of physical nearness to other people with whom we do not share a close relationship [14]. The question is whether in a real world context, members of a company would react in the same way taking into consideration that people from different hierarchy levels or people with hidden conflicts might get together in a PEM project.

5.5 Limitations

The study presented in this paper has some limitations. First, the modeling sessions took place in a lab of the university. The participants involved did not work together in a company and had no professional relationships. Nevertheless, the sample comprised mostly persons who had no background in modeling as it is typical in PEM projects which adds to the study's representativity. Although we used a fictitious subject, the participants became quickly engaged since most students can relate to a pizza delivery service. Our findings do only concern goal modeling. Participants' behavior during modeling business processes and further perspectives is still to be investigated. Moreover, the facilitator did not determine any structure during the session in order to not add an additional influence to the setting and the participants' work behavior. The results of our study might have been different if the facilitator would have guided the procedure more intensively. Nevertheless, we offer insight to how workspace is used when working purely collaboratively without establishing personal territories and how this might be connected with individual and collective feelings of ownership. Moreover, even with a more structured proceeding, the space offered on the tabletop would still have been restricted, and maybe still too little to allow personal territories. The modeling editor itself may also have had an influence on the participants' behavior, particularly with respect to the model components' size. However, we still have to make sure that all elements remain readable to the team members.

We have suggested a particular way of depicting areas where the participants were active on the screen. Our decisions of how to illustrate the level of activity and temporal flow were based on existing methods and adapted to our project. There are certainly further approaches to be explored. Lastly, we used a small sample because of the considerable effort involved with the kind of evaluations we performed. Also, a bigger team size would not have changed the results with regard to the absence of personal territories as the space on the tabletop would have been even less per person. In fact, we present one of few studies of territorial behavior on tabletops where more than two persons are working together, additionally considering ownership feelings. In fact, commitment is not easy to produce in a study setting like ours. Psychological ownership, however, as a determinant of affective commitment is to be attained by ensuring feelings of control towards the target, familiarization with the target, and investing the self [10], which can be implemented in a modeling session to maybe a limited, but still a certain extent. To assess psychological ownership, we used an established and validated measuring instrument [22].

5.6 Implications

Personal territories may serve modeling participants as a private space where they can work independently on their own ideas that can be shared later with the whole group [6,19]. Giving the participants more space by using a bigger table or by making the elements of the user interface smaller has its drawbacks. Instead, we intend to extend our existing tool concept by adding further devices such as mobile phones or tablets.

Stirna and Persson (2018) suggest a more structured procedure where participants of a PEM session first write down their ideas on cards on their own before sharing them later in a collaborative phase [2]. We would like to follow this concept by letting the additional devices play the role of card stacks where the participants can write down their ideas separately from others. The digital cards may be shared on the tabletop by transferring the data from the additional device to the tabletop. During the digital card writing, the team members might not be completely aware of what the others are doing, however, awareness is particularly important in phases of collaborative working [6,19]. A previous phase of brainwriting where participants note their ideas privately may have several advantages: Not only the loudest will be heard, introverted people may also get a chance to voice ideas. Hierarchy levels of the participants will not interfere either. Moreover, the ideas may be more diverse. Often, when an idea is voiced aloud, it will restrict the other participants' thinking into that direction only. Lastly, the participants write down their ideas right away without being disturbed or being forced to hear everybody else out before they can contribute their suggestions.

We would like to examine whether phases of individual and collaborative working will change the extent of individual and collective ownership feelings, respectively. In our study, we have seen that close collaborative work seems to be connected to higher collective ownership feelings towards the model. Depending on the modeling project's target, one must probably find the appropriate ratio of collaborative and individual work.

We would also like to investigate user behavior and the emergence of territories in the context of process modeling. Process modeling can be considered as more complex than goal modeling since temporal aspects have to be regarded as well. Moreover, in contrast to goal modeling, a division into sub-tasks can make sense in process modeling.

On the whole, the study gives insight to the working behavior on tabletops and helps in extending the state of knowledge about collaborative modeling sessions.

References

1. Sandkuhl, K., Stirna, J., Persson, A., Wißotzki, M.: Enterprise Modeling. Tackling Business Challenges with the 4EM Method, p. 309. Springer, Heidelberg (2014). https://doi.org/10.1007/978-3-662-43725-4

2. Stirna, J., Persson, A.: Enterprise Modeling - Facilitating the Process and the People. Springer, Heidelberg (2018). https://doi.org/10.1007/978-3-319-94857-7
3. Stirna, J., Persson, A., Sandkuhl, K.: Participative enterprise modeling: experiences and recommendations. In: Krogstie, J., Opdahl, A., Sindre, G. (eds.) CAiSE 2007. LNCS, vol. 4495, pp. 546–560. Springer, Heidelberg (2007). https://doi.org/10.1007/978-3-540-72988-4_38
4. Gutschmidt, A.: On the influence of tools on collaboration in participative enterprise modeling—an experimental comparison between whiteboard and multi-touch table. In: Andersson, B., Johansson, B., Barry, C., Lang, M., Linger, H., Schneider, C. (eds.) Advances in Information Systems Development. LNISO, vol. 34, pp. 151–168. Springer, Cham (2019). https://doi.org/10.1007/978-3-030-22993-1_9
5. Gutschmidt, A.: Empirical insights into the appraisal of tool support for participative enterprise modeling. In: Proceedings of the 9th International Workshop on Enterprise Modeling and Information Systems Architectures, Rostock, Germany, 24th–25th May 2018, pp. 70–74 (2018)
6. Scott, S.D., Carpendale, S.: Theory of tabletop territoriality. In: Müller-Tomfelde, C. (ed.) Tabletops-Horizontal Interactive Displays, pp. 357–385. Springer, London (2010). https://doi.org/10.1007/978-1-84996-113-4_15
7. Ryall, K., Forlines, C., Shen, C., Morris, M.R.: Exploring the effects of group size and table size on interactions with tabletop shared-display groupware. In: Proceedings of the 2004 ACM Conference on Computer Supported Cooperative Work. CSCW 2004, New York, NY, USA, pp. 284–293. ACM (2004)
8. Brown, G., Crossley, C., Robinson, S.L.: Psychological ownership, territorial behavior, and being perceived as a team contributor: the critical role of trust in the work environment. Pers. Psychol. 67(2), 463–485 (2014)
9. Barjis, J.: CPI modeling: collaborative, participative, interactive modeling. In: Proceedings of the 2011 Winter Simulation Conference (WSC), pp. 3094–3103 (2011)
10. Pierce, J.L., Kostova, T., Dirks, K.T.: Toward a theory of psychological ownership in organizations. Acad. Manag. Rev. 26(2), 298–310 (2001)
11. Atakan, S.S., Bagozzi, R.P., Yoon, C.: Consumer participation in the design and realization stages of production: how self-production shapes consumer evaluations and relationships to products. Int. J. Res. Mark. 31(4), 395–408 (2014)
12. Gutschmidt, A., Sauer, V., Sandkuhl, K., Kashevnik, A.: Identifying HCI patterns for the support of participatory enterprise modeling on multi-touch tables. In: Gordijn, J., Guédria, W., Proper, H.A. (eds.) PoEM 2019. LNBIP, vol. 369, pp. 118–133. Springer, Cham (2019). https://doi.org/10.1007/978-3-030-35151-9_8
13. Hall, E., Library of Congress Cataloging-in-Publication: The Hidden Dimension. Anchor books. Doubleday (1966)
14. Altman, I.: The Environment and Social Behavior: Privacy, Personal Space, Territory, Crowding. Brooks/Cole Publishing Company, Pacific Grove (1975)
15. Kruger, R., Carpendale, S., Scott, S.D., Greenberg, S.: Roles of orientation in tabletop collaboration: comprehension, coordination and communication. Comput. Support. Coop. Work (CSCW) 13(5–6), 501–537 (2004). https://doi.org/10.1007/s10606-004-5062-8
16. Tang, J.C.: Findings from observational studies of collaborative work. Int. J. Man Mach. Stud. 34(2), 143–160 (1991)
17. Klinkhammer, D., Mateescu, M., Zahn, C., Reiterer, H.: Mine, yours, ours: coordination through workspace arrangements and territoriality in tabletop interaction. In: Proceedings of the 17th International Conference on Mobile and Ubiquitous Multimedia, pp. 171–182. ACM (2018)

18. Tuddenham, P., Robinson, P.: Territorial coordination and workspace awareness in remote tabletop collaboration. In: Proceedings of the SIGCHI Conference on Human Factors in Computing Systems, pp. 2139–2148. ACM (2009)

19. Scott, S.D., Carpendale, M.S.T., Inkpen, K.M.: Territoriality in collaborative tabletop workspaces. In: Proceedings of the 2004 ACM Conference on Computer Supported Cooperative Work, pp. 294–303. ACM (2004)

20. Pierce, J.L., Jussila, I.: Collective psychological ownership within the work and organizational context: construct introduction and elaboration. J. Organ. Behav. **31**(6), 810–834 (2010)

21. Mayhew, M.G., Ashkanasy, N.M., Bramble, T., Gardner, J.: A study of the antecedents and consequences of psychological ownership in organizational settings. J. Soc. Psychol. **147**(5), 477–500 (2007)

22. O'driscoll, M.P., Pierce, J.L., Coghlan, A.M.: The psychology of ownership: work environment structure, organizational commitment, and citizenship behaviors. Group Organ. Manag. **31**(3), 388–416 (2006)

23. Pierce, J.L., Kostova, T., Dirks, K.T.: The state of psychological ownership: integrating and extending a century of research. Rev. Gen. Psychol. **7**(1), 84–107 (2003)

24. Wittenburg, P., Brugman, H., Russel, A., Klassmann, A., Sloetjes, H.: ELAN: a professional framework for multimodality research. In: 5th International Conference on Language Resources and Evaluation (LREC 2006), pp. 1556–1559 (2006)

25. Van Dyne, L., Pierce, J.L.: Psychological ownership and feelings of possession: three field studies predicting employee attitudes and organizational citizenship behavior. J. Organ. Behav. Int. J. Ind. Occup. Organ. Psychol. Behav. **25**(4), 439–459 (2004)

26. Martins, E.: Psychological Ownership in Organisationen: Explorative Untersuchung der Antezedenzen und des Entstehungsprozesses. Rainer Hampp Verlag, Munich (2010)

27. Gutschmidt, A., Sauer, V., Schönwälder, M., Szilagyi, T.: Researching participatory modeling sessions: an experimental study on the influence of evaluation potential and the opportunity to draw oneself. In: Pańkowska, M., Sandkuhl, K. (eds.) BIR 2019. LNBIP, vol. 365, pp. 44–58. Springer, Cham (2019). https://doi.org/10.1007/978-3-030-31143-8_4

28. Olson, I.C., Atrash Leong, Z., Wilensky, U., Horn, M.S.: It's just a toolbar! using tangibles to help children manage conflict around a multi-touch tabletop. In: Proceedings of the Fifth International Conference on Tangible, Embedded, and Embodied Interaction. TEI 2011, New York, NY, USA, pp. 29–36. Association for Computing Machinery (2010)

29. Bachl, S., Tomitsch, M., Kappel, K., Grechenig, T.: The effects of personal displays and transfer techniques on collaboration strategies in multi-touch based multi-display environments. In: Campos, P., Graham, N., Jorge, J., Nunes, N., Palanque, P., Winckler, M. (eds.) INTERACT 2011. LNCS, vol. 6948, pp. 373–390. Springer, Heidelberg (2011). https://doi.org/10.1007/978-3-642-23765-2_26

30. Tang, A., Tory, M., Po, B., Neumann, P., Carpendale, S.: Collaborative coupling over tabletop displays. In: Proceedings of the SIGCHI Conference on Human Factors in Computing Systems, pp. 1181–1190. ACM (2006)

31. Briggs, R.O., De Vreede, G., Nunamaker, J.F., Tobey, D.: ThinkLets: achieving predictable, repeatable patterns of group interaction with group support systems (GSS). In: Proceedings of the 34th Annual Hawaii International Conference on System Sciences, 9 p. (2001)

32. Kolfschoten, G.L., Briggs, R.O., Appelman, J.H., de Vreede, G.-J.: ThinkLets as building blocks for collaboration processes: a further conceptualization. In: de

Vreede, G.-J., Guerrero, L.A., Marín Raventós, G. (eds.) CRIWG 2004. LNCS, vol. 3198, pp. 137–152. Springer, Heidelberg (2004). https://doi.org/10.1007/978-3-540-30112-7_12

33. Zerrouk, M., Anwar, A., Benelallam, I., Elhamlaoui, M.: Collaborative modelling: an MDE-oriented process to manage large-scale models. In: 2017 International Conference on Wireless Technologies, Embedded and Intelligent Systems (WITS), pp. 1–8 (2017)

The DEMO Modeling Language

Validation of DEMO's Conciseness Quality and Proposal of Improvements to the Process Model

Duarte Pinto[1,2](✉) [iD], David Aveiro[1,2,3] [iD], Dulce Pacheco[1,2] [iD],
Bernardo Gouveia[1,2,3] [iD], and Duarte Gouveia[1,2,3] [iD]

[1] Madeira Interactive Technologies Institute, Caminho da Penteada, 9020-105 Funchal, Portugal
{duarte.nuno,dulce.pacheco,bernardo.gouveia}@m-iti.org
[2] NOVA-LINCS, Universidade NOVA de Lisboa, Campus da Caparica,
2829-516 Caparica, Portugal
[3] Faculty of Exact Sciences and Engineering, University of Madeira, Caminho da Penteada,
9020-105 Funchal, Portugal
daveiro@uma.pt, duarte.gouveia@staff.uma.pt

Abstract. The Design and Engineering Methodology for Organizations (DEMO) comprises a set of models and diagrams to represent an organization. While applying DEMO on a project in collaboration with the town council of the city of Funchal, we saw a need for improvements in the Process Model. Thus, in this paper we propose improvements to the current body of knowledge regarding DEMO's Process Model representations, fusing the contents of the Process and Cooperation models. Namely, we propose a semantically richer Process Diagram and a Transaction Description Table, to achieve a more agile and comprehensive solution to depict the essence of organizational reality. Our approach presents the information in a more straightforward and transparent way, which is easier to understand by collaborators. This project also confirmed the known DEMO conciseness metric of allowing a reduction of over 95% in the complexity of representations. One of our main research contributions is that, even though the information is more accessible and easier to grasp in the diagrams we propose, the processes' complexity is still present in the description table.

Keywords: Enterprise engineering · DEMO · Process model · Process diagram · Building code · Building appraisal process

1 Introduction

Organizations implement information systems to improve their effectiveness and efficiency, but the achievement of this goal depends on the capabilities of the information system and the characteristics of the organization [1]. Furthermore, the effective transition of strategy into infrastructure requires extensive design activity on both the organizational design and the information systems design to create, respectively, effective organizational infrastructure and effective information system infrastructure [1]. The

© Springer Nature Switzerland AG 2021
D. Aveiro et al. (Eds.): EEWC 2020, LNBIP 411, pp. 133–152, 2021.
https://doi.org/10.1007/978-3-030-74196-9_8

modeling of an organization requires extensive analysis of its processes and a sound methodology to represent it.

The DEMO (Design and Engineering Methodology for Organizations) is based on the PSI theory of Enterprise Ontology, which studies organizations' operational essence, that is, the construction perspective on enterprises, disregarding all functional aspects [2]. DEMO's Way of Modelling comprises a set of models and diagrams to represent an organization. They are correlated with each other, representing coherent information in a platform-independent way [3]. However, DEMO's Coordination Model and Process Model represent almost the same information (process dependencies in regards to structure and flow control), which can be a burden to keep up to date with every single change when we are modeling complex processes. Applying DEMO to a project in the town council of the city of Funchal allowed us to redefine these models within DEMO and propose improvements to its representations.

This paper is organized into six sections. We start by presenting our research method and motivation, followed by the theoretical foundations. We then proceed to introduce the project and our proposal for a new DEMO's Process Model. We finish with the proposal's discussion and wrap up with a conclusions section.

2   Research Method and Motivation

The design-science paradigm seeks to expand the boundaries of human and organizational capabilities by creating new and innovative artifacts that are expected to solve identified organizational problems [1]. In this work, we followed the Design Science Research Cycles [4], considering the Seven Guidelines for Design Science in Information Systems Research [1]. The Relevance Cycle connects the project's contextual environment with the design science activities [4], motivated by the desire to improve the environment by introducing new and innovative artifacts and building them [5]. In our work, we have clearly defined the problem based on the complexity and ambiguity of the Portuguese Building Code (PBC), regarding municipal urban appraisal requirements and procedures. The PBC allows different interpretations that have originated divergent obligations across the country. In the context of the specific town council of Funchal, we found the need to represent this information in a more straightforward and orderly way, as there was the imminent implementation of a new software to manage the urban appraisal processes. For a successful implementation and parametrization of the new system, thorough models of the process will be of high and essential value for them.

The Rigor Cycle connects the design science activities with the existing knowledge base of scientific foundations, experience, and expertise [4]. This paper summarizes the complex and ambiguous PBC requirements and procedures for municipal urban appraisal into several diagrams and tables based on DEMO and the PSI Theory [6]. Based on this project's practical experience, we saw the necessity of improving the representation and nomenclature of process diagrams and associated tables, thus contributing to the knowledge base with method and tool improvements.

During this practical project's execution, we followed the Design Cycle iterating rapidly between the core activities of building and evaluating the design artifacts and the process of research, incorporating the feedback to refine the design further [4]. We balanced our artifact's build and evaluation phases based on the relevance and rigor cycles.

Our artifact's different iterations were evaluated by a highly experienced team of urban appraisal officers in the criteria of completeness, simplicity, elegance, understandability, and ease of use. The feedback was immediately incorporated into the redesign of the artifact. The results presented in this paper are the final iteration after a series of around ten work meetings with officers over seven months.

In this paper, we propose several improvements in terms of how to represent DEMO's Construction and Process Models in a new kind of diagram and table, while changing the nomenclature of some DEMO concepts to facilitate the communication with officers and their interpretation of the representations.

3   Theoretical Foundations

3.1   PSI Theory

The PSI theory, on which DEMO (Design and Engineering Methodology for Organizations) is based, studies organizations' operational essence, that is, the construction perspective on enterprises, disregarding all functional aspects [2]. The fundamental notion of understanding organizations' operation is the coordination act (C-act) [6], where commitments are raised. Performing a C-act results in creating the corresponding coordination fact (C-fact) and affects the coordination world (C-world) (see Fig. 1). C-acts are how actors enter into and comply with commitments towards achieving a certain production fact (P-fact) [6] and have an effect on the production world (P-world) (see Fig. 1). When active, actors take the current state of the P-world and the C-world into account. C-facts serve as an agenda for actors, which they continuously try to deal with. This is the operational principle of organizations, also known as the *operation axiom* [3].

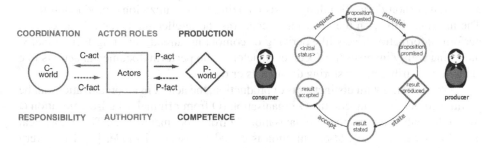

Fig. 1. Depiction of the operation and transaction axioms [3]

According to the PSI theory, every organization's operation is a network of transactions [6]. Each transaction is some path through the complete transaction pattern, which is a universal pattern in all organizations [2]. A transaction is successful if the (final) product is accepted and a production fact (P-fact) starts to exist in the P-world. C-acts are the key elements in (business) conversations, which are the constituting parts of (business) transactions [6]. This interaction between subjects (the initiator or consumer and the executor or producer) follows a certain path along the complete transaction pattern [2, 3] (see Fig. 1).

All transactions go through the four – social commitment – C-acts of *request* [rq], *promise* [pm], *declare* [da] (also known as *state*), and *accept* [ac] (see Fig. 1). The transaction pattern has three phases: (1) the order phase, in which the two actors discuss and negotiate to agree on a product that the executor can promise to bring about in response to the request by the initiator; (2) the execution phase where the executor produces, in fact, the desired result; and (3) the result phase, where the executor declares the product and the initiator accepts that result, thus effectively concluding the transaction. This sequence, known as the basic transaction pattern, only considers the regular flow where everything happens according to the expected outcomes (see Fig. 1). All these five mandatory steps must occur to make a new P-fact. The complete transaction pattern also considers other c-acts, including revocations and rejections that may happen at every step of the regular flow [6]. Therefore, it is considered universal [6] and is also known as the *transaction axiom* [3].

Transaction steps are the responsibility of two specific actor roles, the initiator and the executor. The actor role determines the authority that the actor may exercise and the responsibility to do so. Because of the inherent connection between an actor role and the transaction kind of which fillers are the executor, the combination of the two is called the transactor *role* (the universal building blocks of business processes) [6].

The PSI theory states that three human abilities play a significant role in an organization's operation: (1) the forma ability that concerns documental actions; (2) the informa that concerns informational actions; and (3) the performa that concerns original actions [6]. This is also known as the *distinction axiom* [3]. Regarding C-acts, the performa ability may be considered the essential human competence for doing any kind of business as it concerns being able to engage in commitments either as a performer or as an addressee of a C-act [7]. When it comes to production, the performa ability concerns the original actors. Those actors perform production acts like deciding or judging or producing new and original (non-derivable) things, thus realizing the organization's production facts. The informa ability, on the other hand, concerns the intellectual actors, the ones who perform informational acts like deriving or computing already existing facts. Finally, the forma ability involves the documental actors, who perform documental actions like gathering, distributing, or storing documents or data.

Corresponding with distinct sorts of production, the actors in an organization can be partitioned into three layers: the O-organisation (O from original), the I-organisation (I from informational), and the D-organisation (D from documental) [2]. The ontological model of an enterprise's O-organisation is called its essential model [2]. Like every ontological model, it is abstracted from implementation, but it is also abstracted from realization, that is, from supporting I- and D-organisation [2]. Yet, it contains everything needed to understand the essence of an enterprise's operation, thus contributing to the generic enterprise engineering goal of intellectual manageability by an unprecedented reduction of complexity [8]. In terms of size, that is, the amount of diagrams, text, etc., the essential model is less than 5% of a 'normal' complete model of an enterprise [9, 10].

By performing P-acts, the subjects in an organization create products. The PSI theory also explains how P-Facts are interrelated. It states that every transaction is enclosed in some other transaction or is a border transaction or a self-activating transaction. The carrying out of a transaction (of whatever kind) can be taken as a generic business process building block, and the C- and P-acts in transactions can be taken as a generic notion of *task* [6]. According to Dietz and Mulder [6], a business process is a sequence of process steps, which are steps in transactions of the transaction kinds that are contained in a business process kind in the O-organisation of an enterprise. This is also known as the composition axiom [3].

3.2 DEMO Methodology

The DEMO methodology is based on the previously explained PSI Theory of Enterprise Ontology. DEMO's Way of Modelling comprises a set of models and diagrams to represent an organization. The referred aspect models are the Cooperation Model (CM), the Action Model (AM), the Process Model (PM), and the Fact Model (FM) [9]. They are correlated with each other, representing coherent information in a platform-independent way [3].

The CM specifies the construction of the organization and its transaction types and is the most concise one. It also states the identified transactor roles (the elements) and the coordination structures (the influencing relationships) between them [9]. There are three coordination structures among transactor roles: the interaction structure, the interimpediment structure, and the interstriction structure [9]. The interaction structure consists of initiator links between transactor roles and transaction kinds (the transactor role implicitly specifies the executor links). The interimpediment structure consists of wait links from actor roles to transaction kinds. A wait link expresses that actors in the connected actor role have to wait for specific progress in transactions of the corresponding transaction kind before proceeding with their work (in their own transactions). The interstriction structure consists of access links from actor roles to transaction kinds, conceived as transaction banks. An access link expresses that actors in the connected actor role have reading access to the contents of the transaction bank (both to the C-facts and P-facts).

The AM of an organization is the ontological model of its operation, that is, the manifestation of the construction over time [9]. For every internal actor role, it contains the rules that conduct the role fillers in doing their work. The action rules guide actors in performing coordination acts (represented in the Action Rule Specifications), and the work instructions guide actors in performing production acts (depicted in the Work Instruction Specifications). The action rules are composed of all the information from the other models, CM, PM, and FM, meaning that all the information about enterprise business is covered in this model, being one of the most important models on the methodology [3].

The PM of an organization is a model of the (business) processes that take place as the effect of acts by actors [9]. The PM of an organization connects its CM and AM, as far as coordination is concerned. It contains, for all internal and all border transaction kinds, the process step kinds as well as the applicable existence laws. For all the transaction kinds, the PM reveals the process step kinds and the applicable occurrence laws, including the cardinalities of the occurrences [9].

The FM of an organization is a model of its organizational products [9]. Regarding the state space, the FM contains entity types, value types, property types, and attribute types relevant for the modeled organization and the existence laws that apply. While regarding the transition space, it represents the event types and the occurrence laws [9].

In this paper and in our project, we use the term *task* for the representations instead of *transaction*, as it is much more easily interpreted and understood by officers not familiar with DEMO and we will use both terms interchangeably.

4 Project Presentation

The project this paper reports on resulted from the city of Funchal's town council's request for a thorough modeling of their urban appraisal process.

The town council of Funchal serves a population of around one hundred and ten thousand inhabitants in a land area of about 76 km^2 and it's divided in three cabinets, nine major departments each with multiple divisions under their tutelage, as well as municipal public water service, municipal firefighters and municipal civil protection.

The urban appraisal process falls mostly under the territory planning department, more precisely in the urban appreciation division, but overlaps with other departments or divisions on occasion such as the treasury department on payments related issues or the legal and inspection department on the inspections/fiscalizations done on the urban operations, rule violations or even restoration of legality.

This process handles the requests regarding permits for all kinds of building construction work, land allotment, and other urban operations within the town. Soon, a new software system to manage this process will be implemented and thorough models of the process will be of high and essential value for successful implementation and parametrization of this future system.

We devised our representations by analyzing information from multiple national and local legislation and regulations, as well as from a series of project meetings with officers of Funchal's town council. But the main focus and source of information was the PBC, the main piece of legislation on urbanization that all town councils need to comply with. Our representations consist of two artifacts; (1) a Process Diagram and (2) a Transaction Description Table. Both are DEMO-based, so in our approach, the focus was to find original transactions, although some informational and documental ones were also specified due to legal obligations and the need to make them explicit in the model. We identified 393 transactions, which were grouped into 13 scopes of interest (SoI) corresponding to the respective set of procedures of the global urban appraisal process. Out of these 13 SoI, seven were analyzed in greater detail up to now, regarding rules specifying process structure and flows. Namely, 695 dependencies between transactions were determined 280 originating transactions, 68 waitings for transactions, and 347 target transactions as shown in Fig. 2. Officers were stunned in multiple meetings where the study development was presented by the sheer number of modeled elements and the complexity of their day-to-day work processes, but very happy to see how its huge complexity could be summarized into 19 pages of diagrams.

Outside the 13 identified SoI, 13 other transactions were identified (e.g., permits for local tourist accommodation, etc.), but they were few in number, unrelatable to each

Scope of Interest	Total Transactions	Originating transactions	Waitings for transaction	Target transactions	Total dependencies
1. Urban operations exempt from prior control	5	4	0	6	10
2. Prior Information	10	13	1	12	26
3. Urban operations carried out by Public Administration	16	21	4	23	48
4. Prior communication	43	58	7	68	133
5. Licencing	88	128	43	171	342
6. Use permit for buildings or spaces	17	19	3	20	42
7. Taxes and compensations	33	37	10	47	94
8. Inspection / Fiscalization	37				
9. Rule violations	6				
10. Urban operation offences	9				
11. Restauration of legality	63				
12. Embargo	12				
13. Right to information	41				
Others	13				
Total	393	280	68	347	695

Fig. 2. Scopes of Interest synthesis

other and quite simple, often consisting of just one action and one payment. In the next subsection, we describe the SoI 3. *Urban operations carried out by the Public Administration* used as an example to show our proposals of improvement to DEMO representations of the CM, PM, and AM.

4.1 Urban Operations Carried Out by the Public Administration

In this section, we describe the procedure of appraising urban operations carried out by the public administration. This procedure, compared to most of the other SoI, is one of the less complicated ones and follows a sort of streamlined "happy flow" scenario making it a good fit for a paper with a strict page limit.

Urban operations carried out by the public administration occur when either the national government, the regional government, or some other local authority, which includes the town council of Funchal, its civil parishes, and institutions associated with them, decide to carry out some building/construction work. Much like any citizen, the process starts with the public entity submitting an application. The operations can be of three distinct kinds: 1) that are not allotments (regardless of the public entity promoting them); 2) allotment operations and urbanization work carried out by local authorities and their associations (those authorities being the town council itself, any of its parishes, any of their associations or local public companies); and 3) allotment operations and urbanization work promoted by the state (national or regional government and their public companies).

When a public administration entity carries out an urban operation, it is required that the town council issues a non-binding prior opinion about it. This has to be issued up to 20 days after the application. If this deadline is missed, it is considered to be a tacit approval and the process continues. Nevertheless, if the opinion is given in time, as it is non-binding, the process may still continue regardless of it being favorable or unfavorable.

In the case of allotment operations and urbanization work carried out by local authorities and their associations, it is mandatory to get an authorization from the town assembly. Because this step may occur before the application is submitted, we modeled it as an optional task in this context. However, a mandatory step is the public discussion that has to be announced eight days before its start date and must last at least fifteen days. The public discussion is also a mandatory task in allotment operations and urbanization work promoted by the state. However, for this kind of operation, the town council executive committee must be heard within 20 days after the application submission date and their opinion is binding.

In our representation, the initial appraisal process tasks appear as optional, as its execution depends on the requested operation. The mandatory restrictions mentioned in the previous paragraph must be specified in the action rules.

If not tax-exempt, the tax value calculation must occur and is later communicated to the requester. The fees due to urban operations may be calculated by the applicants and paid by them prior to the submission of the application. In those cases, the town council later confirms the due amount and informs the applicant. This is called a self-payment (by the initiative of the applicant). However, for operations carried out by the public administration, the calculation of the correct amount is a previous mandatory step. If the applicant is the town council itself, a payment makes no sense and, instead of the self-payment, there is an integration of the cost of the operation in the town council's budget. At a later date, if there was a previous payment, the amount is revised to guarantee that the correct fees are paid.

A liability statement must be sent to the town council by the applicant. This can be done simultaneously with the payment procedure or after it. After the payment, the entity must obtain a display sign with the commence and completion dates of the urban operation, that is publicly displayed at the construction site. After getting the sign, it has to be publicly displayed at the worksite. The applicant, having publicly announced the commence and completion dates of the urban operation and paid the due fees (in the case of not being the town council itself), must communicate to the town council the effective commencement date, with identification of the person in charge of its execution, at least five days before that date.

By then, if needed, a public road occupancy permit due to construction work might be requested. During the whole duration of the construction work, the construction site is subject to random inspections realized by the town council inspectors. When the operation is complete, like in other kinds of urban operations, the entity responsible for the operation can then apply for a use permit. This concludes the process of appraisal of an urban operation carried out by the public administration.

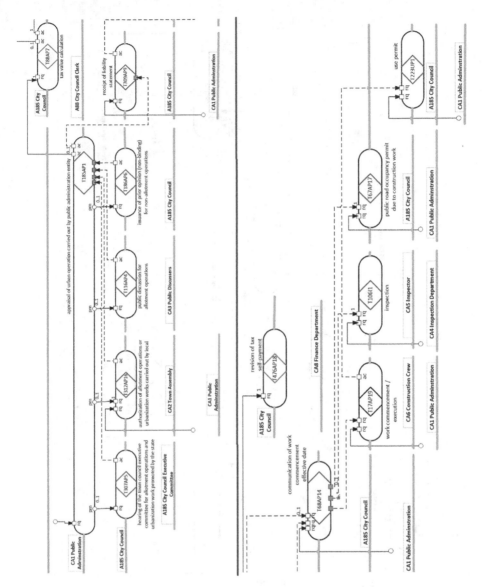

Fig. 3. PSD - Urban operations carried out by Public Administration (parts 1 and 3)

In Fig. 3 and Fig. 4, we present this process in the current DEMO Process Structure Model (PSD) notation. The overall result of the model were 18 transactions (two as a reference to other processes), 32 actors (10 of them unique), 16 wait connections, 8 causal connections, and 11 starts of process (although 10 of them were in the middle of what we identified as the process, but the PSD notation has no solution for those cases).

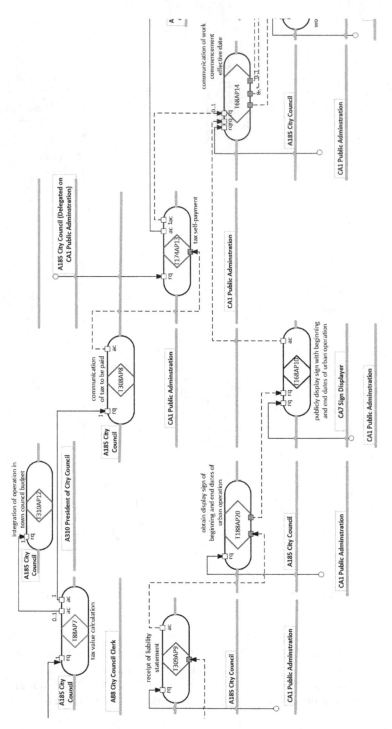

Fig. 4. PSD - Urban operations carried out by Public Administration (part 2)

In the next section, in Fig. 6, we see the depiction of this process using the new notation we propose for the DEMO's Process Model which fuses the contents of the Process Model together with those of the Cooperation Model. We propose that the Process Model is extended with the features we now present and that the Cooperation Model should be renamed to its previous name: Construction Model. We argue that the CM model should show only the composition of transactions in a process as per the composition axiom. Our proposal for the new Process Model is explained in the next section.

5 Proposal for a New DEMO's Process Model

This section presents the Process Diagram and the Transaction Description Table that constitute our vision for a new Process Model within the DEMO methodology. These two new artifacts were created out of the need for a more agile and comprehensive solution to compile and present the essence of organizational reality, when compared to the traditional DEMO models. Having two models (CM and PM) replicating/splitting the same information (process dependencies regarding the structure and flow control) can be a burden to keep up to date with every single change. This can be especially hard when modeling complex processes, with many tasks, with multiple team members working in parallel, and with regular interactions with officers. Therefore a single diagram that we named Process Diagram seemed like the perfect solution to present all the information that we deemed visually necessary to comprehend the process concisely, while still being easy (enough) to understand by any of the officers. Understandably, we couldn't fit all the process information in that single diagram. For that, we also created a Transaction Description Table, where we could add the more text-intensive relevant information, like the descriptions of each transaction, their conditions for taking place, their rules, their time constraints, amongst others. To facilitate collaborative work and easy access to the models by stakeholders, for the diagram we used the tool diagrams.net and, for the table, a google spreadsheet. Next, we explain each of these artifacts in greater detail.

5.1 Process Diagram

Before we present the resulting Process Diagram in Fig. 5 we explain the meaning of each symbol used in the process diagram of Fig. 6.

To keep track of the source of information behind each task, each symbol includes a reference to the source. In the case of the PBC the particular article in the legislation. Besides this reference, tasks are also accompanied by a specific numbering started with "T" that contains the identification (ID) attributed to each transaction in the Transaction Description Table. This grants traceability between the diagram and table, but also in other elements developed in this project but not presented in this paper due to lack of space.

In Fig. 6, we present the diagram of the SoI #3 described previously, split into two parts, side by side (repeating the two bottom tasks at the start of the second side to facilitate the understanding of the connections).

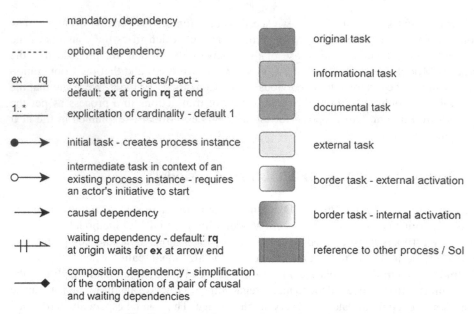

Fig. 5. Process Diagram - Shapes description

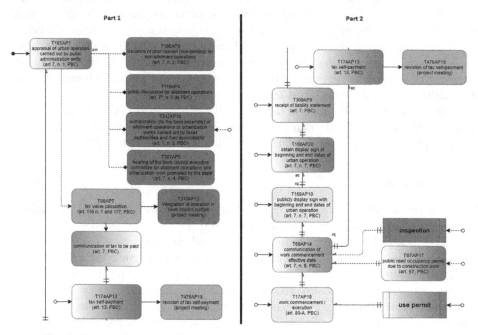

Fig. 6. Process diagram - Urban operations carried out by Public Administration

The resulting model is composed of 16 tasks, 9 ontological, two infological, three datalogical, and two external tasks (relevant to the process). Of the modeled tasks, 7 are border tasks, 6 with external activation (meaning that an external actor is responsible by their request and acceptance), and one with internal activation (meaning that an internal actor requests them and accepts them but the promise, execution, and state are performed by an external actor).

The model also has two references to other processes (one of which with external activation).

Concerning connections between tasks, the end result was one initial task, four composition dependencies, four causal dependencies (three of them conditional), 10 wait dependencies (three of them conditional), and 10 intermediate tasks (three of them conditional) in the context of the process that requires an actor initiative to start.

Although not present in this model, the actors were not forgotten and are represented in the Transaction Description Table presented in the following section.

5.2 Transaction Description Table

In the Transaction Description Table, a detailed description of each task is provided in a structured way, explained as follows. We remind that we use the terms transaction and task as synonyms. For each task, we can find its description (often a direct copy from the text in the legislation), the conditions or rules that need to be verified for the subsequent task(s) to be executed, and time constraints.

In the Transaction Description Table, the information is distributed in the columns as it follows:

#1 ID: unique identifier

#2 Source: source document, in this project, mostly the piece of legislation where the task was identified;

#3 Section: the place (article or section) in the source document where the task is mentioned;

#4 Scope of Interest: scope of that group of tasks (e.g., Licencing, Prior Communication, etc.);

#5 Name: task name (e.g., public discussion for allotment operations);

#6 Task Kind: used to classify the task in original (O), informational (I), documental (D), or external (E);

#7 Executor: organizational position/function (internal or external) responsible for executing the task;

#8 Description: a textual description with task details (in this project, often a copy of the relevant legislation, but may contain other relevant information);

#9 Originating task(s): list of task(s) originated by the current one. A task may be the start of a process, a consequence of another task, a part of another task (composition dependency), or an intermediate task that requires actor's initiative to deploy (e.g., "public discussion for allotment operations" is an optional task originated on "appraisal of urban operation carried out by public administration entity" but, when requested, must be concluded for the completion of the "appraisal of urban operation carried out by public administration entity");

#10 Waits for task(s): used if a task, after its commence, needs to wait for the conclusion of another task to proceed (e.g., when the applicant is the state promoting an allotment operation, the task "appraisal of urban operation carried out by public administration entity" must wait for the completion of the task "hearing of the town council executive committee for allotment operations and urbanization work promoted by the state");

#11 Target task(s): tasks originated as a consequence of another task. It may be created upon its conclusion, but also in any transaction pattern step (request, promise, execution, state, or acceptance). Not all tasks have target task(s);

#12 Conditions/Rules: describes the conditions and rules followed in order to execute the current task and/or target task(s), (e.g., "If the "Receipt of liability statement" has been received, the applicant may "obtain display sign of beginning and end dates of urban operation"");

#13 Temporal constraints: identify deadlines or other temporal restrictions regarding tasks (e.g., the "issuance of prior opinion (non-binding) for non allotment operations" must take place within 20 days after the application).

Figure 7, Fig. 8, and Fig. 9 depict the first two tasks in the Transaction Description Table of the urban operations carried out by the public administration that exemplifies the structure presented above.

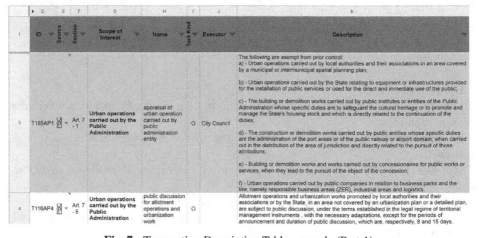

Fig. 7. Transaction Description Table - sample (Part 1)

In creating the Transaction Description Table, the traceability and navigation between tasks were primary concerns. On one hand, this is due to the inherent sequencing between originating and target tasks and, on another hand, because some tasks have their execution halted until others finish. The implementation of the navigation feature was done at a google spreadsheet level with the development of a script that automatically links the transactions present in the "Originating task(s)", "Target task(s)", and "Waits for task(s)" columns to the respective entry in the Transaction Description Table. Interested stakeholders may then follow the process flow in whichever manner they find appropriate, while having the added capability of inspecting and following a link to the piece of legislation that supports the existence of the task itself (i.e. the linked "Source" column). This navigable "spreadsheet method" was highly appraised by the town council officers

	L	M	N
1	Originating task(s)	Waits for task(s)	Target task(s)
2			
3	initial process task	(opt) T186AP6 issuance of prior opinion (non-binding) for non-allotment operations (opt) T116AP4 public discussion for allotment operations (opt) T312AP16 authorization (by the town assembly) of allotment operations or urbanization works carried out by local authorities and their associations (opt) T307AP5 hearing of the town council executive committee for allotment operations and urbanization work promoted by the state	(opt) T186AP6 issuance of prior opinion (non-binding) for non-allotment operations (opt) T116AP4 public discussion for allotment operations (opt) T312AP16 authorization (by the town assembly) of allotment operations or urbanization works carried out by local authorities and their associations (opt) T307AP5 hearing of the town council executive committee for allotment operations and urbanization work promoted by the state (opt) T88AP7 tax value calculation T309AP9 receipt of liability statement
4	(opt) T185AP1 appraisal of urban operation carried out by public administration entity		(opt) T185AP1 appraisal of urban operation carried out by public administration entity

Fig. 8. Transaction Description Table - sample (Part 2)

	O	P
1	Conditions/Rules	Temporal Restraints
2		
3	If the operation is not an allotment, requires the issuance of a prior opinion by the city council (non-binding) (T186OUPPAP6). If the operation is an allotment, requires a public discussion for allotment operations (T116AP4) and a authorization (by the town assembly) of allotment operations or urbanization works carried out by local authorities and their associations (T312AP16) or a Hearing of the town council executive committee for allotment operations and urbanization work promoted by the state (T307AP5) The authorization (by the town assembly) of allotment operations or urbanization works carried out by local authorities and their associations (T312AP16) may take place before the urban operation request. In that case the document should be added to the process on its request. If aproved and the operation is subject to tax the tax value must be calculated (T88OUPPAP7) and the receipt of liability statement may occur (T309OUPPAP9)	
4	After concluded the public discussion, the appraisal of urban operation carried out by public administration entity (T185AP1) may continue	public discussion announcement: 8 days before the discussion. duration of public discussion: 15 days.

Fig. 9. Transaction Description Table - sample (Part 3)

and now constitutes a very useful tool for their daily work, while the new software system is not implemented.

6 Elaboration and Discussion

The distinction axiom is of particular importance because it lets one focus on the essential aspects of the processes, allowing a higher level, simplified and neutral view of them, maintaining only essential (original) tasks and abstracting how this information is treated (informational tasks) or transmitted (documental task) between the officers, with the exception of cases where this is a legal requirement or it is important to make them explicit for another reason.

This abstraction of material/technical details of how a task is performed (manually or with computer support) or how a fact is supported (only on paper or in digital support) allows greater flexibility in the implementation. This also makes it possible to identify possible operational optimizations, namely, opportunities for automation and optimization that would not be possible with the traditional requirements gathering approach. For example, tasks with an informational/documental nature are more likely to be targets of full digital/computer automation.

The PBC and the associated documents are spread in different files that sum up to 387 A4 pages. Our work of synthesizing this complexity resulted in the identification of thirteen SoI. The tasks involved in those SoI were represented in diagrams occupying a total of 19 A4 pages. This shows that our approach was able to present the information more straightforwardly and transparently, easier to be understood not only by the officers involved in these processes but also by any citizen that needs to do building work. It represents a reduction in the number of pages needed to describe these requirements of over 95%. This confirms this common DEMO statistic as purported by [9] and [10]. Even though the information is more accessible and easier to grasp in the diagrams, the PBC's complexity is still present in our description table representing the legal requirements and procedures truthfully.

One of the main contributions of our research is that the representation of the PBC in the devised diagram and table allows a different organization of the information which makes it much easier to understand and find the relevant information at any point in the urban appraisal process. Before our project, the urban appraisal officers had a hard time finding exactly where each urban operation application was and which steps were still missing to continue or finalize the process. With our work, the urban appraisal officers can now easily check the path that each urban operation application should follow, according to the applicant's request. At any point, it is also easily verifiable which are the steps that the urban appraisal application needs to go through still to get the construction permit. Our new version of representing the Process Model solves several issues regarding current DEMO models, explained next.

The current Coordination Structure Diagram is not easy to grasp by newcomers and has extensive line clutter, as visible in the simple example of GloLog enterprise in Fig. 10 depicting a logistics process with "transactor" elements which combine the notion of transaction and the actor that executes it. Transaction was already a "strange" word for people non-familiar with DEMO and transactor seems even worse. Collaborators in an

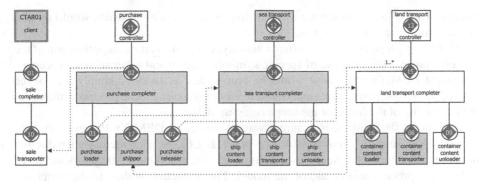

Fig. 10. The interimpediment structure in the GloLog enterprise [11]

organization relate much more with common terms such as *task*. The way we depict the PM (Fig. 6) is semantically richer by: presenting task names, much closer to day-to-day operations rather than "transactor names". We clearly separate the concerns of process composition, task causation, and task waiting. The composition perspective is represented by the connectors with diamonds; the causal by connectors with arrows; and the waiting by the connectors with double-crossed lines.

We solve the problem of "isolated" transactions in a process being able to be started by initiative of both internal or external actors without a need for a management or self-activation transaction - in the relatively simple process depicted in this paper, this would lead to a lot of unneeded tasks and connectors as there are many instances of these "isolated" transactions. The solution we propose is basically replicating the special "external activation connector" presented in some DEMO models of the past. In processes that imply an interaction between actors in different organizational systems, it's essential that we can express that some tasks can start "independently" in the context of an existing process instance.

We propose a simpler way to express border transactions with color gradients which can easily and rapidly make us understand which tasks are initiated by internal actors and executed by external actors and vice versa.

It is also clear that, regarding links between tasks, dashed means optional and non-dashed mandatory. Using numbers at the end of connectors to represent this essential concept is harder/slower to interpret as compared to the line expressing the concept. This is the main differentiation in most connections. Numbers should be used to reflect cardinalities higher than one.

It is interesting that, at least in this case, the waiting links form a tree of dependencies between many tasks that can be started independently and autonomously. We can also express the c-acts involved in all links, as well as cardinality. Furthermore, the network of dependencies expressed with our new syntactics and semantics appears to be able to be directly converted to a Petri-net. Petri-nets enable concurrency of tasks and non-determinism on the order they will be performed. Optional transactions in the network of dependencies correspond to the enactment of rights (or permits) that responsible actors might choose to use or not. It follows the old Roman law tradition that states that the option to act corresponds to an actor's right. These optional dependencies are much easier to handle in a Petri-net than with a simpler state-machine, which would require non-deterministic state transitions.

Our newly proposed notation offers a new layer of depth in the comprehension of the modeled process with the use of specific symbols to represent other related processes. In current DEMO's PSD those would be represented as tasks or simply with some connector to some transaction step. Our new way of depicting these processes improves the readability of the limits of the scope being modeled.

If we directly compare the current way of modeling DEMO's Process Structure Diagram (Fig. 3 and Fig. 4) with our new proposal (Fig. 6), we can notice a great reduction in the representation complexity even though we have the same 18 transactions (or 16 tasks and 2 process references) of the model. This reduction is due: to the better use of space of the task/process symbols as opposed to the PSD's transaction symbol; the reduction of the represented connectors, from 35 to 28 and the removal of the explicit representation of actor roles. It is important to differentiate border transactions thus our special symbols with color gradients to clearly depict external activation (external initiating actor) or internal activation (external executing actor). The TDT is a much better place to represent the concrete actor roles and organizational functions.

And our TDT ends up being a thorough Action Model by specifying both Action Rules Specification (columns "Originating task(s)", "Target task(s)", "Waits for task(s)" and "Conditions/Rules") and as well as some work instructions (task descriptions often include this).

Our practical experience in this project made clear that the term "task" is easier to understand by organization officers and, therefore, we propose that the DEMO methodology should consider replacing the word "transaction" with "task", at least in the representations used in day-to-day work.

Our proposals and claims led to very interesting discussions during the conference which made clear that there is a strong need to improve the way to present and communicate DEMO models. From these discussions we had the idea to propose the development of a new Enterprise Engineering theory: the *X-theory*, taking the CHI letter from the Greek alphabet and standing for **C**ommunication of **H**uman-readable-representations and **I**nterpretation theory. Currently, DEMO's representations and symbols are not grounded in any theory and the work presented in this paper constitutes initial empirical work in the direction of a clear separation between the meta-model aspects of DEMO and the presentation of much more friendly representations of its models to stakeholders/organizations that are easier to interpret. We should strive to make the notation and language used more colloquial so it can be understood with a simple explanation of a few minutes instead of requiring an introduction of complex theoretical subjects. Our future work in real-world applications of DEMO will provide further analysis and development of this theory.

7 Conclusions

In this paper, we propose a new way of representing and tooling the DEMO's Process Model, which fuses the Process Model contents with those of the Cooperation Model. We argue that the Cooperation Model should only show the composition of transactions, as depicted in the composition axiom [3] and that it should be renamed to its previous name: Construction Model.

We propose the new artifacts of Process Diagram and Transaction Description Table that constitute our vision for a new Process Model within the DEMO methodology. These two new artifacts come out from the need for a more agile and comprehensive solution to compile and present the essence of organizational reality when compared to the traditional DEMO models.

The single diagram that we named Process Diagram presents all the information that we deemed visually necessary to comprehensively depict the process while still being easy (enough) to understand by any officer. We also created a Transaction Description Table, where we could add more text-intensive relevant information in a structured way. Our new representation of the PM is semantically richer by presenting task names closer to day-to-day operations, while it clearly separates the concerns of process composition, task causation, and task waiting. This also solves the problem of the "isolated" transactions and clearly expresses, with color gradients, the tasks that are initiated by internal actors and executed by external actors and vice-versa. It makes clear that, regarding the links between tasks, dashed is optional and non-dashed mandatory. The composition perspective is represented by the diamonds, the causal by arrows, and the waiting by the double-crossed lines. We can also express the c-acts involved in the dependency links, as well as its cardinality.

This work reveals that our approach can present the information more straightforwardly and transparently, easier to be understood not only by the officers involved in these processes but also by any citizen who needs to do building work. It confirms the typical reduction of over 95% in the number of pages necessary to describe organizational reality, confirming previous studies with the DEMO methodology. Even though the information is more accessible and easier to grasp in the diagrams, the Portuguese Building Code's complexity is still present in our description table, representing the legal requirements and procedures in a comprehensive way.

One of our main research contributions is that the representations of reality in the devised diagram and table are organized in a way that makes it much easier to understand and find relevant information at any point in the process.

Although the present study provides valuable insights, there are a few limitations that should be recognized and these provide threads for future research. Due to the limited time and resources, we applied these diagrams to the urban appraisal division of the town council of the city of Funchal that is highly structured due to the applicable law requirements. Therefore, future work should explore these diagrams further by applying them to other organizations, especially in areas that do not have such strict regulations. These additional efforts will further confirm the validity of our work. Also, due to space and time constraints, this paper does not include a formal evaluation of the current and newly proposed representations, done by the town council officers, but preparation of such evaluation are underway and will be submitted for publication soon.

Acknowledgments. Special thanks to the officers from the town council of Funchal that contributed with their fruitful insights and feedback.

This work is supported by the Regional Development European Fund (INTERREG MAC), projects Dynamic eGov MAC2/5.11a/359 (MAC-2014-2020) and FiiHUB MAC2/2.3d/335 (MAC-2014-2020).

References

1. Hevner, A.R., March, S.T., Park, J., Ram, S.: Design science in information systems research. MIS Q. **28**, 75–105 (2004). https://doi.org/10.2307/25148625
2. Dietz, J.L.G., Mulder, H.B.F.: The enterprise engineering theories. In: Dietz, J.L.G., Mulder, H.B.F. (eds.) Enterprise Ontology. TEES, pp. 23–48. Springer, Cham (2020). https://doi.org/10.1007/978-3-030-38854-6_4
3. Dietz, J.L.G.: Enterprise Ontology: Theory and Methodology. Springer, Heidelberg (2006). https://doi.org/10.1007/3-540-33149-2
4. Hevner, A.R.: A three cycle view of design science research. Scand. J. Inf. Syst. **19**, 87–92 (2007)
5. Simon, H.A.: The Sciences of the Artificial. MIT Press, Cambridge (1996)
6. Dietz, J.L.G., Mulder, H.B.F.: The PSI theory: understanding the operation of organisations. In: Dietz, J.L.G., Mulder, H.B.F. (eds.) Enterprise Ontology. TEES, pp. 119–157. Springer, Cham (2020). https://doi.org/10.1007/978-3-030-38854-6_8
7. Dietz, J.L.G.: On the nature of business rules. In: Dietz, J.L.G., Albani, A., Barjis, J. (eds.) CIAO!/EOMAS -2008. LNBIP, vol. 10, pp. 1–15. Springer, Heidelberg (2008). https://doi.org/10.1007/978-3-540-68644-6_1
8. Dietz, J.L.G., Mulder, H.B.F.: The ALPHA Theory: Understanding the Essence of Organisations. In: Dietz, J.L.G., Mulder, H.B.F. (eds.) Enterprise Ontology. The Enterprise Engineering Series, pp. 227–257. Springer, Cham (2020). https://doi.org/10.1007/978-3-030-38854-6_11
9. Dietz, J.L.G., Mulder, H.B.F.: The DEMO methodology. In: Dietz, J.L.G., Mulder, H.B.F. (eds.) Enterprise Ontology . The Enterprise Engineering Series, pp. 261–299. Springer, Cham (2020). https://doi.org/10.1007/978-3-030-38854-6_12
10. Aveiro, D., Pinto, D.: Devising DEMO guidelines and process patterns and validating comprehensiveness and conciseness. In: Bider, I., et al. (eds.) BPMDS/EMMSAD -2014. LNBIP, vol. 175, pp. 408–423. Springer, Heidelberg (2014). https://doi.org/10.1007/978-3-662-43745-2_28
11. Dietz, J.L.G., Mulder, H.B.F.: The OMEGA theory: understanding the construction of organisations. In: Dietz, J.L.G., Mulder, H.B.F. (eds.) Enterprise Ontology. TEES, pp. 193–225. Springer, Cham (2020). https://doi.org/10.1007/978-3-030-38854-6_10

Evolving the DEMO Specification Language

Mark A. T. Mulder[1,2]([⊠])(iD) and Henderik A. Proper[3,4](iD)

[1] TEEC2, Hoevelaken, The Netherlands
markmulder@teec2.nl
[2] Radboud University, Nijmegen, The Netherlands
[3] Luxembourg Institute of Science and Technology (LIST), Belval, Luxembourg
e.proper@acm.org
[4] University of Luxembourg, Luxembourg City, Luxembourg

Abstract. This paper reports on the current state of the DEMO Specification Language (DEMOSL). The Design and Engineering Methodology for Organisations (DEMO) is a principal methodology in Enterprise Engineering (EE), while the DEMOSL defines the accompanying integrated modelling landscape.

DEMO provides a method to produce so-called essential models of organisations, which are highly abstracted ontological models. For the DEMOSL this implies that it should enable the integration of the different models used in organisations when they apply DEMO, while also enabling tool support, visualisation, as well as the exchange of models. This paper describes the state of the meta-models, as referenced in the MU-theory, for the modelling and visualisation of DEMO models. The purpose and examples of six of these models and meta-models are discussed, along with extensions of the visualisation of the DEMO models. Moreover, modelling rules are presented that guide the modeller and tool developer in creating diagrams and tables with their respective elements and connections.

1 Introduction

The aim of this paper is to report on the current state of the DEMOSL. The DEMO [3] is a principal methodology in EE [4], while the DEMOSL defines the accompanying integrated modelling landscape.

DEMO provides a method to produce so-called essential models of organisations, which are highly abstracted ontological models. The first step in applying DEMO is producing the so-called essential model of an organisation. An essential model comprises the integrated whole of four aspect models: the Construction Model (CM), the Action Model (AM), the Process Model (PM) and the Fact Model (FM). Each of these models is expressed in terms of one or more diagrams and accompanied by one or more cross-model tables.

The DEMOSL defines the accompanying integrated modelling landscape. As such, it should allow for the integration of the different DEMO models used in

© Springer Nature Switzerland AG 2021
D. Aveiro et al. (Eds.): EEWC 2020, LNBIP 411, pp. 153–172, 2021.
https://doi.org/10.1007/978-3-030-74196-9_9

organisations when applying DEMO, while also enabling tool support, visualisation, as well as the exchange of models.

The DEMOSL, as discussed in this paper, involves a further elaboration and refinement of the earlier version reported in [9]. The elaboration and refinements are, amongst others, based on experiences with the establishment of an integrated tool environment which supports the creation and management of DEMO related models [10].

The remainder of this paper is structured as follows. Section 2 will briefly visit the research methodological background of the research project. Since DEMO's modelling landscape is largely founded on the underlying Model Universe (MU) theory [3], Sect. 3 will summarise the relevant elements of this theory. Using this as a background, Sect. 4 provides an overview of the different models that play a role in the DEMO modelling landscape. Section 5 is dedicated to the discussion of the meta-models and how they have been used in the current tool environment. This is followed (in Sect. 6) by a reflection n the experiences with the implementation of the meta-models in an operational tool environment. This discussion will also highlight some of the refinements and improvements that had to be made in DEMO's meta-model and earlier versions of the DEMOSL to make them operationalisable in a tool environment. Finally, before concluding, Sect. 7 provides an outlook for future research.

2   Research Background

The research effort as reported on in this paper, aims to improve the DEMOSL specification. The DEMOSL is available in a number of versions and at the moment the reported research project commenced, the latest version was 3.7. Moverover, this version had already undergone an initial validation [9].

Originally, the DEMOSL was designed to better understand the concepts that need to be included in DEMO models. However, for the development of automated tool support for DEMO, more details and specificity are needed than is included in the original DEMOSL. This includes e.g. details about the graphical layout of diagrams, exchange of models between tool environments, as well as the specificity of the actual models. As such, the goal is the creation of a version of the DEMOSL that is complete enough to automatically validate the rules and restrictions involved in DEMO modelling using automated tools.

The resulting specification is divided into four kinds of models, and four associated meta-models. These four model kinds need to comply with the requirements as stated in [10]. The required meta-models for the tooling have been iterated to specifically fulfil the following three requirements (see [10]):

1. The tool must support the interchange of models.
2. The tool must support the creation of all four aspect models of DEMO.
3. The tool must allow for model verification against the DEMO meta-model, DEMOSL.

Next to these requirements, the meta-models need to be "build" on top of the MU theory, which is a foundational part of DEMO [5] and was known in a previous iteration of DEMO as *Factual Knowledge* [3].

From a research methodological perspective, the research effort as reported on in this paper, uses the Design Science Research (DSR) approach [1,12]. In design science terminology, the DEMOSL is an artefact. In applying the design science research approach, the development of the DEMOSL is rooted in the existing EE and DEMO body of knowledge (enabling *rigour*), while allowing for the iterative improvement and refinement of the artefact in terms of experiments and cases (enabling *relevance*). The latter involve(d) experiments in terms of the implementation of DEMOSL in an enterprise-grade tool environment [10], as well as the application in real-world cases.

3   MU Theory

The MU-theory provides the theoretical foundation of the notions of model, modelling, and modelling language as used in DEMO. The most recent version of the MU-theory has been presented in [5].

Given the aim of the reported research to further evolve the accompanying DEMOSL, the MU-theory is considered as a fixed and pre-defined part of the knowledge base (in design science terms). In this section, we highlight some of the key elements of the MU-theory that are relevant to the understanding and positioning of the remainder of the paper.

The MU-theory theory adopts Apostel's [2] definition of model: *"Any subject using a system A to obtain knowledge of a system B, is using A as a model of B."* This definition conveys the basic understanding of the notion of model as being a role [5].

A key part of the MU-theory is the General Conceptual Modelling Framework (GCMF), as depicted in Fig. 1. The MU-theory uses the term complex to refer to systems in the general sense, as used in Apostel's [2] definition of model. However, since DEMO uses its own (more specific) definition of system, the term *complex* is preferred when speaking about modelling in general (as is the case for the MU-theory).

The basic thinking underlying the GCMF is based on the semiotic triangle by Ogden and Richards [11]. In line with this, the MU-theory refers to the phenomena we observe and interact with in reality as *concrete complexes*, while the conception of these complexes an actor harbours in their mind is referred to as the *conceptual complexes*, and a resulting symbolic representation (such as a diagram, a narrative description, or an XML document) as *symbolic complexes*.

When combining this with Apostel's definition of a model, then one can state that when such a complex A is used to obtain knowledge of a complex B, then A is said to be a model of B. As a corollary to this, one can (using the terminology from the MU-theory) distinguish between *concrete models*, *conceptual models* and *symbolic models*.

The MU-theory states that the creation of a conceptual complex needs a prescription, called a *conceptual schema*. It is furthermore assumed that a *conceptual complex* can only be created in the mind of some actor observing a

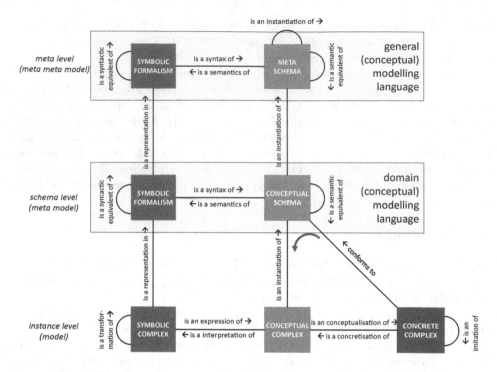

Fig. 1. The general conceptual modelling framework, adopted from [5]

domain, if they already have a *conceptual schema* in terms of which they can observe the world. This is indicated by the red curved arrow in Fig. 1. As such, a *conceptual schema* limits the observable world (of an actor). The MU-theory also states that a modelling language essentially involves a combination of a conceptual schema and a corresponding symbolic formalism that provides the symbolic representation of the conceptual schema.

The DEMOSL is targeted at the schema level of Fig. 1. In other words, it should provide a symbolic formalism corresponding to the conceptual schema(s) used by the different model (and diagram) kinds within DEMO. As illustrated in Fig. 1, the MU-theory also identifies a meta level involving a meta schema and corresponding symbolic formalism. This is where, in our case, we will find UML class diagrams and XML Document Type Definitions (DTDs) to define the DEMOSL.

The MU-theory also provides global guidelines on how to create the various levels of complexes and schemas. Finding a lower level from a higher level can be accomplished by deduction, which also provides a good method for the verification of models. Induction can be used to derive the meta level from examples. In doing the latter, it can be helpful to transform graphical languages into structured textual languages, called verbalisation. We used both deduction and induction methods to create meta-models and DEMO information models which we will describe in the next sections.

4   Perspectives on DEMO Models

Before we proceed to a discussion of the meta-models involved in the DEMOSL, we need to distinguish between three perspectives on the models used when applying DEMO. These are illustrated in Fig. 2.

The first perspective is the *methodology perspective*. Even though it provides a thorough theoretical basis, the DEMO methodology book [5] was primarily written to teach learners (students and practitioners) to create models in accordance with the DEMO way of thinking, and draw (human to human) communicable models to reason about the organisation. Since the book puts the priority on "doing", when introducing the different model kinds, there was no need for a strict meta-model. Furthermore, the formalisation(s) provided in the book aim to support didactic goals rather than the development of automated modelling tools. As such, it was never meant to provide a detailed formalisation and meta-models, that would enable the development of, and automated support for, the methodology. As discussed in [7], different meta-modelling and formalisation goals will/should also result in formalisations with different level(s) of detail/specificity.

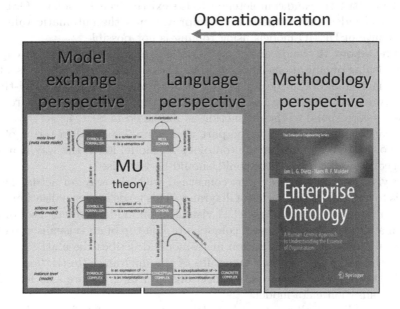

Fig. 2. DEMO model perspectives

When using DEMOSL as base for tool development, then it should indeed provide a more complete and detailed formalisation and meta-model; taking us to the *language perspective*. This is the perspective where it should be possible to (automatically) reason about models and meta-models, to e.g. support model verification. This requires the formalisation of the language definition in a format that lends itself better for automatic processing [7]. It also requires the completion and operationalisation of the ontological meta-models as included in the methodology perspective; in particular the rules and constraints to be applied to the actual models.

The last *model exchange perspective* concerns the exchange and storage of model information. Reasoning about models is only possible when everybody has the same notation of the model and the notation enables the reasoning in the meta-model.

The notation used must be the same across different modelling tools. Therefore, the meaning of the elements and attributes must be well defined. Moreover, the notation must enable the reasoning within the exchange model to be able to check consistency of this model. In addition, the internal consistency needs to be correct and needs to be checked before the model can be converted back to the language perspective.

5   Overview of the Meta-models

In this section the new meta-models will be presented. These meta-models add information, structure and completeness to the existing version of DEMOSL. Our research concluded that without these improvements the automatic validation and exchange of DEMO models using tooling is not possible.

Figure 3 shows the landscape of meta-models that together have the capability of modelling organisations using DEMO. The landscape is depicted as a three dimensional framework, projected on top of the framework from the MU-theory.

The two levels that have been projected on top of the framework from the MU-theory correspond to the distinction as discussed in Sect. 4.

The language perspective is the part that is implemented in terms of software, in order to reason about the (ontological) model itself, the way it may be exchanged, as well as how these could/should be visualised.

The visualisation perspective is concerned with the way an actual DEMO model is to be visualised in terms of diagrams. This leads to a visualisation model conform a visualisation meta-model. A visualisation model involves a set of visualisation attributes (position, size, colours, etc.) on top of an (visualised part of) ontological model. The visualisation meta-model describes these attributes and contains the scripting and data structure of the diagrams. Restrictions on the allowed elements, attributes, and connections in a diagram are also formalised in the visualisation meta-model.

Below, we discuss all mentioned models and meta-models from right to left, from the top to the bottom of Fig. 3.

5.1   High Level Ontological Meta-model

The high level ontological meta-model of DEMO is depicted in Fig. 4. The diagram shows the existing property types and concepts in black. The new property types and concepts that result from this research have been added in red. This

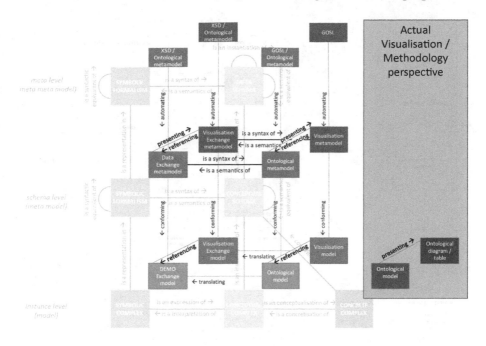

Fig. 3. Meta-model set

high level ontological meta-model is the base for the ontological meta-model of Sect. 5.2.

The high level ontological meta-model is the meta-model that is closest to the meta-model that lists all ontological principles of DEMO models [3]. For example, ontologically, the Composite Actor Role (CAR) cannot be an initiator of a transaction kind because an underlying elementary actor role must be the initiator. Therefore, this property type does not exist in the high level ontological meta-model.

5.2   Ontological Meta-model

In contrast with the high level ontological meta-model, the ontological meta-model (see Fig. 5) contains all implementation attribute types and property types for the DEMO meta-model. The ontological meta-model also includes property types between the concepts.

The example mentioned in Sect. 5.1 about the CAR not being an initiator is not valid in this ontological meta-model. Whenever one designs a CAR that initiates the transaction, this property type instantiation must be present in the model and needs a representation in the ontological meta-model. Therefore, the ontological meta-model also has the property type 'AR is an initiator of TK' from the CAR to the Transaction Kind (TK). Furthermore, mathematical rules have been designed to make sure only the correct property type instantiations can be present in the final ontological model.

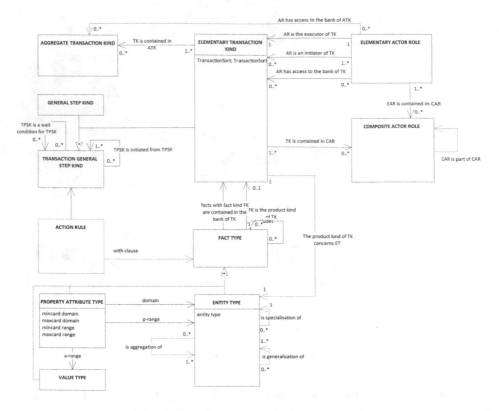

Fig. 4. High level ontological meta-model

The table shown in Table 1 provides all allowed Property Types between the objects of this meta-model.

5.3   Data Exchange Meta-model

The concept of a data exchange meta-model is intertwined in the concept of the ontological meta-model. We describe the data exchange meta-model in terms that a computer can understand.

We choose to represent the data exchange meta-model in XML Schema Definition (XSD), which is a commonly used technique. The alternative structure, XML Metadata Interchange (XMI), has no broad implementation and, therefore, we rejected it as a candidate. The data exchange meta-model represents all entity types and property types of the ontological meta-model. This data exchange meta-model is unambiguously readable for a computer. The proposal of a DEMO exchange format [13,14], based on DEMO 2, is a good start for our exchange meta-model. Despite the current version of DEMO, at moment of writing, is version 4, the modelling itself has not changed and is equivalent to DEMO 2. No attempt has been done to upgrade the proposed formats to DEMO

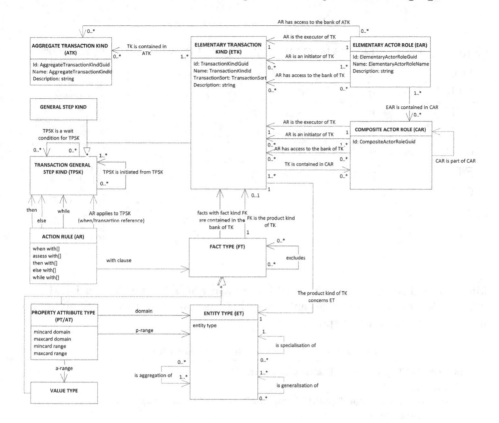

Fig. 5. Ontological meta-model

3 before. Above all, we have based our research at DEMOSL version 3.7, and, therefore, this version is an upgrade of the existing format. DEMO 4 introduces a new element but does not invalidate DEMO 2 or DEMO 3 models and, thus, the choice for these older models are still valid. In future research this exchange model has to be adapted to the features of DEMO 4. The existing paper [14] proposes a data exchange meta-model for the FM and the CM. The XSD for CM proposes the storage of the id, name, initiator(s), executor, and information link and result type. This information is based on older DEMO specifications and, therefore, lacks essential information from the current version. We will build this XSD structure for every element type in the new DEMOSL proposal structure.

The first structure is the name element. The whole DEMO model has a name. Every component has an internal id. We will not mention these attributes while using the data meta-model, but we will model it.

The next structure is a Global Unique IDentfier (GUID) element. A GUID identifies all types and kinds within the exchange model and is a 128-bit number used to uniquely identify information in computer systems.

Another structure are rule elements. Rules restrict the naming of the elements used in e.g. a CM. One of the rules we will mention in this paper is the transaction

Table 1. Element property types

To → / From ↓	ETK	ATK	EAR	CAR	ET	CET	TPSK	AR
ETK	–	c	e	ce	–	–	–	–
ATK	–	c	–	–	–	–	–	–
EAR	ia	a	–	c	–	–	–	–
CAR	ia	a	–	c	–	–	–	–
ET	o	–	–	–	xsrg	–	–	–
CET	o	–	–	–	–	–	–	–
TPSK	c	–	–	–	–	–	iy	tlwh
AR	–	–	–	–	W	–	–	–

Property Types
[c] contained in
[o] concerns
[i] initiator
[e] executor
[a] access to bank
[s] specialisation
[r] aggregation
[g] generalisation
[t] then
[l] else
[w] while
[h] when
[W] with
[x] excludes
[y] wait
[f] role of

kind name. The name is built up of lower case words as specified in DEMOSL [6]. The XSD notation enables enforcing this rule. Note that we allow giving no name for practical use purposes.

Listing 1.1. XSD example: Transaction kind

```
<xs:complexType name="TransactionKind">
  <xs:sequence>
    <xs:element name="Identification" type="TransactionKindId"></
        xs:element>
    <xs:element name="Name" type="TransactionKindName"></xs:element>
    <xs:element name="TransactionSort" type="TransactionSort" default="
        unknown"></xs:element>
  </xs:sequence>
  <xs:attribute name="Id" type="TransactionKindGuid" use="required"/>
</xs:complexType>
```

This exchange rule set described in XSD can sufficiently restrict field content for each TK. The full set of XSD specification is already available for evaluation purposes to some research groups. The full specification with examples will be available to the public at the end of the research program. More information on the location of this specification will be published on multiple sites[1].

The CAR is the embodiment of multiple actor roles at once. This concept allows for modelling the unknown actor role or the 'don't want to know' actor role. In the DEMO methodology the concept of Scope of Interest (SoI) is used to restrain the modelling effort to a selected portion of the organisation. Absent from the DEMOSL meta-model [6], is the SoI itself. To be able to model this concept it could be added, but closer examination of the concept reveals that CAR represents the same information and is, therefore, used for this concept.

---

[1] http://demo.nl and http://teec2.nl.

5.4   Visualisation Meta-model

Communicating a graphical representation of a DEMO aspect model is not trivial. We could choose to communicate the image format in BitMaP image file (BMP), Portable Network Graphics (PNG) or Scalable Vector Graphics (SVG) formats. These formats would give the model interpreter a visualised representation, but would lack the underlying linked model information. We could also transform the graphical representation into a standard commercial format like Microsoft PowerPoint XML Presentation (PPTX) or Microsoft Visio XML Drawing (VSDX), but that could cause vendor lock-in. Instead of these formats, we chose to create only the essential attributes of the kinds and types of the diagram. This point of view is new compared to DEMOSL [6], which only describes visual properties and the exchange format [14] that does not address any visuals.

When we represent elements in a visualised graphical format, the location of the element on the diagram is an essential property. The location type attribute is available for purposes that might differ between software implementation. Next, the size, on the other hand, is used to visualise elements within a diagram. Finally, we define a line as a visualised connection between two or more points. It has a starting point, an endpoint and optionally several midpoints to create a path.

The table shown in Table 2 provides all allowed Property Types between the objects of this meta-model, while below we discuss more specific visualisation details of the various aspect models.

Construction Model – The Organisation Construction Diagram (OCD) is a diagram that expresses a part of the CM. More specifically, it contains the TK, Aggregate Transaction Kind (ATK), Elementary Actor Role (EAR) and CAR concepts. The visualised property types are the initiator, executor and access property types (see Table 2).

The representation of the OCD is used for the communication of the CM. The OCD allows TK, ATK, EAR, CAR as valid elements and initiator, executor and interstriction as valid property types.

The visualisation of the transactions and their products is a table with four columns called the Transaction Product Table (TPT). The transaction kind identification, the transaction kind name, the product kind identification and the product kind formulation. The first two columns can be filled by transaction kind attributes Identification and Name. The last two columns are the properties Identification and Name of the Independent Fact Kind. These two elements have a one-on-one relation and always exist.

We argue that *the concept of SoI is equivalent to the concept of CAR within modelling the CM*. When starting to model an organisation, the first actor inside the SoI is a composite actor role. The methodology describes that this actor role stays in place until one is able to retrieve the information to redesign the internal actor roles of this composite actor role into a white-box model. The CAR does not vanish. The CAR becomes equal to the SoI [9]. Therefore, the only difference

Table 2. Diagram entity and property types

Diagram → Entity Types ↓	OCD	PSD	TPD	OFD	ARD	RHD	AFD	..
ETK	X	X	X	X	–	–	–	–
ATK	X	–	–	–	–	–	–	–
EAR	X	X	–	–	–	X	X	–
CAR	X	X	–	–	–	X	–	–
ET	–	–	–	X	–	–	–	–
CET	–	–	–	X	–	–	–	–
TPSK	–	X	X	–	X	–	–	–
AR	–	–	–	–	X	–	–	–
Property Types ↓								
[c] contained in	–	–	–	–	–	X	–	–
[o] concerns	–	–	–	X	–	–	–	–
[i] initiator	X	X	–	–	–	–	–	–
[e] executor	X	–	–	–	–	–	–	–
[a] access to bank	X	–	–	–	–	–	–	–
[s] specialisation	–	–	–	X	–	–	–	–
[r] aggregation	–	–	–	X	–	–	–	–
[g] generalisation	–	–	–	X	–	–	–	–
[t] then	–	–	–	–	X	–	–	–
[l] else	–	–	–	–	X	–	–	–
[w] while	–	–	–	–	X	–	–	–
[h] when	–	–	–	–	X	–	–	–
[W] with	–	–	–	–	X	–	–	–
[x] excludes	–	–	–	X	–	–	–	–
[y] wait	–	X	–	–	–	–	–	–
[f] role of	–	–	–	–	–	–	X	–

between an SoI and a CAR is its appearance in the diagram. The boundary transactions of the SoI are the interacting transactions in the diagram.

One could still argue that an SoI could be smaller than all transactions that interact with the CAR. This can be illustrated with an extra transaction to CA0 in the construction model. The question that remains is whether the CAR, used as SoI is the same in the diagram as in the model. In practice the SoI never exceeds the diagram boundaries and therefore, de-facto, the CAR can be used for the same purpose. When using the CAR as SoI some nice features for the hierarchy of actor roles appear.

This being said, combined with the ability to nest CARs it becomes clear that an EAR within multiple CAR is not modelled as a construction. It is possible to model this hierarchy as a functional structure, though this is not ontological.

Process Model – In the Process Structure Diagram (PSD) the initiation of the first request is done using the relation 'is initiated from'. This would be sufficient if a step is always initiated from the same step. When, instead of the promise-step, another step is used for initiation this cannot be modelled. Therefore, the relation has to be remodelled as a self-reference in Transaction Process Step Kind (TPSK) 'TPSK is initiated from TPSK'.

The PSD is a diagram that contains elements from the PM. More specifically it contains the TK, EAR and CAR. The visualised relations are the call-link and the wait-link relations. The Transaction Pattern Diagram (TPD) is a diagram that contains elements from the PM. More specifically it contains the TK and TPSK. The visualised relations are the process order, call link and the wait link relations (see Table 2).

Fact Model – The DEMOSL ontological model has some concepts that have made it directly to the ontological model of the fact model. Fact Type and Entity Type have been added to the data model in the same form. Other concepts will be removed or reduced because of the following reasoning. First, the Constructed Entity Type is a concept that allows reasoning about the specialised entities derived from an Entity Type. In a less conceptual model this results in the Entity Type like the generalisation relation between Constructed Entity Type and Entity Type already suggests. The same holds for a generalisation and aggregation of this constructed entity type. Both relations end in the Entity Type Set which, in turn, is an Entity Type concept on its own. This leaves the three relations as self-relations on the Entity Type. Next, the Event Type concept is a data perception of the process events of transaction kinds and TPSK. Events are related to C-acts and C-facts and only concern a concept in the P-world. Therefore, the concerns relation is created between the elementary transaction kind and the Fact Type concept.

The Object Fact Diagram (OFD) is a diagram that contains elements from the FM. More specifically it contains the Independent P-Fact Kind (IFK), Entity Type (ET) and Attribute Type (AT). The visualised relations are the reference, specialisation, aggregation and the concerns relations (see Table 2).

Action Model – The AM is the aspect model with the largest number of details about the enterprise. These details build on the CM, PM and the FM. Therefore, references to these aspect models should be used in order to keep the AM consistent with the other aspect models. Traditionally the Action Rules Specification (ARS) is specified in a natural language, restricted by a partially grammar. This allows for freedom of expression while being readable by humans. Though the advantage of the readability is large, the disadvantage of the not-strict natural language makes it difficult, and at this moment even impossible, to do an automated model verification and validation. Where the three other aspect models always have been described in a graphical way, the AM has been described within a grammar construction. This complicates communication towards different users of these models. All aspect models should have a textual and graphical representation of at least the most essential features of the model.

We added a graphical representation to the AM and improved the grammar of the ARS. All grammar references to other elements of the DEMO model have been connected in the action model.

The AM is the least developed and used aspect model of DEMO. For automation we need this model to represent all details about business rules and their relations to facts and processes.

The AM has no graphical representation in DEMO 3.7. One might argue that the separation of the event part, assess part and result part are actual AM graphical representations due to the fact that these sections of the grammar are often visualised with a background colour in educational slides. Nevertheless, these representation is not more or less that the colouring of a grammar in a modern integrated developing environment. The existing AM has four essential features.

1. Linked to a TK, it needs parameters (with-clause) to verify that all essential information is present to perform the step.
2. Linked to another step, it has to wait for other TKs to finish.
3. Inner conditions have to be checked.
4. Based on the conditions the linked follow-up actions have to be triggered.

Except for the feature three, the features have a connection to other parts of the model. Connections can be visualised as a line, like it has been done in the other three aspect models.

Let us define the connections for the AM.

- With – The with-clause connects several attributes of entities (from the FM) to either the agendum-clause, while clause of action clause. These connections will be represented with an solid line with a winged arrow head. The with connection can connect to the when, while and action clauses.
- While – The while clause connects a different transaction step (from the PM). This connection will be represented with a dotted line with a solid arrow, just like the wait link in the PSD.
- Action – The action clause connects a transaction step with another step. This is the same connection as a call link in the PSD.

Figure 6 gives an impression of the visualisation of this Action Rules Diagram (ARD). While not all arrows have been drawn to the right specifications, this early representation does give a instantiated view on the meta-model.

When we follow the example of Fig. 6, and start at the TPSK1 placed on the top of the diagram, we can see the process unfolding. For the TPSK1 the

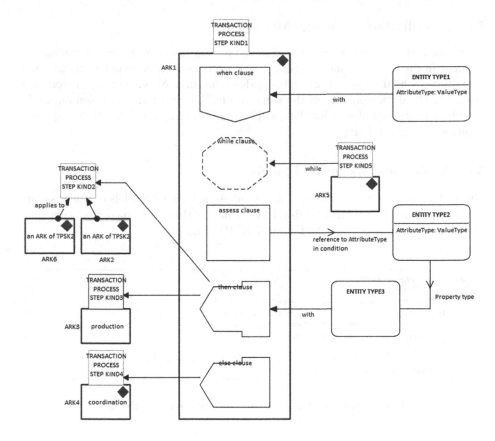

Fig. 6. ARD representation example

Action Rules Kind (ARK) ARK1 is the action rule that needs to be evaluated. In the when clause the required information can be expressed as entity and attribute types. In the following step, the while clause, the process can wait on the completion of the TPSK 5. When these steps have been completed the assess clause is evaluated whether the conditions, that reference the information in ET2, are true. When these conditions are evaluated the then clause triggers TPSK2 and the ARKs 2 and 6 are evaluated.

Action Rule Specification – The information in the existing AM is not detailed enough to validate a model. After analysing the existing, published action specifications we created a grammar that closely represents the existing examples and matches the wishes of the expert group that helped to create the exchange model. The verbalisation used in the DEMOSL grammar of the AM can also be specified in relations to the other aspect models. These relations are described in the ontological model.

5.5   Visualisation Exchange Meta-model

All element that have been described in the previous section have a visualisation element in the exchange meta-model. The structure of the visualisation elements is similar to the data exchange meta-model structure. All visualisation elements reference the data elements in the same model. The visualisation elements add the visualisation attributes for the specific diagram to that information (e.g. size, location, waypoints) (Fig. 7).

5.6   Models and Exchange Models

Due to the origin of the research topics, publishing created models is not possible. One of the cases was modelling dutch NEN norms that confirmed that this type of organisation can be modelled using DEMO (Fig. 8).

```
<xs:complexType name="TransactionKindElement">
  <xs:sequence>
    <xs:element name="ReferenceId" type="TransactionKindGuid"/>
    <xs:element name="Initiator" type="xs:boolean"/>
    <xs:element name="Location" type="Location"/>
    <xs:element name="Size" type="Size"/>
  </xs:sequence>
  <xs:attribute name="Id" type="DiagramElementGuid" use="required"/>
</xs:complexType>
```

Fig. 7. Visualisation exchange TransactionKindElement

Exchanging DEMO models with other tools also needs other tools with the same meta-model implementation. The only tool that has this meta-model in place is a gamification tool. This information exchange has been tested successfully (Fig. 9).

6   Reflection

The research effort as reported on in this paper, took the description of DEMOSL 3.7 as its starting point. In DSR terminology, the meta-model that was created from this specification was the first iteration of the DEMOSL artefact. Using all model from the DEMO book [3], and associated course material, we created a second iteration.

Based on the meta-model of the second iteration artefact, a tool was created [10], which has been used in practice to model organisations. In doing so, all missing modelling elements have been added to the model and to the tool and used in successive cases. After more than seven real live cases we are convinced that the CM, PM and FM are fairly complete to hold all elements and property types needed for modelling DEMO.

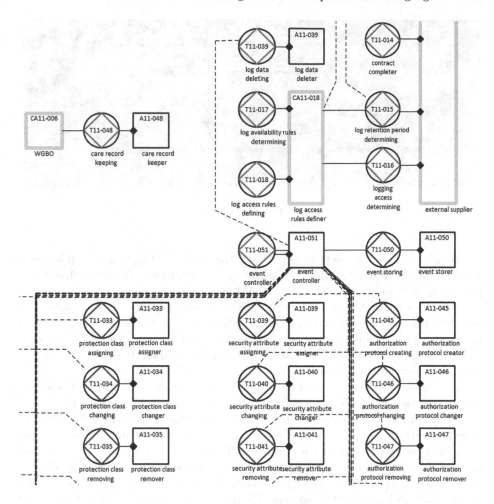

Fig. 8. Partial NEN example

The AM was not complete enough, but has improved a lot compared to the original version. These are not only elements that could be missing in the tool and the meta-model, but often challenge the theory as well because the obvious parts of DEMO can be modelled with more ease than before.

A major challenge in DEMO visualisation remains the potential variety of stakeholders [8]. The more types of stakeholders the larger number of viewpoints might be needed. To aid in bridging the gap between stakeholders in practice, we added a functional concept to the construction model. This is the functional value that the organisation gives to the construction model in its organisation. This one-on-one functional translation is the first step to connect the functional business and construction domains of DEMO.

Fig. 9. Gamification scene

We also did our first steps in developing the eXtended Organisational Essence and Revealing (XOER) method. Modelling all viewpoints at the same time looks promising as it helps modelling and thinking.

During practical use of DEMO models, we encountered some diagrams that were needed to fully represent the model. First, there is the Actor role Function Diagram (AFD). This diagram can be represented in an Actor role Function Table (AFT), but that representation has limited readability. The AFD is the graphical equivalent of the AFT.

The AFD is a diagram that contains elements from both the CM and the implementation world. More specifically it contains the EAR and CAR.

Summarizing these reflections, we made adjustments in the DEMOSL to reflect practical needs in DEMO modelling and to enable automation of the modelling and validation of these models. Furthermore, we added steps in the methodology to cover a wider perspective of the modelling needs that do not necessary belong to the ontology domain, but surely are adjacent and often more visible to business stakeholders. We find the extensions to DEMOSL to be relevant and useful.

7   Future Research

The upcoming iteration of XOER, on which the work has been started as we write this paper, will help us to make this method describable and educable. It will also be subject to an expert group for validation of the meta-model and the used representations.

In a parallel track we are also adding the concepts that are needed for the implementation of the (DEMO-based) VISI[2] standard for the Dutch construction sector; which are now part of the current meta-model.

---

[2] https://www.crow.nl/downloads/pdf/contracteren/visi/visi-systematiek-doelstellin gen-grondbeginselen-be.aspx.

More research is needed on the visualisation of the created DEMO models. A current project is used to investigate the influence of projecting well-known concepts on the explanation and visualisation of DEMO concepts. Although these concepts might not be completely correct, it might improve the acceptability of DEMO as a methodology.

8   Conclusion

In this paper, we discussed the current state of the DEMOSL. In the context of a design science based research effort, the DEMOSL is being refined and extended such that it can serve as a base for automated tool development. We have now reached a stage where the meta-model is sufficient to automate the modelling and validation of the model. Furthermore, the extension of the DEMOSL makes it more comprehensible for people to create information models that support modelling in or with DEMO.

As a next step the meta-models will be extended even further to completely support DEMO 3 and the successor DEMO 4. Development on the methodology needs support in the meta-models, information and automation.

References

1. Aken, J.V., Andriessen, D.: Handboek ontwerpgericht wetenschappelijk onderzoek. Boom Lemma (2011). In Dutch
2. Apostel, L.: Towards the formal study of models in the non-formal sciences. Synthese **12**, 125–161 (1960)
3. Dietz, J.L.G.: Enterprise Ontology - Theory and Methodology. Springer, Heidelberg (2006). https://doi.org/10.1007/3-540-33149-2
4. Dietz, J.L.G., et al.: The discipline of enterprise engineering. Int. J. Organ. Des. Eng. **3**(1), 86–114 (2013)
5. Dietz, J.L.G., Mulder, J.B.F.: Enterprise Ontology - A Human-Centric Approach to Understanding the Essence of Organisation. The Enterprise Engineering Series, Springer, Heidelberg (2020). https://doi.org/10.1007/978-3-030-38854-6
6. Dietz, J.L.G., Mulder, M.A.T.: Demo specification language, vol. 3, p. 7 (2017)
7. Hofstede, A.H.M.T., Proper, H.A.: How to formalize it?: Formalization principles for information system development methods. Inf. Softw. Technol. **40**(10), 519–540 (1998)
8. Lankhorst, M.M., Torre, L.V.D., Proper, H.A., Arbab, F., Steen, M.W.A.: Viewpoints and visualisation. In: Enterprise Architecture at Work - Modelling, Communication and Analysis, 4th edn. The Enterprise Engineering Series, pp. 171–214. Springer, Heidelberg (2017)
9. Mulder, M.A.T.: Validating the demo specification language. In: Enterprise Engineering Working Conference, pp. 131–143. Springer, Heidelberg (2018). https://doi.org/10.1007/978-3-030-06097-8_8
10. Mulder, M.A.T., Proper, H.A.: Towards enterprise-grade tool support for DEMO. In: Grabis, J., Bork, D. (eds.) PoEM 2020. LNBIP, vol. 400, pp. 90–105. Springer, Cham (2020). https://doi.org/10.1007/978-3-030-63479-7_7

11. Ogden, C.K., Richards, I.A.: The Meaning of Meaning - A Study of the Influence of Language upon Thought and of the Science of Symbolism. University of Cambridge, Oxford, United Kingdom, Magdalene College (1923)
12. Recker, J.: Scientific Research in Information Systems: A Beginner's Guide. Springer, Heidelberg (2012). https://doi.org/10.1007/978-3-642-30048-6
13. Wang, Y.: Transformation of DEMO models into exchangeable format. Master's thesis, Delft University of Technology, Delft, The Netherlands (2009)
14. Wang, Y., Albani, A., Barjis, J.: Transformation of DEMO metamodel into XML schema. In: Albani, A., Dietz, J.L.G., Verelst, J. (eds.) EEWC 2011. LNBIP, vol. 79, pp. 46–60. Springer, Heidelberg (2011). https://doi.org/10.1007/978-3-642-21058-7_4

Fact Model in DEMO - Urban Law Case and Proposal of Representation Improvements

Bernardo Gouveia[1,2,3](✉) (iD), David Aveiro[1,2,3] (iD), Dulce Pacheco[1,2] (iD),
Duarte Pinto[1,2] (iD), and Duarte Gouveia[1,2,3] (iD)

[1] Madeira Interactive Technologies Institute, Caminho da Penteada, 9020-105 Funchal, Portugal
{bernardo.gouveia,dulce.pacheco,duarte.nuno}@m-iti.org
[2] NOVA-LINCS, Universidade NOVA de Lisboa, Campus da Caparica,
2829-516 Caparica, Portugal
[3] Faculty of Exact Sciences and Engineering, University of Madeira, Caminho da Penteada,
9020-105 Funchal, Portugal
daveiro@uma.pt, duarte.gouveia@staff.uma.pt

Abstract. This paper reports the findings and insights obtained from the application of a DEMO-based methodology in a collaboration project with the town council of Funchal, city of Madeira Island, on the subject of the Portuguese Building Code of law. As agreed with the council, one of the goals of this project was to model the universe of discourse of their Urban Appraisal Department. Its activity is subject to very complex legal restrictions encompassing several knowledge domains such as architecture, engineering, etc. The unique circumstances and requirements of the project motivated a novel version of DEMO's Fact Model. Specifically, 510 surveyed facts, composed of 65 concepts and 445 composing attributes along with their rationale, were specified in two main artifacts presented in this paper: the Fact Diagram and the Fact Description Table. Moreover, 567 combinations between 119 types of application deliverables and 21 types of urban operations - all of which potentially subject to future changes - were considered as instances of concepts in type-square structures related to application deliverable management. Our main research contributions are the synthetization and expressive power of the improved Fact Model, which allowed us to overcome the complexity and intricacies of legislation and create representations that are easily understood and productively discussed by the full range of stakeholders regardless of their technical prowess, experience, or background.

Keywords: Enterprise engineering · DEMO · Fact model · Fact diagram ·
Building code · Building appraisal process

1 Introduction

Contemporary information and communication systems are key to organizations' success and can be a major driver of organizational changes and transformations [1]. The effective transition of strategy into infrastructure requires extensive activity on both the

© Springer Nature Switzerland AG 2021
D. Aveiro et al. (Eds.): EEWC 2020, LNBIP 411, pp. 173–190, 2021.
https://doi.org/10.1007/978-3-030-74196-9_10

organizational design and the information systems design to create, respectively, effective organizational infrastructure and effective information system infrastructure [2]. Organizations implement information systems to improve their effectiveness and efficiency, but the achievement of this goal depends on the capabilities of the information system and the characteristics of the organization [2].

The DEMO (Design and Engineering Methodology for Organizations) is based on the PSI theory of Enterprise Ontology. It studies the organizations' operational essence [3]. DEMO's Way of Modelling comprises a set of models and diagrams to represent an organization. They are correlated with each other, representing organizational reality in a coherent and platform-independent way [4]. However, we argue that the current syntax and semantics of DEMO's Fact Model is too complex and cluttered, being difficult to interpret by laymen. Applying DEMO to an Urban Appraisal Department, subject to very complex and strict legal requirements and procedures, allowed us to refine improved representations for the Fact Model while respecting the main theories and concepts behind DEMO.

This paper is organized into six sections. We start by presenting our research method and motivation, followed by theoretical foundations. We then proceed to introduce our practical project, followed by the presentation of our proposal for a new way to represent DEMO's Fact Model. We then proceed to a discussion section and wrap up with some conclusions.

2   Research Method and Motivation

According to the design-science research, an artifact's building helps to better understand a design problem and its solution [2]. However, as technical knowledge grows, IT has been applied to new areas [1], making the design of useful artifacts complex due to the need for creative advances in domain areas in which existing theory is often insufficient [2]. Nevertheless, the resultant IT artifacts extend the boundaries of human problem solving and organizations' capabilities by providing both intellectual and computational tools [2].

In this work, we took into account the Seven Guidelines for Design Science in Information Systems Research [2] and followed the Design Science Research Cycles [5]. The Relevance Cycle connects the project's contextual environment with the design science activities [5]. We have defined our work's scope based on the intricacies of the Portuguese Building Code (PBC). The requirements and procedures for municipal urban appraisal are very complex with many vague and ambiguous elements and, consequently, the PBC is applied ambiguously across the country. An orderly way of representing all concepts would aid the officers at urban appraisal departments in their daily tasks and might even facilitate the legislator's work, especially when introducing changes to the law. The Rigor Cycle connects the design science activities with the existing scientific foundations, experience, and expertise [5], ensuring an innovative artifact. This paper presents two artifacts built to thoroughly identify the facts necessary for urban appraisal processes according to the PBC. The Design Cycle iterates rapidly between the core activities of building and evaluating the design artifacts and processes of the research, incorporating the feedback to refine the design further [5]. Artifacts presented in this paper were the target of several iterations of improvement which, in turn, were assessed in the criteria of completeness, simplicity, elegance, understandability, and ease of use by a highly experienced urban appraisal team. Their feedback was repeatedly incorporated into the redesign of the artifact until the current interaction presented in this paper.

3 Theoretical Foundations

3.1 PSI Theory and DEMO Methodology

DEMO (Design and Engineering Methodology for Organizations) is based on the PSI theory, which studies organizations' operational essence, that is, the construction perspective on enterprises, disregarding all functional aspects [3]. According to the PSI theory, every organization's operation is a network of transactions [6]. Coordination acts (c-acts) are the key elements in (business) conversations, which are the constituting parts of (business) transactions [6]. This interaction between subjects (initiator and executor) follows a certain path along the complete transaction pattern [3, 4]. Performing a c-act results in creating the corresponding coordination fact (c-fact) and affects the coordination world (c-world). C-acts are how actors enter into and comply with commitments towards achieving a certain p-fact [6]. P-facts affect the production world (p-world). When active, actors take the current state of the p-world and the c-world into account. This is the operational principle of organizations, also known as the operation axiom [4]. All transactions go through the four C-acts of request [rq], promise [pm], declare [da], and accept [ac]. This sequence, known as the basic transaction pattern, only considers the regular flow where everything happens according to the expected outcomes. All these five mandatory steps must occur to origin a new production-fact (p-fact). The complete transaction pattern also considers other c-acts, including revocations and rejections that may happen at every step of the regular flow [6]. This is called the transaction axiom [4] and is universally applied [6].

DEMO's Way of Modelling comprises a set of models and diagrams to represent an organization. The referred aspect models are the Cooperation Model (CM), the Action Model (AM), the Process Model (PM), and the Fact Model (FM) [7]. They are connected to each other through the central concept of transaction and represent organizational reality coherently and in a platform-independent way [4]. The CM specifies the organization's construction and transaction types and is the most concise one [7]. The AM of an organization is the ontological model of its operation, that is, the manifestation of the construction over time [7]. The action rules are composed of all the other models' information, being one of the most important models on the methodology [4]. The PM of an organization is a model of the (business) processes that take place as the effect of acts by actors [7]. The PM of an organization connects its CM and AM, as far as coordination is concerned. The FM of an organization is a model of its organizational products [7]. In systemic terms, it is a specification of the state space and the transition space of the production world [7]. Regarding the state space, the FM contains entity types, value types, property types, and attribute types relevant for the modeled organization and the existence laws that apply. While regarding the transition space, it represents the event types and the occurrence laws [7]. The FM of an organization connects its CM and AM, as far as production is concerned. An FM is expressed in an Object Fact Diagram

(OFD), supplemented by Derived Fact Specifications and, optionally, by Existence Law Specifications.

3.2 MU Theory

The Model Universe Theory (MU Theory) is, generally, about models and modeling and, in particular, about conceptual modeling [8]. It proposes the GOSL (General Ontology Specification Language), a first-order logic language for specifying the state space and the world's transition space. It is the successor of WOSL (World Ontology Specification Language), presented in [9], which in turn was inspired by ORM [12]. In Fig. 1, we have the FM's OFD of Case Library taken from [10]. We use it to explain GOSL as it is central to this paper's research contribution.

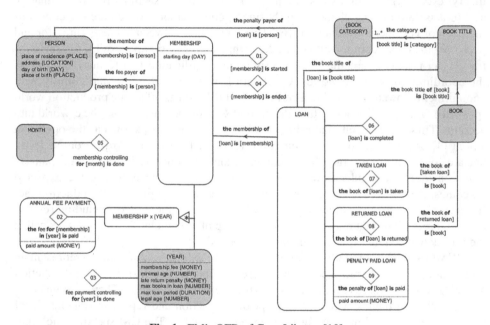

Fig. 1. FM's OFD of Case Library [10]

The GOSL syntax is as follows. The round rectangles (without diamonds inside) (e.g., "PERSON", "MEMBERSHIP", "MONTH") represent entity classes, thus extensions of entity types. In these rectangles, we can also represent the accepted domain and range of the accepted values (e.g., "place of residence {PLACE}" of an entity "PERSON"). When the name in the round rectangle is between { }, it represents a Value Type instead (e.g., "{YEAR}"). Lines with an arrow in the middle can be considered as collections of separate mappings from elements as seen between "LOAN and PERSON ("the penalty payer of [loan] is [person]"). In terms of cardinality, the ends of connectors generally mean 1. If a range string is present (e.g., 1..*) it denotes the minimum and maximum cardinality applying to that end (e.g., a "BOOK CATEGORY" can be related from 1 to an undetermined number of instances of "BOOK TITLE"). Diamonds represent event types (i.e., the p-facts of transactions) that apply to each class (e.g., "[membership] is started" affects class "MEMBERSHIP"). Triangles with a " +" sign inside are generalizations. There is no example in Fig. 1, but a good example is that of "VEHICLE" being a generalization for "CAR", "BOAT", or "AIRCRAFT". A "*" sign inside means aggregations (e.g., "MEMBERSHIP a { YEAR}" is an aggregation of "MEMBERSHIP" and "{YEAR}"). The dashed lines with an arrow at the end are specializations (e.g., we could have "STUDENT" or "ELDERLY" as a specialization of "PERSON"). The round rectangles with diamonds inside are also specializations of entities but in the form of event type (e.g., "PENALTY PAID LOAN" is a specialization of "LOAN").

3.3 Type Square Pattern

The type square pattern [11] addresses the challenge that object-oriented programmers often face of not knowing beforehand the number of subclasses that are needed to model the system effectively. The type square pattern derives from the type-object pattern applied twice. Firstly, to separate the entities (instances) from their entity types and then, secondly, to separate properties (values) from their property types. It simply turns known and unknown subclasses into simple instances of a generic "Entity Type" class. Likewise, the instances of the sub-class itself become instances of a generic "Entity" class, as depicted in Fig. 2.

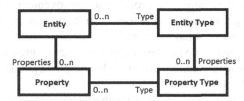

Fig. 2. Type square pattern [11]

A reported advantage is the possibility of subclass creation through dynamic and runtime instantiation of the generic "Entity Type" class. Instances of the subclass can then be created similarly by instantiating the "Entity" class. Likewise, State definition for subclasses and their respective instances is the Property and Property Type classes' responsibility. The proliferation of a considerable number of subclasses is also minimized, albeit at the cost of implementing the logic of the system at instance level.

4   Project Presentation

This paper is based on a study requested by the town council of the city of Funchal, to model their urban appraisal process.

It is the responsibility of the municipality's urban appraisal division, which is under direct tutelage of the territorial planning department, to handle the requests regarding permits for all kinds of building construction work, land allotment, and other urban operations within the city of Funchal.

Being the capital of Madeira, an autonomous region with its own political and administrative statute, Funchal's territorial planning is regulated not only by the Portuguese legislation in general, but also by regional decrees and local adaptations to the citywide urban planning scheme, all of which have a significant impact on how urban appraisal is conducted.

A new software system to manage the urban appraisal process will soon be implemented, and thorough models of the process and related information will be of high and essential value for successfully implementing and parametrizing the future system.

The challenge was to identify, structure, and describe every kind of fact that can influence the life cycle of urban appraisal process instances in a comprehensive fashion. The information to be modeled ranged in type (e.g., dates or documents), size (e.g., a simple completion date or a full-blown allotment plan), and granularity (e.g., the liability statement included in a demolition plan). It was surveyed from various sources including legislation, regulations, internal documents, or meetings with officers of the urban appraisal division. It is to be noted that, although the request was focused on the current state of the urban appraisal process (AS-IS), the intention was also to collect insights regarding insufficiencies and possible deadlocks, that could surface and be adequately addressed within the created (TO-BE) models.

Being a DEMO based approach, the FM of the urban appraisal "world" was formulated into representations composed of two artifacts: (1) Fact Diagram (FD) and (2) Fact Description Table (FDT). We stress that these artifacts are variants of DEMO's Object Fact Diagram (OFD) and constitute our proposal of improvements to the representations of DEMO's FM. We argue the need to incorporate in the current representations new and different graphical elements, a rationale, and associated semantics. On one hand, current representations of the FM do not easily capture these features and, on another hand, present unneeded information adding dispensable complexity. Our concrete proposal is discussed in detail in Sect. 5.

Considering that 65 concepts and 445 attributes were identified, in a total of 510 facts, the ontological model of the urban appraisal "world" was split into a set of logical conceptual domain scopes (CDS), making it more intelligible and manageable by all stakeholders. These CDS are #1 Concepts of the Urban Appraisal Process; #2 Concepts related to the Urban Appraisal Process; #3 Concepts of the Urban Appraisal Procedure; #4 Concepts of Application Deliverable Management; #5 Concepts of Urban Operation; and #6 Concepts related to the Urban Operation. Due to space and confidentiality constraints, we will not present all CDSs, we will focus uniquely on one example, the *Concepts of Application Deliverable Management* (CADM), detailed below.

4.1 Application Deliverable Management

The CADM involves all the procedures related to the deliverables handed by a stakeholder to the town council while applying to obtain a permit for an urban operation (e.g., building work). It also involves how the officers of the urban appraisal division manage these deliverables. Furthermore, enclosed in the CADM, are the posterior actions of adding more documents to the application, either by the applicant's initiative or following the town council's request.

The Portuguese law Decree n. 113/2015, issued on 22 of April, has each urban operation's application requirements and constitutes an essential and important piece of information to all stakeholders. It is basically a set of lists of deliverables required for the application to obtain a permit for different types of urban operations. However, a mix of technicalities expressed in natural language in different knowledge domains (such as architecture, law, and civil engineering) make it hard to grasp for those who lack expert knowledge in these areas. Besides national and regional legislation, several procedural adaptations realized by the town council's services which aim to facilitate internal application deliverable management are changeable over time and may introduce entropy and misinterpretations between interested parties. Ideally, application deliverables are handed over in a timely fashion by the applicant and are subject to prior analysis where missing elements are identified before being forwarded to a more thorough technical analysis for validation against approved urban planning criteria schemes.

This allows the urban appraisal division to identify missing documents according to the requested type of urban operation and inform the applicant quickly. However, some deliverables are optional, some have variations on their content and granularity, which makes it a process with many subtleties. Also, there are some exceptions to the rule that must be considered on a case-by-case basis. All these specificities need to be addressed. If all the needed deliverables are handed during the established period, a technical analysis is initiated. In this manner, the validity of application deliverables (particularly of the architectural, construction, building, and allotment plans) are assessed and lackluster documents are subject to enhancement requests. Consequently, every application deliverable has to be maintained and classified according to its analysis and life cycle (e.g., accepted, enhancement, incomplete, change).

In the following section, we present our CADM's Fact Model's representations, along with our proposal for improvements to the model.

5   Proposal for a New DEMO's Fact Model

When representing the FM of this project, we faced a challenge, as the terms *entity* and *property* relate to, respectively, *institutional entities* (e.g. regional government, civil protection service) and *properties* (e.g. land, house) in the urban appraisal domain. This ambiguity also happens in other domains. To overcome this issue, we used the generic terms *concept* and *attribute* and consider them both as *facts*. We argue that DEMO should adopt this nomenclature. Thus, while communicating with stakeholders, we made clear that, while modeling, we are capturing the relevant types of facts in the domain of urban appraisal: the concept types and the attribute types, of which instances of these are handled in their daily operation. In this project, we identified a total of 510 fact types with 445 attribute types aggregated in 65 concept types. To effectively communicate with stakeholders and understand the domain, we needed to first only represent the concepts, their relationships, and respective cardinalities. This effort resulted in a generic, global, and synthetic view of all the urban appraisal domain's concepts, while abstracting from their attributes. We call this representation the FD which can have two different views: the Concept and Relationships Diagram (CRD) and the Concept Attribute Diagram (CAD) explained in the following sections.

5.1 Concept and Relationship Diagram

As mentioned, we selected the CAMD to illustrate our proposal for a new vision of an FM for DEMO. Its CRD is depicted in Fig. 3.

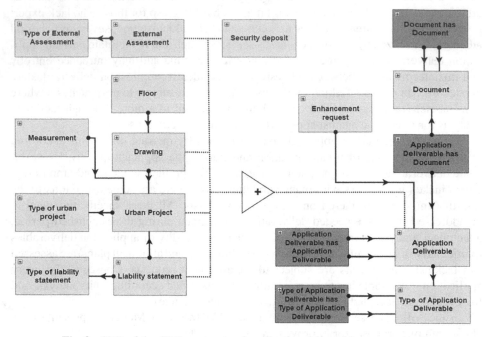

Fig. 3. CRD of the CDS: concepts of application deliverable management

While validating with the urban appraisal officers our view of their main concepts (65 in the whole model), it was essential to abstract from the attributes. Otherwise, we would have too much information in a cluttered diagram. At this level, we just needed to depict which major concepts exist and how they relate in terms of cardinality and obligatoriness in their relationships. We use arrows to express relationships, which will always consist, in practice, of an attribute in one concept whose instances will be a reference to instances of the other concept. We miss the notions of reference and dependency laws that were part of the FM in DEMO Version 2 [4] as we consider they are essential to represent important domain restrictions.

We recover the notion of explicit representation of dependency laws with a dark filled circle, the original notation of this kind of law used in [4] and originally coming from the ORM standard [12], on which DEMO's GOSL is inspired. Attaching this symbol to a concept in one connector means that an instance of this concept, in order to exist, depends on an instance of the concept at the other end of the connector. For example, an instance of an *Application Deliverable* (e.g., a particular architecture project delivered in a particular application for urban appraisal) cannot exist without a reference to an existing instance of *Type of Application Deliverable* (e.g., the architecture project type).

However, the notion of binary and ternary fact types of the mentioned previous version of the FM was more difficult to interpret and explain. As ternary fact types are rare and should be avoided (and easily converted to a new concept plus three new binary fact types), and the binary fact types are essentially of three types (one-to-one, many-to-one, and many to many), we adopt the following standard for each of these cases with examples from the project case:

1) one-to-one relationships are represented by a connector with two arrow symbols in the middle, e.g., an urban operation can have one (and only one) permit and a permit is associated with one (and only one) urban operation (note: this example is not shown in Fig. 3 for space reasons, but was taken from another part of the project case);
2) many-to-one relationships are represented by a connector with only one arrow pointing to the side "one" of the relationship, e.g., an instance of *Application Deliverable* has one (and only one) *Type of Application Deliverable*. However, the other way around, a *Type of Application Deliverable* can be associated with multiple (potentially zero) instances of *Application Deliverable* as shown in Fig. 3;
3) many-to-many relationships are represented with an intermediate concept depicted with a darker color; this concept will have many-to-one relationships with the concepts participating in this many-to-many relationship; both of these relationships will have dependency laws on the side of this intermediate concept; e.g., an application deliverable can have one or more documents associated with it; and one document can be associated with one or more application deliverables as shown in Fig. 3.

Compared to the current version of the FM, we also slightly change the notation of the specialization/generalization relationship by using a connector with a pointed line, instead of a dashed line (e.g., the specialization of *Application Deliverable* into its several more specific concepts). In practice, this specialization implies that a series of one-to-one relationships exist between the more specific concepts and the higher order concepts, with a dependency law on the side of every specific concept.

5.2 Concept Attribute Diagram

With the main concepts and relationships known, one also needs to identify the attributes that belong to each concept, considering that at least one transaction in the enterprise's processes has to create values for it. This is better done in the FDT, presented in the next section. Regarding the diagram representation, the ability to inspect which attributes each concept possesses has been highly useful. So we propose the Concept Attribute Diagram (CAD), which can be considered a variation or "expansion" of the CRD presented previously.

In the CAD, a concept is represented by a collapsible box whose expansion discloses its attributes, one per line (Fig. 4). The value type of an attribute is specified to the left of the line, whilst to the right, the name of the attribute and eventually a list of possible values, usually for categorical value types. A brief description of each value type follows in the next section.

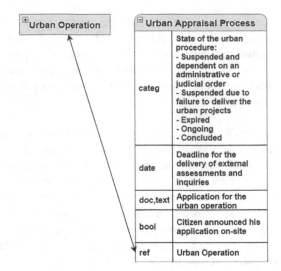

Fig. 4. Some attributes of the Urban Appraisal Process concept in the CAD

5.3 Fact Description Table

The Fact Description Table (FDT) presents details of relevant information not shown in the diagrams. Every concept in the diagram is mirrored into this table, along with a description of every attribute. Traceability is the primary motivation for this artifact because not only the source that supports the existence of the attribute is referenced by means of an external link (in this case, a link to a shared pdf containing legislation), but there are also multiple references to the transactions that are responsible for creating or updating values of the attribute at hand. The transaction list is navigable and provides rich information of DEMO's CM perspective but is left out of this paper because of space constraints.

Automatic maintenance of the transaction references and its legal source in the FDT is assured by programming the supporting google spreadsheet with the capability to reflect changes to DEMO's CM perspective directly in the FDT table. Moreover, if new transactions are added to the CM these will be available for selection in a dropdown list. Once a transaction is selected in the FDT, a trigger automatically links it to the CM, and the source of legislation is updated.

To facilitate communication and interpretation by officers, in the representations of DEMO models we replace the term *transaction* with the term *task* and these can be considered synonyms in the next explanations.

We now explain the meaning of the elements in each column of which examples are presented in Fig. 5. The first two columns simply present the names of the concepts and attributes that belong to each concept. The 3rd column specifies the value type of an attribute which can be any the following options: 1) *category* - an enumerated set of allowed values which, in turn, are listed in the double role column called Referenced concept/Category values; 2) *reference* - a link to another concept specified in the previously mentioned double-role column; we can consider it as the same as a foreign key

Concept	Attribute name	Value Type	Referenced Concept / Category values	Description	Source - task 1	Step	Task 1 (creates or updates the attribute)
Concepts of Application Deliverable Management							
Application Deliverable	Application Deliverable			The "Deliverable" concept specifies the instances that are handed over to the Municipality's services as part of the management of deliverables procedure. Supports the preliminary analysis task by making it possible to discriminate which deliverables were effectivelly delivered.	RJUE - Art. 11	Ex	T197CP5 Preliminary analysis of urban planning / building process (preliminary assessment)
Application Deliverable	State of the application deliverable	category	Change	This attribute holds the the state of deliverables (e.g. if it is the initial handing over of the element, if it is an enhacement or if this element has already been accepted): Possible options for the state of the deliverable are presented as follows: - Initial: the initial delivery; - Change: a change (potentially unsolicited) of a given deliverable; - Improvement: a new iteration of a deliverable following an enhacement request; - Conditionally Accepted: the deliverable was accepted minus some impending changes which are yet to be delivered; - Accept: an accepted deliverable; - Incomplete: the deliverable has flaws in its components;	RJUE - Art. 11	Ex	T197CP5 Preliminary analysis of urban planning / building process (preliminary assessment)
Application Deliverable	Justification for an otherwise obligatory deliverable	document		According to the Decree No. 113/2015 of April 22nd there may be deliverables which are exceptionally considered unnecessary to hand over for a particular urban operation.	RJUE - Art. 11	Ex	T197CP5 Preliminary analysis of urban planning / building process (preliminary assessment)
Application Deliverable	Type of deliverable	reference	Type of Application Deliverable	From the analysis of Decree No. 113/2015 of April 22nd, a survey of types of deliverables was promoted. Given that upon delivery, there is a need to maintain which types of deliverables were actually handed over, the correspondence between what was delivered and the type of deliverable is implemented in this attribute.	RJUE - Art. 11	Ex	T197CP5 Preliminary analysis of urban planning / building process (preliminary assessment)

Fig. 5. Fact description table (FDT)

attribute in the world of databases; 3) *document* - a reference to a document that might exist physically and/or in an Electronic Document Management System (EDMS); 4) *text* - any kind of text from a simple string or name, to a description or even the result of optical character recognition (OCR) on some document; 5) *doc & text* - an abbreviated way to specify that a certain attribute is of value type document and a reference will be kept to the document, together with the full text obtained from its OCR processing; 6) *number* - a quantity expressed as an integer or a floating-point number; 7) *date* - a timestamp; 8) *boolean*. The column *Description* explains the rationale for the specification/identification of an attribute as part of a concept. Because descriptions are specified in natural language, this column represents a common understanding that facilitates communication and discussion among stakeholders. The *Task N* columns hold links to the transactions that can create/update values of the attribute at hand. The *Step* columns are a shorthand indication of which step of the transaction pattern the attribute is created or modified, in regard to the *Task N* at hand. Columns *Source task N* provides, for each of the tasks identified, a link to the information source that justifies the existence of the respective attribute. In this project, the vast majority of these links refer to a certain legislation article and/or section.

Navigation in the FDT is facilitated by an underlying organization of concepts that are grouped according to the CDS to which they pertain. Likewise, attributes are grouped together under the grouping of the concept to which they pertain. We used the respective google spreadsheet functionality which made this artifact very easy to navigate even while aggregating a huge amount of information regarding the 445 identified attributes.

5.4   Type Square Pattern Application

The basis of part of our solution regarding application deliverable management is a 2-level Type Square pattern [11]. At the Entity-Type level, we model what is stated in the Decree n. 113/2015, issued on 22 of April, i.e. that different types of urban operations may require different types of application deliverables in order for the application to be carried out successfully. This level is depicted by the concepts enclosed by the bottom red rectangle of Fig. 6. At the instance-level, we model what is delivered by applicants in practice, i.e. which application deliverables were effectively handed over to urban appraisal officers and are to be tracked for application deliverable management purposes for a particular urban operation. This level is depicted by the concepts enclosed by the top green rectangle of Fig. 6.

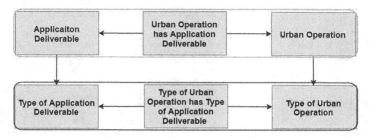

Fig. 6. Type square pattern at the entity-type and instance level.

It is important to emphasize how this solution simplifies the conceptual model while addressing the intricacies and complexities of legislation written with technical terms and natural language. Because the law is also mutable over time, new types of application deliverables or urban operations can be integrated at runtime with additional instances of these entity types. In our study, this solution allowed for the 119 types of application deliverables to be considered as instances of the *Type of Application Deliverable* concept and the 21 types of urban operations to be considered as instances of the *Type of Urban Operation* concept. It became clear that the Type Square pattern prevented the need to model a "combinatorial explosion" of associations between these types by considering them as instances of *Type of Urban Operation has Type of Application Deliverable* and not as separate concepts. The processing of application deliverables is far from a linear task. Certain application deliverables are optional, some are contained within others and alternatives between application deliverables can be equally accepted by the city council's services.

A by-product of the legislation analysis and this double type square pattern application was the so-called *Application Deliverable Matrix*, with an excerpt depicted in Fig. 7. This matrix specifies the allowed subset of 567 combinations of types of urban operation with types of required application deliverable, out of a total of 2499 possible combinations.

Before the implementation of the future software system, this matrix, also implemented in a google spreadsheet, constitutes a highly valuable tool for the urban appraisal officers to develop their work, especially the ones handling the initial applications.

Deliverable	Prior information Allotment Operations	Prior information Urbanization Work	Prior information Edification Work	Prior information Demolition Work	Prior information Change in the authorization for the use of buildings or fractions	Prior information Other Urban Operations	Licensing Allotment Operations
Blueprints & Graphical Representations							
Blueprint in a 1:1000 or greater scale, containing the technical elements of the urban operation	☐	☐	☐	☐	☐	☑	☐
Blueprint indicating the yielding areas for implantation of green spaces, road infrastructure and equipment for collective use	☐	☐	☑			☐	☐
Blueprint identifying the yielding areas to be transferred to the municipal domain	☐	☐	☐			☐	☑
Blueprint identifying the accessible routes	☐	☐	☐			☐	☑
Blueprint of the current situation in a 1:1000 scale or greater	☐	☑	☐			☐	☑
Blueprint of the local infrastructure and connections to the general infrastructure	☐	☐	☑			☐	☐

Fig. 7. Application deliverable matrix.

It will also constitute an essential source of information for the implementation and parametrization of future software.

5.5 Representation in the Current Fact Model

The Fact Model for the Application Deliverable Management is depicted using the GOSL notation in Fig. 8 and Fig. 9. The central entity class in the diagram is the Application Deliverable. It is a generalization of the entity classes whose domain and range are

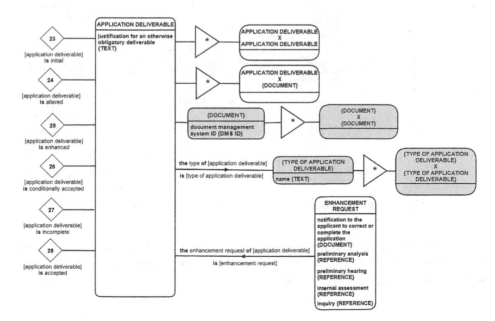

Fig. 8. Application deliverable management in GOSL notation (part 1)

fundamental to the modelling effort and the discussion among stakeholders as shown in Fig. 8. The specialized entity classes, namely Security Deposit, External Assessment, Drawing, Urban Project, and Liability Statement have mappings to other relevant entity classes or value types.

The traceability of application deliverables, their types and respective documents, was specified with aggregations in Fig. 9. For example, in order to track which documents constitute and pertain to an application deliverable, the "APPLICATION DELIVERABLE X DOCUMENT" aggregation is used. In the same manner that certain application deliverables may contain other application deliverables, documents may hold other documents. These facts are detailed in the "APPLICATION DELIVERABLE X APPLICATION DELIVERABLE" and "DOCUMENT X DOCUMENT" aggregations.

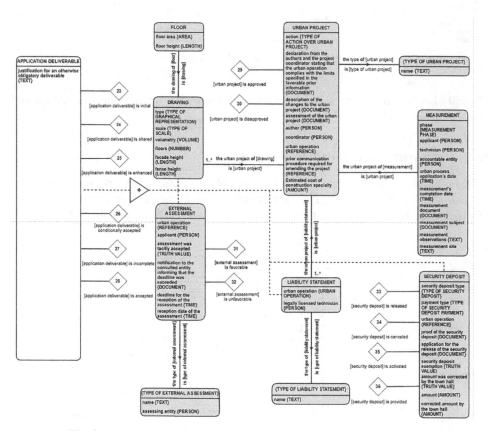

Fig. 9. Application deliverable management in GOSL notation (part 2)

Regarding the CADM in GOSL, nine entity classes, of which one is a generalization and five were specializations, four aggregations, twenty event types, and five value types were found, totaling thirty-eight graphical elements.

6   Elaboration and Discussion

This practical project showed the importance of using artifacts whose vocabulary is closer to the day-to-day operations and common lexicon. We started by using DEMO's traditional representations of the FM. However, these were difficult to grasp by those without DEMO knowledge and imposed communication barriers. Therefore, to discuss and validate our models with the stakeholders, we had the need to change and refine them, while addressing in a satisfactory way all the detail and complexity of the domain being analyzed. Our refinements were directed by these five practical requirements of this project: 1) provide insight and overview of the huge complexity of the legislation regarding application documents for the urban appraisal process, in a way that could be easily understandable/intelligible by all stakeholders; 2) provide traceability in all modeled artifacts regarding their composing elements; 3) make the rationale for each fact explicit; 4) clear reference to applicable legal rules; 5) provide a diagram with the simplicity of elements capturing the relevant concepts and their attributes along with their value type and their dependencies, and how they relate in a set of logical scopes.

One essential tool while modeling this very complex urban appraisal domain was that of the type square pattern. From this and other projects, we verify that, often, the type instances (e.g., instances of the *type of urban project* or *type of application deliverable*) end up fixed in program code or as an attribute in some table. However, a new instance of that type will cause a combinatorial effect that may increase operational and/or software complexity. As depicted in Fig. 6, just six concepts implementing two pairs of type squares were enough to encompass a huge space of hundreds of possible combinations of application deliverables needed in certain urban operations.

Looking at the diagram of such a simple case as that of the Library presented in Sect. 3.2, it is evident that the current format of the OFD in GOSL has too many different elements, symbols, and text, making it very difficult to be interpreted by officers without experience in DEMO, in fact the experience we got, while presenting a first GOSL diagram to the town council officers. GOSL revealed to be an impractical representation solution for the complex domain we were confronted with. Looking at Fig. 8, the CADM in GOSL notation amounts to a total of thirty-eight graphical elements. This total does not even include the specification of exclusion laws between event types which should be represented for the OFD to be complete. In comparison, the newly proposed FM contains eighteen graphical elements in the CRD.

Layering the representations in the Concept and Relationships Diagram (CRD) with the Concept Attribute Diagram (CAD) along with the Fact Description Table (FDT) allows for greater synthetization in the CRD and leaving more detail towards the FDT. This tradeoff promotes inclusion and facilitates the interpretation and discussion of the underlying organization among stakeholders.

It is essential to know which steps of a transaction are responsible for creating values for each attribute. Current DEMO's OFD shows only the p-fact associated with each class, while any transaction step may create original facts, that is, values that are instances of attributes. It creates unneeded complexity in the OFD to include event types. But they are, of course, an essential part of the FM perspective. Our solution solves two problems: it reduces the complexity of the diagrams and presents further important detail, while allowing the specification, not only of the transaction responsible for originating the fact, but also of its respective step, and also of possibly other transactions/steps that might create it/update it.

Including attributes of concepts in the diagram can be excessive, especially in projects whose magnitude is similar to the one being discussed, where 445 attributes were identified. However, it is useful to be able to quickly inspect the attributes of a concept. So, it was decided to provide the functionality of making the concept symbols expandable/collapsible to provide that capability. Also regarding complexity handling, and just like in DEMO's CM which includes Scopes of Interest (SoI), we saw the need for the creation of scopes for the concepts which we call CDS, i.e. aggregate concepts that are closely related or form natural domain clusters and facilitate navigation both in the FD as well as in the FDT.

It is common knowledge that the human brain interprets graphical symbols or images faster than words composed of characters. Our approach is to have a minimal set of symbols to represent the main and more common restrictions in the FD. We argue that cardinalities are better represented with arrows pointing to the one side of relationships and that dependency laws are better represented in the ORM way and not within a cardinality's numbers as in the current GOSL way.

GOSL proposes a relatively large number of "predefined value types", some of them visible in the Library example. We consider this another unneeded complexity and that it is better to restrain the possible value types to the minimum possible, closer to the notion of sort in GOSL. The possible sorts of GOSL are *ordinal, interval, ratio, absolute, boolean,* and *categorial*. We basically agree with these sorts and that they should be considered the main basic value types but using slightly different terminology. And, as previously presented, we include the following complementary ones: *document* (can be physical, digital, etc.), *text* (any kind of string, like names or long descriptions), and *reference* (a "pointer" to a concept instance).

Domain-specific value types such as the type of graphical representation or the measurement phase in Fig. 9 were represented inline in their respective entity class and not separately because it would needlessly make the diagram expand its size even more. In fact, claims of clutter, mainly regarding text, and the need for a cleaner representation with simplified semantics was reported by the officers of the urban appraisal division. These claims reinforce the need for a simpler notation, one where the essence of a property isn't semantically or visually impaired by the notions of value type, sort, base type, measuring unit or dimension.

GOSL and the associated DEMO's FM strive for a "pure" ontology where signs and/or names should not be part of the ontology [8]. We strongly disagree with this stance which we think is even contradictory to DEMO and PSI Theory's approach, which is a language-based one, considering communication as the central notion and the thread on which organizations are woven [4]. In real life and operation of organizations, references (e.g., process numbers), names, and descriptions associated with daily concepts and their instances, are essential aspects to be taken into account and facilitate communication and interpretation in an organization's operation. The value types we present in this paper may need to be refined/perfected but were shown to be useful in this practical project and enough to encompass the 445 identified attributes.

We were cautious about the elements we selected to include in our proposal for our new FD, as we intend to have a direct derivation of an implementable database relational schema. That is, the chosen symbols and syntax allow a direct transformation of this diagram into related tables in a database system. Our proposal for this new way of representing DEMO's Fact Model has a hybrid nature merging elements of DEMO's OFD, traditional ER-diagram, and relational schema. It represents the universe of discourse in a semantically richer way facilitating discussion and communication regardless of the stakeholder's technical prowess, experience, or background.

7 Conclusions

One of the goals of Enterprise Engineering and Ontology is the capability of directly realizing an information system based on the ontological models, or automatically transforming them into program code [13]. If we want such capability, it is important that the models themselves are designed in a way that facilitates their implementation, which goes against one of the premises of DEMO theories that we also disagree with: that all models should be abstracted from implementation. Before some intense discussions in the CIAO! community initiated by us some years ago, the claim was that DEMO models were implementation independent. Thanks to these discussions the claim was changed to use the term "abstracted", but in a way that we are not satisfied yet. Indeed, DEMO's higher-level models should be abstracted from implementation. But at some point, we have to deal with the real complexities of the real world and these will always influence, sometimes to a very high degree, even the higher-level models, what to say from the more detailed models. We claim that this new Fact model could be considered a derived representation from the existing GOSL Fact model, enhanced and enriched with valuable information from various sources. And, therefore, this is a valuable contribution to the professional world, derived from but not a replacement of the GOSL based Fact model.

With this project and associated research presented in this paper, other papers to come, and previous work [14, 15], we are striving towards the goal of being able to directly execute and run an information system from models [16]. This project and its practical research results is a step in this inspiring direction.

Although the present study provides valuable insights, there are a few limitations that should be recognized, and these provide threads for future research. Due to the limited time and resources, we only applied these diagrams to the urban appraisal division of the town council of Funchal, which is highly structured due to the applicable law requirements. Therefore, future work should test the validity of these diagrams further by applying them to other organizations, especially in areas that do not have such strict regulations. These additional efforts will further confirm the validity of our work.

Acknowledgments. Special thanks to the officers from the town council of Funchal that contributed with their fruitful insights and feedback.

This work is supported by the Regional Development European Fund (INTERREG MAC), projects Dynamic eGov MAC2/5.11a/359 (MAC-2014–2020) and FiiHUB MAC2/2.3d/335 (MAC-2014–2020).

References

1. Markus, M., Majchrzak, A., Gasser, L.: A design theory for systems that support emergent knowledge processes. MIS Q. **26**, 179–212 (2002). https://doi.org/10.2307/4132330
2. Hevner, A.R., March, S.T., Park, J., Ram, S.: Design science in information systems research. MIS Q. **28**, 75–105 (2004). https://doi.org/10.2307/25148625
3. Dietz, J.L.G., Mulder, H.B.F.: The enterprise engineering theories. In: Dietz, J.L.G., Mulder, H.B.F. (eds.) Enterprise Ontology: A Human-Centric Approach to Understanding the Essence of Organisation, pp. 23–48. Springer, Cham (2020). https://doi.org/10.1007/978-3-030-388 54-6_4
4. Dietz, J.L.G.: Enterprise Ontology: Theory and Methodology. Springer, Heidelberg (2006). https://doi.org/10.1007/3-540-33149-2
5. Hevner, A.R.: A three cycle view of design science research. Scand. J. Inf. Syst. **19**, 87–92 (2007)
6. Dietz, J.L.G., Mulder, H.B.F.: The PSI theory: understanding the operation of organisations. In: Dietz, J.L.G., Mulder, H.B.F. (eds.) Enterprise Ontology: A Human-Centric Approach to Understanding the Essence of Organisation, pp. 119–157. Springer, Cham (2020). https://doi.org/10.1007/978-3-030-38854-6_8
7. Dietz, J.L.G., Mulder, H.B.F.: The DEMO methodology. In: Dietz, J.L.G., Mulder, H.B.F. (eds.) Enterprise Ontology: A Human-Centric Approach to Understanding the Essence of Organisation, pp. 261–299. Springer, Cham (2020). https://doi.org/10.1007/978-3-030-38854-6_12
8. Dietz, J.L.G., Mulder, H.B.F.: The MU theory: understanding models and modelling. In: Dietz, J.L.G., Mulder, H.B.F. (eds.) Enterprise Ontology: A Human-Centric Approach to Understanding the Essence of Organisation, pp. 71–94. Springer, Cham (2020). https://doi.org/10.1007/978-3-030-38854-6_6
9. Dietz, J.L.G.: A world ontology specification language. In: Meersman, R., Tari, Z., Herrero, P. (eds.) OTM 2005. LNCS, vol. 3762, pp. 688–699. Springer, Heidelberg (2005). https://doi.org/10.1007/11575863_88
10. Dietz, J.L.G., Mulder, H.B.F.: Exercise: case library. In: Dietz, J.L.G., Mulder, H.B.F. (eds.) Enterprise Ontology: A Human-Centric Approach to Understanding the Essence of Organisation, pp. 349–366. Springer, Cham (2020). https://doi.org/10.1007/978-3-030-38854-6_16
11. Yoder, J.W., Balaguer, F., Johnson, R.: Architecture and design of adaptive object-models. SIGPLAN Not. **36**, 50–60 (2001). https://doi.org/10.1145/583960.583966
12. Halpin, T.: Object-role modeling: an overview (2002). http://www.orm.net/pdf/ORMwhiteP aper.pdf
13. Dietz, J.L.G., Mulder, H.B.F.: Exercise: case rent-a-car. In: Dietz, J.L.G., Mulder, H.B.F. (eds.) Enterprise Ontology: A Human-Centric Approach to Understanding the Essence of Organisation, pp. 323–348. Springer, Cham (2020). https://doi.org/10.1007/978-3-030-38854-6_15
14. Figueira, C., Aveiro, D.: A new action rule syntax for DEmo MOdels based automatic worKflow procEss geneRation (DEMOBAKER). In: Aveiro, D., Tribolet, J., Gouveia, D. (eds.) EEWC 2014. LNBIP, vol. 174, pp. 46–60. Springer, Cham (2014). https://doi.org/10.1007/978-3-319-06505-2_4
15. Andrade, M., Aveiro, D., Pinto, D.: Bridging ontology and Implementation with a new DEMO action meta-model and engine. In: Aveiro, D., Guizzardi, G., Borbinha, J. (eds.) EEWC 2019. LNBIP, vol. 374, pp. 66–82. Springer, Cham (2020). https://doi.org/10.1007/978-3-030-379 33-9_5
16. Andrade, M., Aveiro, D., Pinto, D.: DEMO based dynamic information system modeller and executer (2018)

Enterprise Engineering Practice

An Enterprise-Engineering Based Approach to Develop Enterprise Capacity

Andreas de Boer and Marné De Vries

Department of Industrial and Systems Engineering, University of Pretoria, Pretoria, South Africa
andreas@adbconsult.co.za, Marne.DeVries@up.ac.za

Abstract. Significant progress has been made in the South-African early childhood and Grade R spheres. However, South-Africa has a long way to go to meet the needs of majority of its children. Institutional capacity (IC) refers to the administrative and managerial aspects of an Early Childhood Development Centre (ECDC). Failure to build this capacity impacts the quality of services delivered to the most vulnerable children in our society. The purpose of this article is to extract knowledge from the institutional capacity knowledge area, as well as the enterprise engineering body-of-knowledge as a baseline for developing an enterprise capacity development approach (ECDA) for early childhood development centers. The ECDA should be useful to South-African ECD administrators, if they intend to develop enterprise capacity, leading to the improvement in quality of services delivered. ECDA is the main contribution of this article. As a second contribution, we validate its completeness when compared to existing IC literature, as well as its comprehensiveness in terms of eleven approach design principles. Finally, we provide a partial demonstration of ECDA's heuristic at a real-world ECDC in South Africa.

Keywords: Enterprise engineering · Institutional capacity · Early childhood development · Quality · Education service · Public sector

1 Introduction

The number of working parents, including single-parent families and families with both parents employed is rising, creating an ever-growing need for quality child care, according to Experthub [1]. The department of social development, department of basic education, and department of health, all have the mandate to develop an integrated approach for services for children aged from birth, up to, but not including Grade R, formally classified as the early childhood phase. In South-Africa, Atmore et al. [2] classify early childhood development (ECD) centers in three distinct facility types, namely (1) public schools, (2) registered community-based ECDCs, and (3) unregistered community-based ECDCs. Public schools typically cater for grade R only, whilst community-based centers accommodate children from birth, up to and including grade R. There are approximately 25,254 centers nationally and 1,354,274 children access these centers [3]. The ECD goal is to provide developmentally-stage-appropriate quality ECD services to all infants, young children and their caregivers by 2030 [3].

© Springer Nature Switzerland AG 2021
D. Aveiro et al. (Eds.): EEWC 2020, LNBIP 411, pp. 193–212, 2021.
https://doi.org/10.1007/978-3-030-74196-9_11

Significant progress has been made in the South-African early childhood and Grade R spheres. However, South-Africa has a long way to go to meet the needs of the majority of its children [2]. Various challenges exist within the early childhood sector, including infrastructure availability, nutrition, various different ECD curricula, ECD teacher skill level, administrative and management function (also called institutional capacity), and limited government funding [2]. Of particular interest is institutional capacity, and the inability of ECDCs to execute its purpose effectively. Imbaruddin [4] defines institution as enterprise and capacity as the ability of an enterprise to pursue its objectives, indicating that intuitional capacity (IC) is a prerequisite for delivering *quality services,* as assessed by customers. IC is not a new concept in the public sector performance arena, but not well defined or researched in the ECD sector [5]. Aligned with literature, in this article, IC refers to the *administrative and management function* that is currently lacking at many ECDCs and should be realized via multiple design domains. Yet, the management function is a function that relates to multiple ECDC functions.

The provision of early childhood development services is deemed a right to all children. In addition, ECD services must be provided because they afford a foundation for good child outcomes as well as national developmental outcomes necessary to address South Africa's two key development challenges namely poverty and inequality [6]. The department of social development [6] states that the public provisioning of early childhood development thus embraces a continuum of responsibilities, and its objectives are to ensure:

- All services necessary for the optimal survival, growth, development and protection of infants and young children to their full potential are available in sufficient quantities and through a sufficient number of appropriate spaces in sufficiently close proximity so that all children have an equal opportunity to participate in or make use of the ECD services.
- All services that are provided are of a sufficiently high quality and are age- and stage-appropriate to the needs and context of the children in question to ensure universal quality outcomes for all children receiving the service.
- Early childhood development programs are appropriately designed to ensure the delivery of quality, age and stage-appropriate, and inclusive services.
- The environment, infrastructure (including ICT), and materials supporting the delivery of all early childhood development services are safe, healthy and enable the delivery of age-appropriate quality services.
- There are a sufficient number of appropriately qualified practitioners to provide age-appropriate, inclusive plus quality early childhood development services.
- Measures are implemented to ensure that the cost of the services do not preclude children living in poverty and the qualifications and number of early childhood development practitioners, including the design of the programs and services, address the needs of children with disabilities.
- Appropriate management, coordination, monitoring and evaluation systems are in place to adequately plan for, measure, monitor and improve availability, quality and equity of ECD access.

Literature indicates that the ECD environment is complex, and there is a need for fresh new thinking to evolve ECDCs. A case is made to act and think more systemically to deliver higher quality programs and ECDC services that are sustainable over a longer period of time. IC has an impact on the quality of the ECDC, and the need is greater than ever to scale up an approach to meet increased demand of early childhood care in South-Africa. In a study conducted by Hayden [7], specific focus was placed on addressing the gap in understanding the director's role, administration, and management functions in childcare and preschool settings. It is becoming increasingly clearer that process components which make up the adult work environment, have a powerful effect upon quality care in child care centers, and that the center director plays a central role.

Atmore [8] and Van Heerden [9] indicate that community-based ECDCs lack IC, i.e. proper administrative and management systems, to meet the minimum standards set by the department of social development. Financial management of many of the community-based ECD facilities is poor, whereas more than 50% of these centers do not have many of the necessary administrative documents and structures in place [8]. The department of social development commissioned a national audit of registered ECDCs in 2013, and the scope included conditional and unregistered centers outlined in their report [10]. ECDCs across South-Africa are sub optimal, indicating that less than half of all registered centers having nothing more than staff attendance records or job descriptions [10]. This class-of-problems has already been validated via a systematic literature review (SLR) in [11].

The SLR also indicated that numerous ECD quality frameworks and IC development frameworks exist, each focusing on different performance areas and functions. We also indicated that existing frameworks, contain a mix of concerns, functions and structural/design aspects in a disparate way. Enterprise engineering (EE) could be useful to re-structure existing concepts in a consistent and useful way.

Enterprise engineering (EE) emerged as a new discipline to encourage comprehensive and consistent enterprise design [12]. Since EE is multidisciplinary, various researchers study enterprises from different perspectives, which resulted in a plethora of applicable literature and terminology, but without shared meaning [13]. The enterprise evolution contextualization model (EECM), is a metamodel for existing enterprise design approaches. Since EECM is descriptive, rather than prescriptive, approach design principles (ADPs) provide prescriptive guidance on developing new enterprise design approaches.

This article applies existing approaches, i.e. Hoogervorst's approach and existing IC approaches, guided by ADPs, to develop an enterprise capacity development approach (ECDA), assisting ECD Directors to develop EC. ECDA will enable development of all ECDA functions, but also focus on a similar scope than IC, namely the *administrative and management* function. Addressing the lack of applying IC and EE within the South African ECD sector, this study synthesizes existing knowledge by developing the ECDA.

The article is structured as follows. Section 2 presents action design research as an appropriate research methodology to develop the new artefact, called ECDA. As a theoretical foundation for developing ECDA, Sect. 3 provides background on method engineering, Hoogervorst's enterprise engineering approach, and general principles to develop a new approach. Section 4 presents the constructional components of ECDA, validating its comprehensiveness in Sect. 5, and demonstrating ECDA's heuristic in Sect. 6. Section 7 concludes on ideas for future research.

2 Research Method

Action design research (ADR) combines the strengths of two existing research paradigms, i.e. design science research and action research, facilitating an iterative process for designing and evaluating an artefact within a real-world setting [14], also suggested as an appropriate research methodology for EE-related studies [15]. We now define the four main stages of ADR and indicate their application within the context of this study:

Problem Formulation: ADR studies are initiated by a practice-inspired problem and serves as an inspiration for research efforts [14]. The problem formulation, presented in Sect. 1, indicates that community-based ECDCs lack IC, i.e. proper administrative and management systems, to meet the minimum standards set by the department of social development. This class-of-problems, validated using a systematic literature review, also features as a problem instance at a South African ECDC [11].

Building, Intervention, Evaluation: This stage consists of recursive cycles of building, intervention and evaluation, since an increased understanding of the organizational context also influences the selection and design of the artefact [14]. Evaluation is not separate from building. Rather, decisions about designing and reshaping the artefact and intervening in organizational work practices should be interwoven with ongoing evaluation [14]. Using a participative approach, also extracting from existing theory, i.e. method engineering, approach design principles, Hoogervorst's enterprise engineering approach, and IC approaches (presented in Sect. 3), we *built* a new approach, namely ECDA (presented in Sect. 4). Section 5 indicates how ECDA incorporated existing IC approaches within ECDA's heuristic. For *intervention*, we demonstrate ECDA's heuristic at a real-world ECDC, presented in Sect. 6. As indicated in Sect. 7, future work will further *evaluate* whether ECDA's iterative application will also improve the quality of services as ECDCs.

Reflection and Learning: This stage runs parallel to the first two stages. The learning from conceptualizing a solution for a particular problem instance, is used to address a broader class-of-problems [14]. For this study, learning from the first two stages contributed towards the packaging of ECDA for addressing a class-of-problems, rather than only a single problem instance.

Formalizing of Learning: The purpose of this stage is to generalize outcomes that would address a wider class-of-problems [14]. In Sect. 7 we provide ideas for future research to further evaluate and validate the ECDA for its use within other industries.

3   Background Theory

Method engineering and situational method engineering focus on formalizing the use of methods for systems development [16]. Even though method engineering and situational method engineering focus on formalizing methods for systems development, we believe that their concepts are also applicable to the development of an enterprise approach, and more specifically, ECDA. Formal techniques have been incorporated into situational method engineering, in particular metamodeling approaches at various scales, from full method to single fragment descriptions [16]. Multiple dimensions of modelling exist, in particular models can be stacked in terms of their abstraction level. Metamodels provide the means of defining the rules at a higher level of abstraction, and this in essence acts as an introduction to the abstraction levels adopted in this particular study. The General Conceptual Modelling Framework, provided by Dietz and Mulder [17], assists in explaining how the ECDA was constructed.

With reference to Fig. 1, we believe that the enterprise evolution contextualisation model (EECM) is a meta model for enterprise design approaches, since EECM was developed inductively as elaborated in Sect. 3.1. Both Hoogervorst's approach, discussed in in Sect. 3.2, and IC development approaches, introduced in Sect. 3.3, are *instantiations* of EECM. Using EECM as a common frame of reference, we developed ECDA, enriched

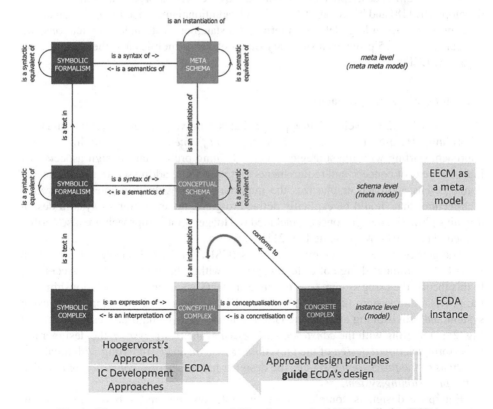

Fig. 1. The general conceptual modelling framework of [17], applied to ECDA

by Hoogervorst's approach as well as existing IC development approaches. Since EECM is not prescriptive on developing a new enterprise design approach, we use approach design principles to provide additional guidance during ECDA's design. ECDA has to be implemented at a real-world ECDC as an ECDA instance, as indicated in Fig. 1. In Sect. 6, we partially demonstrate ECDA's heuristic at a real-world ECDC.

3.1 EECM and Approach Design Principles

Since EE is multidisciplinary, various researchers study enterprises from different perspectives, which resulted in a plethora of applicable literature and terminology, but without shared meaning [13]. Addressing the knowledge fragmentation, the enterprise evolution contextualization model (EECM) inductively abstracted knowledge from multiple existing enterprise design approaches to create a metamodel for enterprise design approaches [13]. EECM indicates that existing enterprise design approaches consist of four main components: (1) Concept of the enterprise and paradigm of creating value; (2) Three dimensions to define the scope of evolution (design domains; concerns & constraints; and enterprise scope); (3) Supporting mechanisms & practices to enable the desired evolution across three dimensions; and (4) Approach classifiers that influence selection of appropriate mechanisms and practices [13].

Since EECM is descriptive and not prescriptive, eleven approach design principles, developed by [18] and based on EECM, provide additional guidance for approach development. Each principle is defined in terms of a statement, rationale, implications and measures. Section 5 provides a summary of the eleven principles and their application regarding ECDA.

3.2 Hoogervorst's Approach

Hoogervorst [19, 20] developed an approach that is iterative, emergent, creative and non-algorithmic. He uses a *generic system development framework* to explain his iterative approach, starting with the strategic context, defining preliminary design aspects that indicate areas of concern and requirements that need to be addressed in system design domains. His approach emphasizes the importance of design principles (also called architecture) that should be explicitly defined to guide the evolution of system design domains [20]. The design concepts included in Hoogervorst's approach are also further refined via a codebook, presented in [21].

The generic system development process (GSDP), a kernel theory, adapted from Dietz [22], facilitates design of different systems within the enterprise [20]. According to this theory, the using system (e.g. the environment) has a functional relationship with the provisioning system (e.g. the enterprise). For this particular combination of using system and provisioning system, the GSDP consists of two main phases, indicated in Fig. 2: (1) Starting with the *constructional design* of the *using system*, the designer has to perform *functional design* of the *provisioning system*; and (2) Starting with identified *functions* of the *provisioning system*, the designer has to perform *constructional design* of the *provisioning system*.

Enterprise design is complex, since multiple systems and sub-systems need to be designed, often concurrently, especially when enterprise constructs already exist.

As indicated by Hoogervorst [20], enterprise designers need to define appropriate design domains for a particular enterprise. Using the GSDP as a means to demarcate design domains, De Vries [23] identifies four main design domains for enterprise design: (1) organization, (2) information, communication and technology (ICT), (3) infrastructure/facilities, and (4) human skills & know-how.

3.3 IC Development Approaches

A systematic literature review on existing IC approaches indicated that multiple frameworks already exist, each highlighting different design facets, multiple design levels and performance factors [11].

Bloom [24] describes an ECDC as a dynamic and an open social system, indicating that a systems approach for describing early childhood centers can lead towards a better understanding of the impact of change and can assist administrators to better understand the significance of their day-to-day roles and responsibilities. Bloom includes six components to enable effective ECDC design: (1) environment; (2) people; (3) structure; (4) processes; (5) culture; and (6) outcomes. Imbaruddin [4] (extended by [25]) identified three levels of capacity development: (1) the system, (2) the entity, and (3) the individual. Bergin-Seers and Breen [26] aim to close a gap in research, specific to the performance of ECDCs from a viability perspective, suggesting a performance framework that includes environmental factors, center performance, organizational factors and the leader/manager role within the center. The five dimensional framework by Grindle and Hilderbrand [27] includes a systemic method to analyze determinants of administrative competence, consisting broadly of the action environment, public sector institutional context, task network dimension, organizational dimension, and lastly human resources. Scheepers [28] describes the elements and sub-elements of IC as follows: (1) strategic leadership, (2) human resources, (3) financial management, (4) infrastructure, (5) program management, (6) process management, and (7) inter-institutional linkages. The increasing recognition of the importance of the administrator within an ECDC calls for research about this role and about the characteristics of those who assume it. The leadership framework by Nupponen [29] focuses on: (1) relational and pedagogical leadership, (2) intra and interpersonal skills, and lastly (3) education and training to master these traits.

4   Construction of ECDA

Consolidating from Hoogervorst's approach, as well as existing IC development approaches, this section presents the function (in Sect. 4.1) and form (in Sect. 4.2) of ECDA, following guidance from the *approach design principles* presented in Sect. 3.1. Section 5 indicates how we validate ECDA's comprehensiveness by: (1) validating ECDA against eleven approach design principles, and (2) demonstrating how ECDA has synthesised appropriate literature to create a theory-ingrained artefact.

4.1   ECDA Introduction (Function)

ECDA adopts the morphogenic enterprise paradigm from Hoogervorst [20] to address the three essential concepts that fuel and determine enterprise developments: human agency (especially employee agency), reflexivity, and reciprocity. In addition, ECDA also acknowledges that the ECDC is a social system, in accordance with Bloom [24].

Objectives and Intended Value

According to EECM [13], an enterprise design approach has to answer three questions. ECDA answers the three questions as follows:

Why should the ECDC use the ECDA to evolve? ECDA should provide constructional guidance towards the evolution of South African ECDC's, improving the *administrative and management function* associated with *enterprise functions* to increase quality of service delivery. ECDA is comprehensive for the early childhood development context, since it synthesizes knowledge from existing IC approaches, as well as an existing EE approach, i.e. Hoogervorst's approach.

What should the ECDC evolve? ECDA focuses on developing *inside-the-boundary* complexities of an ECDC (as the provisioning system) for the environment (as the using system). Four main design domains are included: (1) organisation; (2) information, communication and technology (ICT); (3) Infrastructure (i.e. facilities); and (4) human skills & know-how. ECDA also acknowledges the existence of *other facets* that evolve at an enterprise, but cannot be designed via a system development process.

How should the ECDC evolve? The ECDC will evolve by applying the ECDA, implementing a key mechanism, namely a *heuristic*.

Scope

Hoogervorst [20] denotes the system to be designed as the *provisioning system*. The *provisioning system* has a functional relationship with its environment, also called the *using system*. Using the *generic system development process* (GSDP), ECDA facilitates constructional design of the provisioning system, as indicated by Fig. 2.

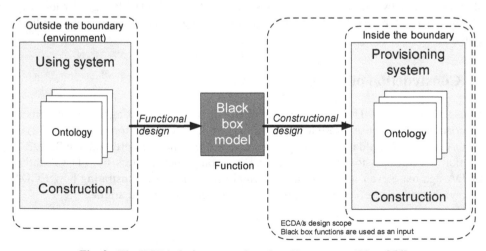

Fig. 2. The ECDA design scope, based on Hoogervorst [20, p 256]

In order to properly define the functional relationship, the wants and needs (*functions*) of the *using system* must be precisely known. In addition, the construction (white-box model) of the using system (i.e. the environment) must be known. Hoogervorst [20] defines *function* as a relationship (R) and not a system property, whereas construction is a system property.

Using [20], we provide two examples within the ECDC context:

F (function): Using system (need, purpose) R Provisioning system (properties)
F (child caregiving): Child (need, purpose) R ECDC (properties)
F (child caregiving): Parent (need, purpose) R ECDC (properties)

Child caregiving as the *function* in the two examples, refers to the operating function of child-caregiving, as well as its management, that should be enabled through various design domains within the ECDC, delivering on various stakeholders' needs and purposes.

Role Players and Users

ECDA will be useful to enterprise engineers as well as design teams. ECDC administrators will find ECDA useful to develop IC in order to improve quality of services delivered. The main user of ECDA will be the early childhood development director/administrator, typically the role accountable for quality of the ECDC operation.

Prerequisites for Using ECDA

The following are identified as prerequisites for using the ECDA: (1) Existence of a problem/deficiency related to the *administration and management* of one or more functions at the ECDC; (2) Need and desire for change clearly established; (3) Buy-in from the director; (4) ECDC functions have already been determined from the environmental (using system) context; and (5) the director is aligned with ECDA's concept of the enterprise, i.e. the morphogenic paradigm defined by Hoogervorst [20] and the social system paradigm presented by Bloom [24].

4.2 ECDA Mechanisms and Practices (Form)

The ECDA adopts a *heuristic* indicated in Fig. 3, using multiple enterprise functions (f_1, $f_2 \ldots f_n$) as main input to perform four main activities via multiple cycles.

A *function* is defined as the utility or capability that must be addressed via enterprise design. Conversely, the enterprise, its design domains or constructs, must operationalize one or more functions [21]. The function should be specified using an adjective(s) + noun, also associating the function with the *entire enterprise* or a *particular design domain or construct*, indicating how an input should be transformed into an output [21].

Next, we present the *heuristic's* four activities in more detail. We used alphabetic letters as a quick reference to the activities, but the alphabetic sequence is not an indication of execution sequence. Once enterprise functions have been identified, the heuristic may either start with A or B. As indicated in Fig. 3, representations of constructional design exist for *current designs* as well as *future designs*. Activities that are associated with *future design* are grey-shaded.

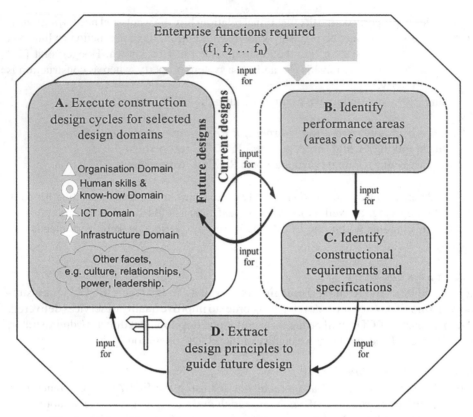

Fig. 3. ECDA's heuristic within the GSDP, based on Hoogervorst [20, p 256]

A: Execute Construction Design Cycles for Selected Design Domains

Design domains are those aspects of an enterprise that approach authors deem important/necessary for design [13]. De Vries [23] suggests that design domains are demarcated in a consistent way, using the generic system development process. ECDA adopts the design domains as described by De Vries [23] as a means to represent an ECDC's constructional design.

As discussed in [23], design domains cannot all be classified as systems. Using the definition provided by [17], a homogeneous system consists of elements that are of a similar kind. When human beings are considered to be social elements, then an organization system's construction can be defined by its kernel elements, boundary elements, environmental elements and structural bonds between elements [17]. Depending on the analyst's purposeful demarcation of a system boundary [30], an organization system thus includes human beings as kernel elements (within the boundary), boundary elements (on the boundary) and environmental elements (outside the boundary). Humans that form part of an organization's construction have structural bonds, since they collaborate to produce new production facts. Likewise, other systems also exist within the enterprise, but their elements are of a different kind. Information, communication and technology (ICT) are constructed from hardware and software elements, whereas infrastructure (i.e.

facilities) are constructed from building-construction elements. The enterprise thus consists of multiple sub-systems, where each of the sub-systems need to be designed, using the *generic system development process* (GSDP). The GSDP that was also illustrated in Fig. 2, starts with the construction of a *using system* to derive black box functions for a *provisioning system*.

Figure 4 provides a simplified view from [23] to illustrate how the GSDP was used, starting from the *using system* (i.e. *the environmental context*) to design the provisioning system (i.e. the *enterprise*). The GSDP is also used to illustrate how multiple enterprise sub-systems are developed concurrently. Each *support* arrow in Fig. 4 represents an iterative GSDP that exists between a using system and a provisioning system.

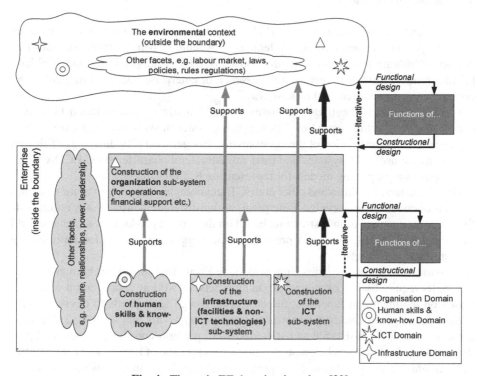

Fig. 4. The main EE domains, based on [23]

Figure 4 illustrates two of the *support* arrows, highlighted in black, with the following interpretation: (1) The *enterprise* (as provisioning system) supports *the environmental context* (as using system); and (2) The *ICT sub-system* (as provisioning system) supports the *organization sub-system* (as using system). Explaining the last-mentioned *supports* arrow in terms of the GSDP, illustrated right next to the *supports* arrow in Fig. 4, the construction of the *organization sub-system* is used as a starting point to perform *functional design* of the *ICT sub-system*. Then, the *functions* of the *ICT sub-system* are used as input to perform *constructional design* of the *ICT sub-system*.

As indicated in [23], the notion of *system* alone is not sufficient to describe the enterprise, its construction and its behavioral complexities. An enterprise consists of many *facets*, such as human skills and know-how, culture, relationships, power and leadership [20]. Figure 4 represents *facets* with cloud-constructs. We believe that some of these facets may also be classified as design domains when it is possible to follow the GSDP to design a future version of the *facet*. Hence, we believe that *human skills & know-how* needs to support the *organization sub-system* and should therefore be designable. Yet, we acknowledge that the GSDP is less useful when other facets, such as culture and power need to be "designed".

Figure 4 includes several grey-shaded constructs to indicate the envisaged design scope for ECDA, including organization, ICT, infrastructure, human skills & know-how, and other facets. Next, we provide ECDA's interpretation and means for representing the four design domains:

(a) Organization. Dietz and Mulder [17] define the o*rganization* of an enterprise as a *social system*, i.e. actor roles, implemented by human beings, form relationships due to collaboration to produce production facts. ECDA adopts Dietz and Mulder's [17] four aspect models to represent the essence of enterprise operation in a coherent, comprehensive, consistent and concise way.

(b) ICT. Software applications, databases and ICT hardware are included [17]. ICT can be designed in the context of different using systems, such as construction of the organization, or construction of the environment. Hoogervorst [20] describes IT design aspects as the use of IT systems and their infrastructural characteristics. ECDA is not prescriptive on suggesting models for representing ICT constructs.

(c) Infrastructure. Facilities and other non-ICT technologies that support actor roles and their production acts are included. Enterprises within different industries may require different representations of infrastructure, based on the type of production acts that should be supported [23]. ECDA is not prescriptive on suggesting models for representing infrastructure constructs.

(d) Human skills and know how - Human skills & know-how constitutes human abilities and skills required when executing production acts, as well as coordination acts [23]. Based on the identified functions, the enterprise design team needs to devise *specifications* for required contextual *knowledge, experience, skills* and *working styles* (e.g. perseverance, stress resistance and self-control) to perform coordination acts and production acts. The three-level capacity development approach of Imbaruddin [4] identifies the *individual (level 3)* as the skills, experience and knowledge that allow each person to perform. Some of these are acquired formally, through education and training, whereas others come informally, through doing and observing. Bloom [24] refers to the people component as a psychosocial subsystem, meaning the interrelation of social factors and individual thought and behavior. The description of this component includes elements such as values, attitudes, motivation, morale, and personal behavior of each individual.

B: Identify Performance Areas (Areas of Concern)

Areas of concern are generic characteristics that the black-box or white-box enterprise properties must manifest [20]. De Vries [21] states that due to the negative connotation to *concerns*, *performance areas* should rather be used. In this context, a *performance area* is a generic characteristic of an enterprise that must be addressed via enterprise design. A *design domain* must operationalize one or more *performance areas*. The performance area must be stated in terms of a variable, that can increase (improve) or decrease (deteriorate) [21].

Within this step, in consultation with ECDA's main user, performance areas or concerns are documented, e.g. internal efficiency, fiscal viability, or quality of caregiving.

C: Identify Constructional Requirements and Specifications

The *constructional requirements* express certain wants and needs that the system construction must fulfil in view of the intended black box properties as well as the performance areas [20].

As indicated by [21], it is difficult to distinguish between *constructional requirements* and *design principles* (used in the next activity, i.e. activity D). Both provide *guidance* on how design of design domains or their embedded constructs must proceed. Usually a constructional requirement is defined for a narrow design scope, i.e. designing one particular construct, such as a software application. If a constructional requirement is generic in nature and applicable to a larger design scope, such as the entire ICT domain, the constructional requirement is transformed into a design principle, as indicated in activity D.

Constructional requirements will be defined by ECDA's main user. The requirements have to be associated with the *performance areas* that were identified and effected through design cycles when (re-)designing the design domains.

Constructional requirements need to be stated in a prescriptive format, using the words/phrases such as *should*, *must* or *may not*. The phrase "must be" is useful to indicate that the prescription needs to be verifiable [21].

D: Extract Design Principles

White box system properties result from the system's construction. Guidance for constructional design is informed by constructional architecture, also called *design principles* [20].

Existing constructional requirements, identified in activity C, will be used during activity D to identify requirements that are generic and useful to guide future development of applicable design domains. We believe that general design principles may also be extracted from IC literature.

5 Validating ECDA's Comprehensiveness

The SLR in [11] indicated that numerous IC development approaches exist, each focusing on different performance areas and functions in a disparate way, as noted in Sect. 1. We include these learnings and contributions within ECDA. Figure 5, a different representation of ECDA's heuristic, indicates how ECDA incorporated existing IC development approaches, previously discussed in Sect. 3.3. The construction design cycle (activity A) adopts an iterative process of suggesting the (re-)design of constructs. This step encapsulates various elements of IC approaches, demonstrating ECDA's comprehensiveness.

ICDA	EE Main design domains	IC within ECD			Other IC approaches		
		Social system Bloom [24]	Performance framework Bergin-Seers and Breen [26]	Leadership framework Nupponen [29]	Three levels of capacity development Imbaruddin [4]	Five dimensional framework Grindle and Hildebrand [27]	IC elements Scheepers [28]
Activity A	Execute construction design cycles for selected design domains						
	Environment	X	X		X	X	X
	Enterprise boundary				X		
	Organisation sub system (Operations)	X	X			X	X
	Organisation sub system (Financial support)	X					X
	Organisation sub system (Skills support)		X	X			
	Organisation sub system (Human support)					X	X
	Organisation sub system (Maintenance)	X					
	ICT sub system	X					X
	Human skills and know-how sub system	X		X	X		X
	Infrastructure sub system	X					X
Activity B	Identify performance areas (areas of concern)						
		X	X	X		X	
Activity C	Identify constructional requirements and specifications						
Activity D	Extract design principles to guide future design						

Fig. 5. ECDA's heuristic, synthesizing existing IC approaches

In Table 1 we also validate the comprehensiveness of ECDA as an enterprise design approach, indicating that ECDA addresses the eleven *approach design principles* from [18].

As indicated in Table 1, the current version of ECDA addresses the eleven principles, except for principles J and K that are only partially addressed. Suggestions for comprehensive demonstrations of ECDA are discussed in Sect. 7.

Table 1. Validating ECDA against the ADPs

Approach design principle	Applied to ECDA
Principle A - Explicit concept of the enterprise: A design approach should indicate how an enterprise is perceived or conceptualized	The ECDC is perceived as social system. Also, it is perceived as a living organism defined within a morphogenic paradigm (see Sect. 4.1)
Principle B – Explicit phenomenon: A design approach should provide evidence for a phenomenon or class-of-problems, i.e. similar kinds of problems	Atmore et al. [2] state that various challenges exist within the early childhood sector, among those are IC identified as a class-of-problems (see Sect. 1)
Principle C – Explicit paradigm of value-creation: A design approach should state a paradigm of value-creation as a testable proposition for addressing an existing phenomenon or class-of-problems	The ECDA, through a heuristic, enables ECD directors to effectively transition from functional requirements to constructional design in order to develop IC

(*continued*)

Table 1. (*continued*)

Approach design principle	Applied to ECDA
Principle D - Explicit means (ways) of demarcating and representing design scope: A design approach should clearly define and motivate the way to demarcate design scope (enterprise scope, design domains, and concerns/requirements) relevant to the approach	ECDA do not demarcate new design domains, but adopts those described in Sect. 4.2 as means to represent the ECDC' constructional design (activity A of ECDA's heuristic).
Principle E – Well-demarcated and well-defended design scope: A design approach should define and defend the intended design scope to achieve the intended value-creation	The ECDA uses the *generic system development process* (GSDP) to facilitate constructional design of the provisioning system (refer to Fig. 2)
Principle F – Representations of design scope: A design approach should clearly define and motivate notation standards that are used to adequately describe/represent the design scope	The organization domain adopts DEMO aspect models [17] as the notation standard, whilst ECDA is not prescriptive for the infrastructure and ICT domains. The human skills & know how domain will be represented by curriculum vitae
Principle G - Approach form and function: A design approach should clearly define the constructs and features of the approach	The ECDA's function is described in Sect. 4.1 and its form (i.e. a heuristic), is presented in Sect. 4.2
Principle H: Justificatory knowledge: A design approach must provide explanatory knowledge that links the paradigm of value-creation with its constructional components	As indicated in Fig. 1, the ECDA is a theory-ingrained artefact, guided by approach design principles (discussed in Sect. 3.1), informed by Hoogervorst's approach (presented in Sect. 3.2), as well as existing IC development approaches (introduced in Sect. 3.3)
Principle I – Approach mutability: A design approach should clearly state possibilities for tailoring the approach, within the pre-defined design scope	The ECDA may be applied to a different sector, industry or operational context than ECD
Principle J – Principles of implementations (conditional): A design approach may incorporate guidance for implementing the approach	Partially: The demonstration of ECDA's heuristic in Sect. 6 provides some guidance in the form of questions per activity (see Table 2)
Principle K – Expository instantiation (optional): A design approach may incorporate an instantiation	Partially: An instantiation of ECDA's heuristic is included in Sect. 6. The instantiation is not comprehensive to cover all the design domains

6   Application of ECDA's Heuristic

In this section, we demonstrate ECDA's heuristic in accordance with Sect. 4.2. Ideally, holistic design requires identification of multiple *functions*, *multiple performance areas* that need to be identified for the entire enterprise and all its *design domains and facets* [20]. In addition, *design principles* need to guide the design of the entire enterprise [20]. ECDA's heuristic supports a holistic approach, but for the purpose of this article, we only focused on a single function, i.e. *child caregiving*, to demonstrate a single cycle of ECDA's heuristic. Table 2 presents ECDA's heuristic on the left-hand side and its application at a real-world ECDC at the right-hand side. We also grey-shaded the parts of ECDA's heuristic that were demonstrated.

Table 2. Scope of demonstrating ECDA's heuristic

ECDA's heuristic – holistic scope	ECDA's application at ECDC
Functions (f, f,...f,) as input.	Single function (f,): *child caregiving*.
B. Identify performance areas (areas of concern).	Single performance area of concern: *quality of caregiving*.
A. Execute construction design cycles for selected design domains – **current design.**	See below.
Organization domain: What is the *current design* of the organization domain? Is it effective in terms of *performance areas*?	The *current design* for the function *child caregiving*, using the Cooperation Model (CM) to represent the *current design* (see Fig. 6). We believe that the *essence* of the current operations is effective in terms of *quality of caregiving*. The problem is that operations are not well supported by ICT.
ICT domain: What is the *current design* of the ICT domain? Is it effective in terms of *performance areas*? Is it effective in supporting the organization domain? If not, what *functions* are needed from the ICT domain?	The ICT domain is currently under-represented by the ECDC. It does not support the organization domain and has a detrimental effect on the *quality of caregiving*. Given the essential design of the child caregiving function, depicted in Fig. 6, the following functions are needed from ICT: • Fact maintenance, i.e. creating, reading, updating and deleting facts associated with child reception, feeding, providing fluids, nappy changing, bathroom assisting, nap attending, temperature measuring, structured skill-development, and go-home preparation. • On-time reporting to the director, highlighting problems, e.g. push notifications where needed. • Daily electronic reporting to parents.
Infrastructure domain: What is the *current design* of the infrastructure domain? Is it effective in terms of *performance areas*? Is it effective in supporting the organization domain? If not, what *functions* are needed for the infrastructure domain? **Excluded for demonstration.**	
Human skills & know-how domain: What are the *current* human skills & know-how? Is it effective in terms of *performance areas*? Is it effective in supporting the organization domain? If not, what changes are needed? **Excluded for demonstration.**	
Other facets: What are the *current* facets? Are they effective in terms of *performance areas*? If not, what changes are needed? **Excluded for demonstration.**	
C. Identify constructional requirements and specifications.	See below.
Organization domain: What *constructional requirements* should be addressed by the *future design* of the organization domain?	Since the current organizational design for *child caregiving* is sufficient, there is no need to identify constructional requirements for the future design of the organisation.
ICT domain: What	Constructional requirements for an ICT solution specify

(continued)

Table 2. (*continued*)

ECDA's heuristic – holistic scope	ECDA's application at ECDC
constructional requirements should be addressed by the *future design* of the ICT domain?	that the solution: • Must be cloud-based. • Must be easy to use. • Must be accessed via single sign-on using fingerprint-identification. • Must be available 100% of the time, accessible on- or off-line. In event of being off-line, data will be uploaded as soon as connectivity is restored. • Must be easily accessible to the primary caregiver, such as a hand-held device. • Must be accessible to multiple users in real time, e.g. parents, the director and caregiver. • Must be the core communication interface between the ECDC and parents.
Infrastructure domain: What *constructional requirements* should be addressed by the *future design* of the infrastructure domain? **Excluded for demonstration.**	
Human skills & know-how domain: The concept of *constructional requirements* is NOT applicable to human skills & know-how. **Excluded for demonstration.**	
Other facets: The concept of *constructional requirements* is NOT applicable to other facets. **Excluded for demonstration.**	
D. Extract design principles to guide future design.	From the constructional requirements that were identified for the ICT solution (Activity C), the following are generic for the ICT domain: • Must be cloud-based. • Must be easy to use.
A. Execute construction design cycles for selected design domains – **future design.**	See below.
Organization domain: What *future design* of the organization domain will address identified *constructional requirements*?	Future design will be the same as the current design, i.e. the essential operations, as depicted in Fig. 6 also represent the future design.
ICT domain: What *future design* of the ICT domain will address organization-supporting *functions* and identified *constructional requirements*?	Although not detailed here, alternative constructs will be compared against the required *functions* and *constructional requirements*. It is possible that existing software solutions exist that may be bought off-the-shelf. Alternatively, a new software application will have to be developed.
Infrastructure domain: What *future design* of the infrastructure domain will address organization-supporting *functions* and identified *constructional requirements*? **Excluded for demonstration.**	
Human skills & know-how domain: What *future* human skills & know-how will support the organization domain? **Excluded for demonstration.**	
Other facets: What should be the arrangement of future facets? **Excluded for demonstration.**	

As indicated in Fig. 3, ECDA's heuristic requires the main user to select a function as main input to perform the four main activities. The function *child caregiving* was selected to demonstrate the heuristic, since its *management and administration* is currently inadequate due to inefficient ICT support in providing timeous feedback to management when new production facts come into existence. Inadequate management has a detrimental effect on one of the performance areas, i.e. *quality of caregiving* (Fig. 6).

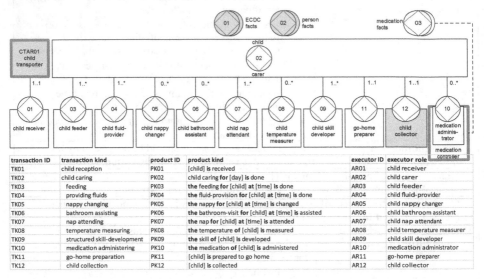

Fig. 6. The ECDC's cooperation model, represented by the coordination structure diagram and transactor product table

The demonstration of ECDA's heuristic in Table 2 excluded theory from IC, even though Fig. 5 provided a mapping to existing IC literature. During ECDA's further development and refinement, we believe that existing IC literature (as mapped in Fig. 5) will be useful to further shape ECDA.

7   Conclusion and Future Research

IC is defined as the ability of an enterprise to pursue its objectives, and is therefore a prerequisite for delivering quality services. IC is not a new concept in the public sector performance arena, but not well defined or researched in the ECD sector.

ECDCs across South-Africa are sub optimal, indicating that *less than half* of all registered centers having nothing more than staff attendance records or job descriptions. Various solutions, frameworks and approaches exist, but none are integrated or constructed in a manner to guide administrators on *how* to develop IC, let alone inform the (re)design of constructs in order to improve quality of services delivered. Thus, ECDA is constructed to *develop* IC that is useful to ECD directors or administrators when they need to improve quality of services.

Metamodels provided the means of defining the rules at a higher level of abstraction, and this in essence acted as an introduction to the abstraction levels adopted in this study. The general conceptual modelling framework was used to explain how the ECDA was constructed as an instantiation of EECM, a metamodel for enterprise design approaches.

ECDA as a theory-ingrained artefact was guided by (1) approach design principles that were derived from EECM, (2) Hoogervorst's approach, and (3) IC development approaches. Through synthesis, it is shown and proven that the plathora of existing solutions and frameworks were effectively integrated within ECDA's heuristic. The heuristic should enable ECDA's main user to systematically (re-)design certain enterprise design domains in order to have an impact on problematic performance areas.

We *demonstrated* ECDA's heuristic within a real-world ECDC, starting with the organisation domain's *current design* and specifying the ICT domain's *future design* to address inefficiencies related to the *administration and management* of the function *child caregiving*. Within its existing theoretical structure, we need to further develop ECDA iteratively and in a participative way to ensure that it is useful within a real-world ECDC context. In future, ECDA could also be tested within a different sector or industry to test its suitability, robustness, mutability and scalability.

In closing, albeit significant progress has been made in the South-African early childhood and Grade R spheres, ECDA as a theory-ingrained artefact has the ability to develop IC, and thus improve the *quality of services* delivered. ECDA is poised to not only have a contribution to the educational domain, but could have a societal impact for the majority of South-Africa's children.

References

1. Experthub: How do I start a child services business? https://www.experthub.info/launch/start-up-industry-specific-qas/how-do-i-start-a-child-services-business/. Accessed 15 Dec 2018
2. Atmore, E., Van Niekerk, L.J., Ashley-Cooper, M.: Challenges facing the early childhood development sector in South Africa. S. Afr. J. Child. Educ. 2(1), 120–139 (2012). https://doi.org/10.4102/sajce.v2i1.25
3. UNICEF: Draft national integrated early childhood development policy. Report (2015)
4. Imbaruddin, A.: Understanding institutional capacity of local government agencies in indonesia. Australian National University (2003)
5. Assefa, T.: Institutional capacity of local government in implementing the national policy on ethiopian women (NPEW): the case of Dilla town. Dilla University (2014)
6. Department of Social Development: Introduction and background to the policy. In: National integrated early childhood development policy. pp. 18–28. Government Printers, Pretoria (2015). https://www.gov.za/sites/default/files/gcis_document/201610/national-integrated-ecd-policy-web-version-final-01-08-2016a.pdf
7. Hayden, J.: Directors of early childhood services: experience, preparedness and selection. J. Aust. Res. Early Child. Educ. 1, 49–61 (1997)
8. Atmore, E.: Early childhood development in South Africa – progress since the end of apartheid. Int. J. Early Years Educ. 21(2–3), 152–162 (2013). https://doi.org/10.1080/09669760.2013.832941
9. Van Heerden, J.: Quality in South African early learning centres: mothers' and teachers' views and understanding. S. Afr. J. Child. Educ. 6(1), 1–11 (2016). https://doi.org/10.4102/sajce.v6i1x.423

10. Department of Social Development: Audit of early childhood development (ECD) centres - national report. Report, Department of Social Development (2014)
11. De Boer, A. C., De Vries, M.: A framework to embed institutional capacity at an early childhood development centre. In: SAIIEneXXXt Proceedings, 30th September – 2nd October 2019, pp. 613–627 (2019)
12. Dietz, J.L.G., et al.: The discipline of enterprise engineering. Int. J. Org. Des. and Eng. 3(1), 86–114 (2013). https://doi.org/10.1504/IJODE.2013.053669
13. De Vries, M., Van der Merwe, A., Gerber, A.: Extending the enterprise evolution contextualisation model. Ent. Inf. Syst. 11(6), 787–827 (2017). https://doi.org/10.1080/17517575.2015.1090629
14. Sein, M., Henfredsson, O., Purao, S., Rossi, M., Lindgren, R.: Action design research. MIS Q. 35(1), 37–56 (2011). https://doi.org/10.2307/23043488
15. de Vries, M., Berger, S.: An action design research approach within enterprise engineering. Syst. Pract. Action Res. 30(2), 187–207 (2016). https://doi.org/10.1007/s11213-016-9390-7
16. Henderson-Sellers, B., Ralyte, J.: Situational method engineering: state-of-the-art review. J. Univ. Comput. Sci. 16(3), 424–478 (2010)
17. Dietz, J.L.G., Mulder, H.B.F.: Enterprise Ontology: A Human-Centric Approach to Understanding the Essence of organisation. Springer, Heidelberg (2020). https://doi.org/10.1007/978-3-030-38854-6
18. De Vries, M.: Guiding the development of enterprise design approaches. S. Afr. J. of Ind. Eng. 27(3), 12–22 (2016). https://doi.org/10.7166/27-3-1621
19. Hoogervorst, J.A.P.: Foundations of Enterprise Governance and Enterprise Engineering - Presenting the Employee-Centric Theory of Organisation. Springer, Berlin Heidelberg (2018). https://doi.org/10.1007/978-3-319-72107-1
20. Hoogervorst, J.A.P.: Practicing Enterprise Governance and Enterprise Engineering - Applying The Employee-Centric Theory of Organization. Springer, Berlin Heidelberg (2018). https://doi.org/10.1007/978-3-319-73658-7
21. Vries, M.: Reducing ambiguity during enterprise design. Require. Eng. 25(2), 231–251 (2019). https://doi.org/10.1007/s00766-019-00320-1
22. Dietz, J.L.G.: Enterprise Ontology. Springer, Berlin (2006). https://doi.org/10.1007/3-540-33149-2
23. De Vries, M.: Towards consistent demarcation of enterprise design domains. In: de Cesare, S., Frank, U. (eds.) ER 2017. LNCS, vol. 10651, pp. 91–100. Springer, Cham (2017). https://doi.org/10.1007/978-3-319-70625-2_9
24. Bloom, P.J.: Child care centers as organizations: a social systems perspective. Child Youth Care Forum 20, 313–333 (1991). https://doi.org/10.1007/BF00757061
25. Davis, A., Lemma, T.: Capacity development: a UNDP Primer. https://www.undp.org/content/undp/en/home/librarypage/capacity-building/capacity-development-a-undp-primer.html. Accessed 15 Apr 2020
26. Bergin-Seers, S., Breen, J.: The performance of long day care centres in rural and remote areas. Aust. J. Early Child. 27(1), 24–33 (2002). https://doi.org/10.1177/183693910202700106
27. Grindle, M.S., Hilderbrand, M.E.: Building sustainable capacity in the public sector: what can be done? Public Adm. Dev. 15(5), 441–463 (1995). https://doi.org/10.1002/pad.4230150502
28. Scheepers, L.A.: An institutional capacity model of municipalities in South Africa. Stellenbosch University, Stellenbosch (2015)
29. Nupponen, H.: Framework for developing leadership skills in child care centres in Queensland, Australia. Contemp. Issues in Early Child. 7(2), 146–161 (2006). https://doi.org/10.2304/ciec.2006.7.2.146
30. Giachetti, R.E.: Design of Enterprise Systems. CRC Press, Boca Raton (2010)

Enterprise Coherence Metrics in Enterprise Decision Making

Joost Bekel[1]([✉]) and Roel Wagter[2]

[1] Radboud University, Nijmegen, The Netherlands
`joost.bekel@ru.nl`
[2] Solventa B.V., Wattbaan 51-1, 3439 ML Nieuwegein, The Netherlands

Abstract. Many organizations still struggle to translate strategy into design. Enterprise Architecture (EA) can be regarded as a key function to facilitate strategy execution. General Enterprise Architecting defines enterprise coherence as 'the extent to which all relevant aspects of an enterprise are connected, in such a way that these connections facilitate an enterprise obtaining/meeting its desired results'. There is a growing need to demonstrate the importance and usefulness in terms of the value that EA represents to an organization. Enterprise coherence is currently not measured within enterprises. Graphs are key to understanding systems on a quantitative and predictive basis. The core for enterprise coherence calculation is a graph of interrelated directions and decisions, which we will call the enterprise guidance graph (EGG). Based on EGG we envision an EC-index that takes decisions and guiding statements as input, and gives enterprise coherence as output. Inspiration for networks derived from natural systems has been used to formulate metrics for organizations. The research encompasses an experiment within an international financial company with circa 3000 employees, to understand first behavior of the developed model in practice. We conclude that an instrument for showing and measuring coherence is valued, and that support is given for quantification through the use of graphs, with enterprise coherence being one of the relevant metrics. This research aims to aid in improving structured enterprise engineering.

Keywords: Enterprise coherence · Enterprise guidance graph · General Enterprise Architecting · GEA · Strategy · Enterprise design

1 Introduction

A key reason for strategic failures is lack of coherence and consistency [1]. Many organizations still struggle to translate strategy into design. A system view on organizations, e.g. [2–4], learns that, since system viability relies on design [5], lack of coherence in design threatens viability of an organization. The value of enterprise coherence drives us to the research effort of quantifying enterprise coherence. This paper describes the background for quantifying enterprise coherence in Sect. 2, research methodology and artefact description in Sect. 3, a case study to measure coherence and its effects in Sect. 4. Section 5 holds conclusions and discussion, and Sect. 6 lists items for further study.

D. Aveiro et al. (Eds.): EEWC 2020, LNBIP 411, pp. 213–227, 2021.
https://doi.org/10.1007/978-3-030-74196-9_12

2 Background

2.1 Role of Enterprise Architecture

Enterprise Architecture (EA) can be regarded as a key function to facilitate strategy execution [6]. EA is a competence to guide the design and build of the organization and its aspects, in terms of e.g. business, information, application, infrastructure, security and governance [7]. EA needs to balance between a large number of concerns, on a large number of aspects, for a large number of stakeholders, and create coherent views on the enterprise and on related decisions, and should focus on methods and tools that provide the requisite coherence and adaptability [8]. Indications are that coherence in organizations is unsatisfactory on average, and even poor when it concerns enterprise design [9]. To translate strategy into enterprise design is one of the key functions of EA, which indicates that EA is still unable to fulfill on its promise.

Within EA, several frameworks exist to bring strategy into enterprise design, e.g. Dietz [6], Simon et al. [10], and Radeke [11]. Enterprise governance, which can be considered as part of enterprise engineering, relates to the competence of enterprise change and adaptation and thus reflects the process towards enterprise design [12]. Several scholars ([6, 13]) recognize the essence of EA in guiding enterprise designs and the role that principles play. Principles, requirements and guidelines can e.g. greatly help in ensuring standards within an enterprise to restrict the design freedom [14].

Under the axiom that lack of coherence will result in poor enterprise performance the General Enterprise Architecting (GEA) [15–19] has coherence governance at the heart of its method. To make coherence within an organization explicit GEA defines connected levels of cohesive elements, including guiding statements, which are defined as internally agreed and published statements, which direct desirable behavior [13]. Guiding statements may include policy statements, (normative) principles and objectives. GEA defines enterprise coherence as 'the extent to which all relevant aspects of an enterprise are connected, in such a way that these connections facilitate an enterprise obtaining/meeting its desired results' [13]. Based on this definition, GEA constructs an Enterprise Coherence Framework (ECF) that consists of a series of cohesive elements and cohesive relationships, which together define the playing field for an enterprise's coherence. Enterprise Coherence is about coherence at the level of purpose, at the level of design, and between the level of purpose and design. In that way the connections on the level of design facilitate the enterprise meeting its results [13]. EA needs tools and techniques that target more directly enterprise coherence [9].

2.2 Measurable Value in EA

There is a growing need to demonstrate the importance and usefulness in terms of the value that EA represents to an organization [18]. Tamm et al. [19] show that the value of EA is in either organizational alignment, information availability, resource portfolio optimization, and/or resource complementarity. Rodrigues & Amaral [20] identified a list of 29 key benefits/value drivers of Enterprise Architectures. While multiple quantifications exist in modern EA (see e.g. [21]), identifying and quantifying the direct and indirect impact of EA in organizations activities is a major challenge. Observation is even that there is currently not a single benefit that can be measurable and, at the same time, be achieved in a short-term period, however quantification of aspects may not be totally impossible [18]. Quantification of enterprise coherence is in its infancy as well. Despite some initiatives, e.g. [9], enterprise coherence is currently hardly measured within enterprises. We argue that measuring is expected to have a number of positive effects, e.g. improved awareness on the importance of steering on coherence, capability to capture design rationales for decisions (e.g. [22]), and higher awareness on the linkage between enterprise decisions. Decision making is known to follow a two stage process: 1) carry out a situation assessment, 2) use a decision method, e.g. intuitive or rational decision making, to come to a course of action. Situation assessment is an attempt to make sense of the present situation [23] and eliminate uncertainty that would otherwise constrain the effectiveness of the decision-making [24]. Connecting with the proper (architecture) guiding statements for the context can be regarded as part of situation assessment and as such improve fast and effective decision-making. Since the latter predicts firm growth and profit and mediates the relation of dynamism, munificence, centralization, and formalization with firm performance [25], there is likely value in (linking to) coherent architectural guidance.

2.3 Graphs as Quantification Method

Understanding the interactions between the components of a system is key to understanding it on a quantitative and predictive basis. Networks (or graphs) are a tool for keeping track of who is interacting with whom, at what strength, when, and in what way [26]. Even when mechanisms are unexplained, the topology of the graph often allows to understand its properties [26]. An earlier effort to quantify enterprise coherence showed that all identified models were graph based [27].

Design inspiration for networks derived from natural systems has been receiving increasing attention. Analogies between ecosystems and food webs and industrial networks, or other human systems that exchange materials and energy, is supported by previous works, for example [28]. Trophic coherence, a measure of a network's hierarchical organization, based on the concept of trophic levels used mainly in ecology [29], has been shown to be linked to a network's structural and dynamical aspects [30]. Trophic coherence is the tendency of nodes to fall into well-defined trophic levels. It has been related to several structural and dynamical properties of directed networks, including stability and spreading processes. Trophic coherence allows for systems to become more stable with size and edge density, and a ground why large, complex ecosystems are observed to be the most stable [28]. Thus, trophic coherence can be regarded as the extent to which a network approaches this state of order [31] which make it useful to relate it to -recursive- structural elements of e.g. GEA. Representations of influence with directed links from basal nodes to nodes higher in the hierarchy can be seen as transport networks (e.g. [32]), where a kind of quantity (whether biomass, energy, or information) originates in the sources and flows through the ecosystem, some of it reaching the sinks [28, 29, 32]. Transport, coherence and stability of the system seem related [31]. Other metrics that transfer from biosystems to industrial and organizational networks are e.g. Link Density, Prey-to-Predator Ratio (P_R), Specialized Predator Fraction (P_S), Generalization (G), Vulnerability (V), Mean Path Length (MPL) [33]. Another known metric is the 'minimal cut' between source and sink nodes that describes how sensible a graph is to loose its connectivity that offers important insights into the structure of the graph [32]. Since it is suggested that a group of (ecological) metrics is better used to come to design rules of a network [33], we took up -next to coherence- also these other metrics in our research.

3   Research Setup

3.1   Artefact

We envision an EC-index [34] that takes decisions and guiding statements (as grounds for decision making) as input, and give enterprise coherence as output. The EC-index dashboard will be enriched with other metrics as well. The EC-index has a target group consisting of Enterprise Architects and Senior Management of organizations of over 750 employees, either national or international, commercial or not-for-profit, with a more permanent character. The context is formed by the aim to support (architectural) governance, by facilitating decision making to come to a more sustainable enterprise. We regard as requirements that the calculation must include enterprise coherence -adhering to a (e.g. GEA) enterprise architecture definition-, be relevant and representative in enterprises of the earlier described target group, and have added value in an enterprise dashboard. Furthermore, it must be end user friendly, both in format and (re)calculation, must be scalable and future proof, and data gathering for calculation must fit the enterprise practice. The core for the calculation is a graph of interrelated directions and decisions [27], which we will call the enterprise guidance graph (EGG). The EGG has enterprise decisions as 'leaves'. The other nodes are 'guiding statements', that, in another view, of course are enterprise decisions as well. NB: This fits the notion of a food-web in which predators are other animal's prey. In terms of coherence we will take the bio-inspired trophic coherence as starting point, and calculate the trophic incoherence parameter $q(EGG)$ as described by Moutsinas et al. [30]. In terms of influence dynamics [30], new decisions trigger change in existing guidelines, and we interpret paths from source (ultimate guideline) to sink (decision) node for now as 'the buy-in for the decision'. This confronts us with the question how to model the interrelationships between guiding statements, and the relationships between decisions and guiding statements. We choose to express expert opinion in a 'Facebook like' as follows: From the point of view of the guiding statement, an expert 'likes' (supports) the decision. With this choice we stay close to the original food web model and provide simplicity.

Current setup of de artefact, serving as a 'Minimum Viable Product'(MVP) is as follows: inputs are collected in Microsoft MS Forms during the assessments, subsequently inserted into matrices in MS Excel, and then exported to R Studio to perform metrics calculations. Graphs were visualized in Gephi to support analysis and basic data manipulation (e.g. deletion of unused nodes). Manipulated graphs were exported as csv to R Studio directly to perform new metrics calculations. Exporting a graph in Archimate 3 language from BizzDesign Enterprise Studio through Excel has been done as a test, with positive result.

3.2 Research Methodology

For the earlier design of the GEA theory and their artefacts the research methodology Design Science (DSRM) of Hevner et al. [35] and Wieringa [36], including the design science research methodology process (DSRM process) of Peffers et al. [37] has been followed. Also, artefact evaluation based on Gregor et al.'s anatomy of a design theory [38] has been used. For the evaluation of theory and artefacts Yin [39] has been applied.

For this artefact we will use these same research methodologies. We will formulate a research problem, that will lead to our research questions and a description of the artefact to develop, and use case study as a mean to strengthen both design and knowledge. The case study in this paper can be interpreted as single case experiments under idealized conditions to aid in developing the artefact [36], with the primary goal to assess whether it is feasible to construct a meaningful quantification of enterprise coherence.

3.3 Problem Statement

The presumption is that in spite of the developments on enterprise coherence governance, enterprises still lack on coherence, and that measurement of enterprise coherence will strengthen the need for moving towards improved enterprise coherence governance, which in turn will promote transparency of decision-making, delivery of reasoned decisions, and respect for proportionality in decision-making. This will improve viability of organizations. Our problem statement is formulated as follows: generic metrics that would allow to assess decisions, architectures, and even enterprises on their coherence is lacking. Based on the principle 'what gets measured gets done', lack of measurement indicates that enterprise coherence gets overlooked within the average organization, which weakens governance.

3.4 Research Questions

The aim is to develop an artefact, that measures enterprise coherence itself. We will call this additional artefact the EC-index. Our research question is: how to quantify enterprise coherence? High level design questions are:

1. How can we measure enterprise coherence for a certain domain at a certain point in time?
2. How does this give clues to improving guidance in enterprise decision making?
3. How can we measure the improvement of decision making?

In terms of the instrument to measure enterprise coherence, more detailed knowledge questions are e.g.:

1. How can trophic coherence be measured on an Object of Study (OoS)?
2. What is the effect of adding, changing or deleting a decision?
3. How does trophic coherence scale, e.g. by aggregating OoS?

This leads us to the hypotheses for this paper as stated in the next section. E.g. limitations and opportunities for enterprise use of bio-inspired, but mathematically generalized, metrics will be part of further study.

3.5 Hypotheses

Our model relies on expert opinion and we take the 'Facebook like' as a basis for graph links. This leads to our first hypothesis.

– Hypothesis 1: the 'like' is intuitive, 'good-enough', and easy to use.

Link Density is the number of links with respect to the number of nodes. We regard this as a measure of maturity of the EGG, and associate this with maturity of this governance practice.

– Hypothesis 2: Link Density will be a measure for coherence governance maturity.

When decisions are taken at the right spot, it may be clear indeed that coherence in the organization is improved. If trophic coherence is higher, i.e. if directions and decisions fall better into the frames where decision makers need and expect them, we expect improved decision making: decisions/guiding statements and decision makers will be a better match on average. We expect the improved decision making to be more thorough on average, which will lead to less rework.

– Hypothesis 3: high EGG trophic coherence means low rework.

The minimal cut of a graph describes how sensitive a graph is to lose its connectivity. We are interested if a decision (sink node) connects to the enterprise's identity and strategy (source node), so in whether there is a path to it. The argument is that if a decision fits an organization's strategic storyline, it is more likely that the decision, once effectuated, does not need to be reversed. Reversal of a decision comes with rework. We focus for now on the size of the minimal cut (i.e. amount of edges or vertices that need to be removed).

– Hypothesis 4: high minimal cut size means robust decisions, with low chance of rework.

In the current experiment we focus on underpinning for these hypotheses.

4 Case in an International Organization

We will use a single case experiment with realistic conditions and expert opinion. This is to understand first behavior of the developed model in practice, and to weed out bad design parts early.

4.1 Object of Study

The organization is an international financial company with circa 3000 employees, with head office in The Netherlands. The organization is subdivided into various business units. The business units are organized in an agile way in terms of value streams. Value streams encompass DevOps teams that focus on the development of a particular functional domain. As Object of Study (OoS) we take decisions made in a DevOps team, and connect with the relevant directional context. This directional context consists of guiding statements with a goal character, e.g. strategic goals and their related objectives, and with a principle character. In the experiment the decision will be connected to the guiding statements, guiding statements will be related to each other, and subsequently coherence (and other) calculations are performed. The outcomes of the calculations are analyzed and discussed. Company policy does not allow to publish the decisions and guiding statements but they are available on direct request to the authors.

4.2 Experiment Setup

In the experiment a network of existing guiding statements (the Enterprise Guidance Graph 'EGG') was constructed to understand their contribution to enterprise decision making. The experiment is also used as a starting point for revitalizing existing principles and guidelines, because for several years this has been neglected, at least methodological application. In this endeavor both a theoretical framework is used as top-down approach to (re)define principles and guidelines, and a 'proof of concept' is setup as bottom-up approach, to understand how principles and guidelines aid in coming to correct decisions, and eventually how decisions may influence existing principles and guidelines. A group of four domain and enterprise architects assessed two decisions against guiding statements and vice versa during a total of three sessions. With individuals from this group semi-structured interviews were held before and after the assessments, in order to get their (change in) expert opinion on the research. Furthermore, semi-structured interviews were held with the Head of Enterprise Architecture on the used framework, with two enterprise architects on the connections between various guiding statements, with a member of the strategic transformation office of the company on the interrelationships between strategic guiding statements and with resulting initiatives. Material from strategic direction, and from a larger base of guiding statements was studied. Finally, use was made from the system JIRA to obtain the initiative context in which the decision was required. The specific decisions under study were brought forward by domain architects that were closely involved in the decision making. The first decision, that we will call ED1, was selected, because intervention on the highest level was required to make the decision pass. The second decision, that we will call ED2, represents a case where an enterprise architect's view overruled the initial preference of the domain architect. Both decisions were well described as formal Architectural Decision conform a structured template, and have a formal status within the organization, which means that they ran through multiple boards in order to be approved. During the sessions the respective decisions were assessed from the point of view of the available guiding statement network. Guiding statements were available on the local domain, on enterprise architecture level, and on strategic level. Decisions were directly assessed from the guiding statements of both the domain level as well as the enterprise architecture level, in order to assess differences in coherence. The total experiment encompassed calculation and analysis of the following cases:

1. Guiding statements for decision ED1
2. Guiding statements for decision ED2
3. Guiding statements for decisions ED1 and ED2 combined
4. Guiding statements with a goal character for decision ED1

No separate goals graph was made for decision ED2, because the method and therefore the result is basically the same as for ED1.

4.3 Results

The experiment lead to results for the cases as described earlier. For decisions ED1, ED2 and ED1 and ED2 combined, the resulting EGGs are shown in Fig. 1, Fig. 2 and Fig. 3.

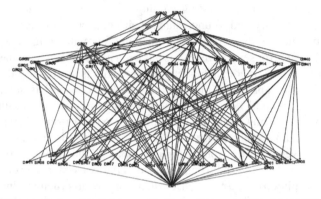

Fig. 1. Enterprise Guidance Graph for Enterprise Decision ED1

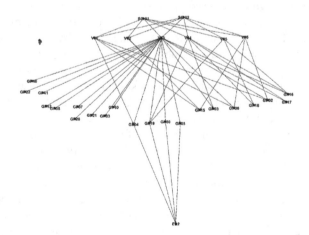

Fig. 2. Enterprise Guidance Graph for Enterprise Decision ED2

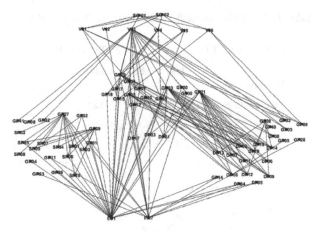

Fig. 3. Enterprise Guidance Graph for Enterprise Decisions ED1 and ED2 combined

Decisions ED1 vs Principle Guiding Statements. The resulting metrics are given in Table 1. We compare the results with targets from food web metrics [33] in order to have a (because of network generalization [30]) -defendable- starting point. This is only a temporary norm, due to the absence of comparing figures. To obtain comparing figures is part of further study. In all cases Link density is poor, which is in line with expectation, since the organization is only restarting principles & guidelines practices and is therefore considered immature at this point. Coherence is good (low incoherence) in all cases. This could be a reflection that the relatively low number of guiding statements that were available, were in fact well attributable to hierarchical levels. At the same time, because of the relatively low numbers, we must consider the coherence figures flattered. For minimal cut we have no figures yet to compare to, however in our interpretation as robustness on buy-in from the top for the decision, we would prefer that it is much larger than 1. A minimal cut of 6 for decision ED1 may be therefore quite good: at least there are multiple paths from source to sink node. The decision ED1 is thoroughly discussed within the organization and reversal is not expected within the next 10 years. In case ED2 minimal cut is substantially lower. The decision ED2 is discussed within the organization, but only with a limited group, and should introduce a new architecture on this point. This architecture is clearly not yet stable, which is indeed expressed in the figures. Minimal cut only applies to single decisions, therefore the combined case we see for now as not applicable.

Decision ED1 vs Goal Guiding Statements. For decision ED1 the resulting EGG is shown in Fig. 4, but then, instead from a principles view, from a goal-view.

The resulting metrics are given in Table 2. We again compare the results with targets from food web metrics. What must be said is that all development activities, in terms of stories and features to realize, are connected to higher level strategic initiatives and ultimately to the enterprises vision and mission. At the same time, connection of decisions to goals is not a institutionalized activity. Therefore, from the view of our case, Link density is poor. Coherence is satisfying which reflects the adequate building up of initiatives towards the top. We expect that application of more decisions will give a rise

Table 1. EGG Metrics for decisions ED1, ED2, and ED1&2.

EGG Metric	ED1	ED2	ED1&2	Target (FW)
Link Density	1.83	1.87	1.63	5.00
Incoherence	0.38	0.40	0.37	0.25
Minimal Cut	6	3	N.A	>>1

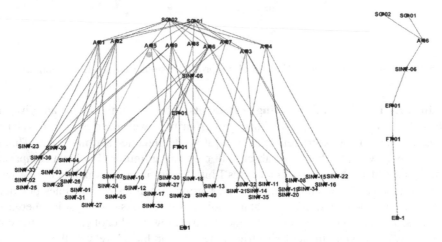

Fig. 4. Enterprise Guidance Graph for Enterprise Decision ED1 vs goals

of coherence against goals. Although we have no comparing results yet, we expect that a minimal cut of 1 is critical. This gives the impression of a decision that reaches goals with only a small basis in the organization.

Table 2. EGG Metrics for decision ED1 vs goals.

EGG Metric	Value	Target (FW)
Link Density	1.13	5.00
Incoherence	0.36	0.25
Minimal cut	1	>>1

4.4 Expert Feedback

As stated, the case study is to aid in developing the artefact, and to see whether it is feasible to construct a meaningful quantification of enterprise coherence. To support this goal, expert feedback was collected using semi-structured interviews with (enterprise) architects. The structure was given with two surveys, of which the results are available with the authors.

The first set of semi-structured interviews led to the following results:

- Enterprise coherence is regarded as important, and it must be defined very clearly what is meant. Interpretations align with the GEA view of level of purpose, level of design and the interrelationships between them.
- The need for coherence is felt for reasons of efficient production with the right initiatives and not too many dependencies, and for understanding of context.
- There is some perceived value in a metric for enterprise coherence, and some believe that this may be possible.
- The percolation concept (paths from source to sink nodes) could be understood by the participants, and the concept is perceived as strong in that it gives some view on and strength of the rationales in the enterprise in relation with decisions.
- However, the value of an instrument that measures coherence, if defined correctly, is regarded as positive. This is with a background of participants that value metrics in general as slightly positive. As critical success factors objectivity and repeatability, and proper use cases where mentioned.

The second survey led to the following results:

- An instrument such as EC-INDEX is regarded as positively influencing architectural practices, and expected to contribute to improved enterprise coherence.
- The model decision to use the 'like' as a way to interconnect guiding statements and decisions is regarded as correct, intuitive, and user-friendly.
- Enterprise coherence, in the bio-inspired 'trophic'/'hierarchical' meaning, and other described metrics, are expected to contribute to recognized enterprise values, more specifically to lower rework, lower number of conflicts, and more consistent and coherent decision making.

5 Discussion

This research aims to help organizations to be more coherent in their decision making, by improving their decision making structure, and measuring these improvements. Since this is a new field in enterprise architecture, where quantification is almost fully absent, this gives rise to a large number of new discussion points. First of all, we look at the hypotheses to validate with the experiment:

- Hypothesis 1: We take the 'like' as a way to incorporate intangible, expert opinion, in the model. We argue that this is an easy, intuitive, and -while based on expert opinion-sufficiently correct way to express influences, at least to start with. The answers to the survey give support to this.

- Hypothesis 2: Link Density as representative for maturity. Link Density is low in all researched cases. The enterprise at hand is on the eve of a new setup of a principles and guideline framework, in the recognition that this has been neglected in the past years. Therefore maturity is expected to be low. The experiment therefore gives support to the hypothesis.
- Hypothesis 3: Low incoherence results in low rework. From the metrics we cannot draw a conclusion on this hypothesis. Expert opinion supports the reasoning that the modeled incoherence parameter will reflect the chance for lower rework. This strengthens somewhat the believe that the bio-inspired measure for (in)coherence, with the proper translation through EGG, can be used to represent 'enterprise coherence', thereby giving a quantification for enterprise coherence.
- Hypothesis 4: Minimal cut as indicative for decision stability. The experiment showed higher minimal cut for the organization wide discussed decision versus the less broad discussed decision. The latter decision was also part of a new architectural setup that is yet immature. Minimal cut gives indication to this case, so we conclude that the results of the experiment give support to this hypothesis.

Other discussion points are:

- We take a graph of the embedding of decision making in organizational guiding statements as a representative model for decision making in the organizations, while there exists large variety in influences on decision making, e.g. power structures, historic behavior, trends. We find this defendable, because the 'EGG' represents the more common, and often rational part of decision making. By improving coherence and other aspects, decision making can be expected to be improved, despite presence of other influences.
- We expect the linking effort to happen in reality. At the same time we concluded that the effort in the experiment was perceived as user unfriendly, and too much. So an issue is how to organize the 'administrative' linking effort, so that the linking is done by a sufficiently knowledgeable set of (local) experts, and that the linking effort per decision can be limited. We conclude that governance is needed, and suggest an architectural framework like GEA to support this 'enterprise coherence governance'.
- Metrics results are directly compared with food-web metrics. While we defend this to some extent, based on the argument that the food-web graph has already been proven to be extendible outside the bio-domain, it is clear that extensive research is required to allow improved benchmarking and propose this for further study.

From the expert interviews we conclude that an instrument for showing and measuring coherence is valued, and that parts of this value are plausible. It is too early to complete the view on applicability and limitations of all metrics, but the experiment fulfilled the goal to aid in development of the artefact, and can be interpreted as giving support for using quantification through the use of graphs, with enterprise coherence being one of the relevant metrics.

6 Further Study

This research aims to help organizations to be more coherent in their decision making. With EGG and the measurement instrument EC-INDEX we made it possible to measure enterprise coherence and some other relevant metrics that give insight in the structure of organizational decision making. Further study should include doing measurements in various domains and organizations, as to understand how metrics compare. This will allow to research the hypotheses as stated in this article. Furthermore, governance on the EGG should be setup. This would allow to give more consistency in measurement and broaden experiments. Finally, the measurement instrument EC-INDEX must be improved in terms of user-friendliness, measurement speed, and portability. This would allow to broaden experiments, and also test coherence measurements in real-life situations.

References

1. Dietz, J.L.G., Hoogervorst, J.A.P.: The unifying role of enterprise engineering. In: Magalhàes, R. (ed.) Organization Design and Engineering, pp. 11–38. Palgrave Macmillan UK, London (2014). https://doi.org/10.1057/9781137351579_2
2. Keating, C.B., Bradley, J.M.: Complex system governance reference model. Int. J. Syst. Syst. Eng. 6(1/2), 33–52 (2015)
3. Keating, K.B., Katina, P.F.: Complex system governance development: a first generation methodology. Int. J. Syst. Syst. Eng. 7(1/2/3), 43–74 (2016)
4. Katina, P.F.: Sustainability of systems of systems. Int. J. Syst. Syst. Eng. 5(2) (2014)
5. Whitney, K., Bradley, J.M., Baugh, D.E., Chesterman, C.W., Jr.: Systems theory as a foundation for governance of complex systems. Int. J. Syst. Syst. Eng. 6(1–2), 15–32 (2015)
6. Dietz, J.L.G.: Architecture: Building Strategy into Design. Academic Service, The Hague (2008)
7. The Open Group: The TOGAF standard, version 9.2, Van Haren Publishing, Zaltbommel (2018)
8. Korhonen, J.J., Lapalme, J., McDavid, D., Gill, A.Q.: Adaptive enterprise architecture for the future: towards a reconceptualization of EA. In: 2016 IEEE 18th Conference on Business Informatics (CBI), Paris, pp. 272–281 (2016). https://doi.org/10.1109/CBI.2016.38
9. Bekel, J., Wagter, R.: Measurement of enterprise coherence by means of the GEA C-Index-a first investigation. In: 2020 IEEE 22nd Conference on Business Informatics (CBI), Antwerp, Belgium, pp. 57–64 (2020). https://doi.org/10.1109/CBI49978.2020.10058
10. Simon, D., Fischbach, K., Schoder, D.: Enterprise architecture management and its role in corporate strategic management. Inf. Syst. E-Bus. Manag. 12(1), 5–42 (2013). https://doi.org/10.1007/s10257-013-0213-4
11. Radeke, F.: Toward Understanding Enterprise Architecture Management's Role in Strategic Change: Antecedents, Processes, Outcomes. Wirtschaftsinformatik Zurich, Switzerland (2011)
12. Hoogervorst, J.: Practicing Enterprise Governance and Enterprise Engineering: Applying the Employee-Centric Theory of Organization. Springer, Cham (2018). https://doi.org/10.1007/978-3-319-73658-7. ISBN: 978-3-319-73658-7
13. Proper, E., Greefhorst, D.: The roles of principles in enterprise architecture. In: Proper, E., Lankhorst, M.M., Schönherr, M., Barjis, J., Overbeek, S. (eds.) TEAR 2010. LNBIP, vol. 70, pp. 57–70. Springer, Heidelberg (2010). https://doi.org/10.1007/978-3-642-16819-2_5

14. Op't Land, M., Proper, E., Waage, M., Cloo, J., Steghuis, C.: Enterprise Architecture: Creating Value by Informed Governance. Springer, Heidelberg (2008). https://doi.org/10.1007/978-3-540-85232-2

15. Wagter, R.: Enterprise coherence governance. Dissertation, Radboud University Nijmegen (2013)

16. Wagter, R., Proper, H.A., Witte, D.: Enterprise coherence in the Dutch ministry of social affairs and employment. In: Bajec, M., Eder, J. (eds.) CAiSE 2012. LNBIP, vol. 112, pp. 600–607. Springer, Heidelberg (2012). https://doi.org/10.1007/978-3-642-31069-0_50

17. Wagter, R., Proper, H.A., Witte, D.: Enterprise architecture: on the use of GEA at the Dutch ministry of social affairs and employment. In: Proceedings of 2012 IEEE 14th International Conference on Commerce and Enterprise Computing (CEC 2012), Hangzhou, China, September 2012, p. 115–119 (2012)

18. Wagter, R., Proper, H.A., Witte, D.: A theory for enterprise coherence governance. In: Saha, P. (ed.) A Systemic Perspective to Managing Complexity with EA. National University of Singapore, Institute of Systems Science (2013)

19. Wagter, R., Proper, H.A., Witte, D.: Enterprise coherence governance in the public sector. In: Proceedings of the 15th IEEE Conference on Business Informatics (CBI 2013), Vienna, Austria (2013)

20. Rodrigues, L.S., Amaral, L.: Stakeholder perspectives on time horizon and quantification of enterprise architectures benefits/value drivers. In: Proceedings of 32nd IBIMA Conference (2018)

21. Tamm, T., Seddon, P., Shanks, G., Reynolds, P.: How does enterprise architecture add value to organisations. Commun. Assoc. Inf. Syst. 28(1), 10 (2011)

22. Rodrigues, L.S., Amaral, L.: Key enterprise architecture value drivers: results of a Delphi study. In: Proceedings of the 21st International Business Information Management Association (IBIMA) Conference, Vienna, Austria, pp. 588–599 (2013)

23. Monahov, I.B.: Integrated software support for quantitative models in the domain of enterprise architecture management. Dissertation, Technische Universität München (2014)

24. Plataniotis, G., De Kinderen, S., Proper, H.A.: Relating decisions in enterprise architecture using decision design graphs. In: 17th IEEE International Enterprise Distributed Object Computing Conference (2013)

25. Flin, R.H., O'Connor, P., Crichton, M.: Safety at the Sharp End: A Guide to Non-technical Skills. Ashgate Publishing Ltd., Farnham (2008)

26. Sniazhko, S.: Uncertainty in decision-making: a review of the international business literature. Cogent Bus. Manag. 6(1), 1650692 (2019)

27. Robert Baum, J., Wally, S.: Strategic decision speed and firm performance. Strategic Manag. J. 24(11), 1107–1129 (2003)

28. Thurner, S., Hanel, R., Klimek, P.: Introduction to the Theory of Complex Systems. Oxford Press, Oxford (2018)

29. Bekel, J., Wagter, R.: Quantifying enterprise coherence – a design based comparison of calculation methods. To be published in: Book of Conference Proceedings of XIV Balkan Conference on Operational Research, Hybrid BALCOR (2020)

30. Mayer, A.L.: Ecologically-based approaches to evaluate the sustainability of industrial systems. Int. J. Sustain. Soc. 1(2), 117–133 (2008)

31. Johnson, S., Domínguez-García, V., Donetti, L., Muñoz, M.A.: Trophic coherence determines food-web stability. Proc. Natl. Acad. Sci. 111(50), 17923–17928 (2014)

32. Moutsinas, G., Shuaib, C., Guo, W., Jarvis, S.: Graph hierarchy and spread of infections. arXiv preprint arXiv:1908.04358 (2019)

33. Klaise, J., Johnson, S.: From neurons to epidemics: how trophic coherence affects spreading processes. Chaos Interdiscip. J. Nonlinear Sci. 26(6), 065310 (2016)

34. Knorn, S., Varagnolo, D., Staffas, K., Wrigstad, T., Fjällström, E.: Quantitative analysis of curricula coherence using directed graphs. IFAC-PapersOnLine **52**(9), 318–323 (2019)
35. Layton, A., Bras, B., Weissburg, M.: Designing industrial networks using ecological food web metrics. Environ. Sci. Technol. **50**(20), 11243–11252 (2016)
36. Bekel, J.: Quantifying enterprise coherence. In: 2019 IEEE 23rd International Enterprise Distributed Object Computing Workshop (EDOCW), pp. 179–183. IEEE (2019)
37. Hevner, A.R., March, S.T., Park, J., Ram, S.: Design science in information systems research. MIS Q. **28**, 75–106 (2004)
38. Wieringa, R.J.: Design Science Methodology for Information Systems and Software Engineering. Springer, Heidelberg (2015). https://doi.org/10.1007/978-3-662-43839-8, ISBN 978-3-662-43839-8
39. Peffers, K., Tuunanen, T., Rothenberger, M.A., Chatterjee, S.: A design science methodology for information system research. J. Manag. Inf. Syst. **24**(3), 45–78 (2007)
40. Gregor, S., Jones, D.: The anatomy of a design theory. J. Assoc. Inf. Syst. **8**(5), 312–335 (2007). Article 2
41. Yin, R.K.: Case Study Research Design and Methods. Sage Publications Inc., Thousand Oaks (2013)

Testing the Concept of the *RUN-Time Adaptive* Enterprise

Combining Organization and IT Agnostic Enterprise Models with Organization Implementation Variables and Low Code Technology

Martin Op 't Land[1,2](✉) [iD], Marien R. Krouwel[1,3] [iD], and Steven Gort[4]

[1] Capgemini Netherlands, PO Box 2575, 3500 GN Utrecht, The Netherlands
{Martin.OptLand,Marien.Krouwel}@capgemini.com
[2] Antwerp Management School, Boogkeers 5, 2000 Antwerp, Belgium
[3] Radboud Universiteit, Comeniuslaan 4, 6525 HP Nijmegen, The Netherlands
[4] ICTU, PO Box 84011, 2508 AA The Hague, The Netherlands
Steven.Gort@ictu.nl

Abstract. Our research program aims at finding and testing methods that allow organizations to become more *RUN-time adaptive* enterprises, with a near-zero time-to-market for new or changed products and services. Indeed, to thrive in increasingly more disruptive environments, an enterprise's IT time-to-market should sustainably no longer be on the critical path of business time-to-market. Earlier research suggests that key elements for such a method are (a) an organization and IT agnostic way of modeling products and services and its collaboration network, using DEMO, (b) a universal transaction pattern of coordination and production acts as atoms for building business processes, and (c) designing the aspects in which organizational adaptivity is desired, in terms of Organization Implementation Variables (OIVs). To test the combined application of these elements in practice, ICTU and Capgemini conducted a Proof of Concept on Social Housing during 5 weeks. The resulting application, built with the Mendix low code platform, showed the ability to reorganize – in this case: reconfiguring accountabilities inside and across organizations – at run-time, without the need to change software. Future research should clarify to what extent such intrinsic application adaptivity can be increased, e.g., by (a) embedding the use of APIs, (b) automated support of all coordination acts in the universal transaction pattern, and (c) parametrizing more OIVs.

Keywords: Time-to-market · Agile · Enterprise engineering · DEMO · Organization implementation · Low code · Intrinsic application adaptivity

1 Introduction

As strategic and operating conditions become increasingly turbulent due to factors such as hyper-competition, increasing demands from customers, regulatory

© Springer Nature Switzerland AG 2021
D. Aveiro et al. (Eds.): EEWC 2020, LNBIP 411, pp. 228–242, 2021.
https://doi.org/10.1007/978-3-030-74196-9_13

changes, and technological advancements, the ability to change with an ever decreasing time-to-market, often referred to as 'agility' [14], becomes an important determinant of firm success [17]. Though change occurs in organizational essence, such as products and services delivered, most of the time change deals with different implementations [5], e.g., the shifting of responsibilities to different parts of the organization. Our research program aims at finding and testing methods that allow organizations to become more *RUN-time adaptive* – as opposed to *DESIGN-time adaptive*, where changes in the design phase typically take weeks to years for transformation projects/programs to change the operation accordingly – enterprises, with a near-zero time-to-market for new or changed products and services – in which the enterprise's IT time-to-market should sustainably be no longer on the critical path of its business time-to-market.

Earlier research [7] suggests that key elements for such a method are (a) an organization and IT agnostic way of modeling products and services and its collaboration network, using the Design and Engineering Methodology for Organizations (DEMO), (b) a universal transaction pattern of coordination and production acts as atoms for building business processes, and (c) designing the aspects in which organizational adaptivity is desired, in terms of OIVs. While this sounds promising, it has only been tested with an undocumented prototype [7]; a traceable and documented implementation for a real case, from product definition to working software, is missing.

To test and document the combined application of these method elements in practice, ICTU and Capgemini conducted a Proof of Concept (PoC) on Social Housing during 5 weeks. This PoC, built with the Mendix low code platform, focuses on flexibility in implementation, starting with drafting the implementation independent collaboration design (with DEMO) – taking the product definition and its Quality of Service as a given, therefore the impact of (formalizing) product variability is out of scope for this PoC. This meant exploring the required organizational flexibility and a possible IT implementation that only depends on the products to be delivered – supporting the universal pattern for communication and collaboration between actors and with known and consciously chosen dimensions of organizational adaptivity, to be changed at *run-time*.

The remainder of this paper is structured as follows. The research design (Sect. 2) introduces the way of thinking and embeds this in a way of working. Next, the actual intervention (Sect. 3) is described as well as its results (Sect. 4), supporting the conclusions and future research directions (Sect. 5).

2   Research Design

2.1   Proposed Method: Way of Thinking

Our Way of Thinking (WoT) strictly separates the concerns of the essence of an enterprise from its organization and IT implementation, while also traceably connecting those concerns. The WoT therefore consists of 4 building blocks and a vision on how they relate. From DEMO we use (1) its universal transaction pattern, applicable to any kind of service delivery, and (2) its notion of an *essential model* that is implementation independent, given that the products and services of a Scope of Interest (SoI) are defined – in which we understand implementation as the assigning of people and means (including Information Technology). For organization implementation choices and its degrees of freedom, we use (3) the notion of OIV. For Information Technology (IT) implementation, we use (4) the concepts of low code. Finally we will express the relationship between these building blocks in terms of linking their metamodels – to be tested in this PoC.

DEMO's Universal Transaction Pattern: the first building block of our WoT is DEMO's universal pattern of collaboration in business processes [6]. DEMO sees an enterprise – any goal-oriented cooperative – as a network of actors that enter into and comply with commitments. Each commitment is raised in a coordination act (C-act) and results in the corresponding coordination fact (C-fact) – e.g., performing a request act concerning some product results in the fact that the product is requested. Coordination acts/facts – the atomic building blocks of organizational processes – about the same product (or production fact (P-fact)), such as "baked pizza pepperoni #125", occur in particular patterns of interaction, called the transaction – the molecular building block of organizations. This *universal transaction pattern* comprises the "basic pattern" (request, promise, declare, accept), but also its "discussion and discourse layers" (decline, reject, and revocations). Every transaction (instance) is of a particular transaction kind – e.g., "pizza baking". A transaction kind concerns one specific product kind – e.g., "baked pizza" – has one specific actor role – e.g., "pizza baker" – as its executor role, and can have multiple actor roles as its initiator role. Note that a subject (human being) can fulfill more than one actor role – e.g., Mario may fulfill both the actor roles "pizza baker" and "stock controller".

DEMO's Essential Model: this second building block of our WoT, also called the *enterprise ontology*, is the highest level white-box model of the construction and operation of an enterprise. Since it only depends on an enterprise's products and services, it is fully independent from the way in which it is realized and implemented – which makes it organization and IT agnostic. DEMO's essential model consists of an integrated whole of four aspect models:

Cooperation Model (CM) models the *construction* of the enterprise; it consists of transaction kinds, associated (initiating and executing) actor roles, access links for actor roles to inspect transaction banks, and wait links from transaction kinds to actor roles;

Process Model (PM) models the *processes* that take place as the effect of acts by actors, by detailing the coordination between actor roles – specifying the state and transition space of the *coordination world* by making explicit the causal and wait links between C-acts from the universal transaction pattern;

Fact Model (FM) is the semantic model of *products* of the enterprise – specifying the state and transition space of its *production world* in terms of entity types with their related product kinds, property types, attribute types and value types, existence laws and occurrence laws;

Action Model (AM) is a model of the *operation* of the enterprise, guiding actors in performing production act (P-act)s (via work instructions) and C-acts (via action rules) – specifying for every C-fact on which the enterprise has to react (agendum kind) one or more action rules.

Organization Implementation Variables (OIVs): the *notion of OIV*, the third building block of our WoT, expresses a degree of freedom in organizational implementation. Indeed, when a product/service is decided upon, and the collaboration network needed for its delivery has been revealed in a DEMO model, still many degrees of freedom exist before an organization can become operational [6, p. 349]. Some examples of the 25 of such OIVs[7] include:

– deciding upon *functionary types* and which actor roles or coordination acts they should fulfill – e.g., the functionary type "cook" that fulfills both the actor roles "baker" and "stock controller"; or the functionary type "deliverer" who is authorized for the transaction kind "transporting" (including the C-acts of promising and declaring the transport), and also for (the C-act of) accepting the customer payment;
– deciding on *order of working* – e.g., should delivery only be done after receiving payment (as common in retail) or is it (also) possible to pay afterwards (more common in B2B); and
– deciding on *work locations & organizational units*, e.g., which branches of the pizzeria do exist, and what functionary types do exist there.

Organization implementations, and therefore the value of OIVs, will change far more often than the products/services they help deliver. E.g., actor roles as "sales" and "baker" are stable notions in a pizzeria, just as the C-act "accept payment"; what might change often is the authority of a functionary type – answering questions such as "shall we combine the actor roles of sales and baker in one functionary type in the first months of opening our new pizzeria branch?" or "shall we take the responsibility for accepting payments away from our functionary type deliverer, now payment accepting is executed automatically by a web agent under the (outsourced) responsibility of a payment service provider?". For a run-time adaptive enterprise it is a priority that frequently occurring changes, typically implementation choices, are not on its critical path; therefore ideally it should be possible to make such changes at run-time, including its impact in software. However, organizationally variability is so large that conscious choices have to be made what organizational changes should be made possible at run-time. Even the simplistic assumption of each of the 25 OIVs able to independently change with 3 values each already creates $3^{25} \approx 3.5 * 10^{11}$ different organizational implementations for each transaction kind – a problem for automation, but even more so for human overview.

Low Code: this fourth building block of our WoT refers to a style of software development and the use of specific platforms. *Low code* development platforms allow the creation of application software through graphical user interfaces and configuration instead of traditional procedural computer programming [4,20].

Depending on the features of the platform being used and the overall system requirements, the developer may or may not have to augment the design with some good old-fashioned code, or the platform may produce an entire working solution with no additional code required [9]. Low code platforms are recent enablers of Model Driven Development [12], that rely on code generation, model interpretation or a combination of both. Claimed benefits of low code include [10, 16] (a) the ability to produce complex and effective software in shorter time, thus shortening IT time-to-market, and (b) less technical skills needed to produce software, as a response to the growing shortage of technical IT people - with low code, business analysts, architects and even end users can build software and prototype new (business) ideas. Example characteristics of such platforms include generation of data models by importing existing spreadsheets or databases and generating interfaces (both screens and API's) for data management, to build upon to enrich the user experience, not only for desktop applications but also for tablet and mobile devices.

Low code platforms rely on the 3 basic concepts *data* (entity), *logic* (or action or (micro)service) and *interface* (screen or API), and their interrelations. Compared to traditional programming languages like Java and .Net, which mainly rely on the concepts of class and method, the metamodel of low code is richer and closer to the business, making it easier to, e.g., connect the information need of an actor role (as described in DEMO's essential model) to a technical interface to retrieve the corresponding data. However, low code introduces IT variability (e.g., changing from one database to another, or from one front-end framework to another) rather than variability in organizational implementation. It is still very easy with these platforms to hard code organization implementation [3], and thus up to the developer to implement concepts to support the required organization implementation variability.

Relationship Between These Buildings Blocks: The relationship between DEMO and OIVs is apparent[7]; some implementation choices will be directly related to the discerned transaction kinds or actor roles, e.g., in relating functionary types to agendum kinds. The relationship between DEMO and low code seems likely: the DEMO FM provides a good basis to model data, the DEMO AM provides a basis to model logic, and interfaces (either screens or API's) provide a way for actors (either human or automated) to enter the system, based on authorizations. The relationship between organization implementation and low code, is where we can add to both existing IT implementations of DEMO models and to low code: to make explicit, also in software, what organization implementation flexibility is required.

2.2   Proposed Method: Way of Working

We will now elaborate a Way of Working (WoW) to develop an application with known organizational flexibility for a small business domain, building on the expounded WoT. We designed our approach to consist of four elements, executed in an agile way, allowing for iteration and continuous improvement:

1. create and validate the essential (DEMO) model of the business domain, using existing materials such as product descriptions, process models, data models and working instructions, next to input of subject matter experts;
2. identify the needed organizational variability for the business domain, in terms of what OIVs should be changeable at run-time – and elicit them in an essential model for the organizational implementation domain;
3. map the essential models – one for the business and one for the organizational implementation – to the low code platform, exploring the mapping from the metamodel of the essential model to the metamodel of the low code platform;
4. establish what organizational flexibility has been achieved.

3 The Intervention

3.1 Context of the Intervention

Many (also governmental) enterprises in the Netherlands face continuous reorganizations to deliver the same products and services by different organizations. Expected benefits vary from a better tuning of services to citizens and firms to simply cost savings. Typical examples include the shifting of social domain responsibilities from national to municipality level, and the emergent collaboration (sharing, sourcing) between municipalities and/or private organizations.

From its mission 'working for a better digital government', the Dutch state governed Foundation ICT execUtion organization (ICTU) is actively promoting a curious and personal government, in which the human dimension is leading in serving the citizen. ICTU therefore starts from the context, lifeworld and terminology of the citizen to address his/her real needs, especially the weakest ones – such as dependent, non-self-reliant and care avoiding people. As a consequence, the government in communication with its citizen should use terminology which is meaningful for the citizen, takes the intention of the citizen as a starting point, and operates from an *Open World Assumption* [18]. Therefore ICTU wants to invest in methods, ICT solutions and platforms that are open for these principles and assumptions, take continuous change and reorganization as a starting point, and can be shared publicly.

As global leader in consulting, technology services and digital transformation, Capgemini invests at the forefront of innovation in its ambition to put its customers in the driving seat for steering business agility. Such agility needs both an agile development process (e.g., with SAFe® [19]) and agile products – with known (in)flexibilities. Because of the stability and objectivity of its essential model, Capgemini has applied DEMO many times as a basis for redesigning organizations and processes [6, 15]. Also Capgemini invested in research on OIVs to professionalize making choices in such redesigns [7]. And because of its great way of creating flexible IT, Capgemini is a supporter of low code technology, having global and local partnerships with many low code platform vendors. The next step is to gain more knowledge about the transformation of DEMO models and chosen organizational flexibility into working and run-time adaptive software.

3.2   Preparing the Intervention

First of all a suitable business domain had to be chosen. We selected Social Housing because of its representativity for ICTU and because of the availability of documentation. In Social Housing two main areas can be discerned, namely (1) the registration of a home seeker as a member, and (2) assigning a house to the member; we decided to focus on the first.

For this PoC we used Mendix [10] as low code platform, not only because it can be used for free during PoCs, but also because of its Model API [11], which enables us to automate the mapping from the DEMO and OIV models to a Mendix application, ultimately also expected to be able to support new products and services to be deployed within minutes. During the PoC we did a manual conversion from DEMO and OIVs to Mendix, in order to gain experience with the process of mapping.

Finally a team, a steering structure and agreements for collaboration during the PoC were established. A team of 4 people (2.5 FTE) – a DEMO expert, a junior business analyst, a senior Mendix developer and a junior Mendix developer, the latter three without previous DEMO- or OIV-knowledge – were dedicated to execute 3 iterations during 5 weeks. The team regularly communicated with the Product Owner, and at the end of every iteration with the steering committee of ICTU and external stakeholders – demonstrating the progress and discussing the course of action for next iteration.

3.3   Executing the Intervention

During the 3 iterations, the work was executed as follows, each iteration ending with a working version of the application and a growing presentation:

1. team and product owner were introduced to one another; one day was spent on education on DEMO and OIVs; then subsequently the CM and FM for Social Housing were built and a start was made with choosing OIVs and building its FM; some basic interfaces for data management were built;
2. then the focus shifted to building a first version of the AM for Social Housing, including the building of some interfaces to handle c-acts;
3. finishing Social Housing's AM and its FM testset and derivation rules, and finalizing the Mendix application.

4   Results of the Intervention

Essential Model of the Social Housing Domain. The DEMO Cooperation Model (Fig. 1) reveals the starting, periodic renewal and ending of a registration. Starting the registration is initiated by the (aspirant) member and executed after at least paying the registration fee. Every year the registration is renewed against payment of a renewal fee. Ending of registration can be initiated by the member (e.g., when moving to another area) or by the Social Housing organization (e.g., in case of non payment of the renewal fee). The model shows that actors in this domain need access to facts about Social Housing costs & terms, and about person & living – intentionally abstracting from who should provide this access and how, sparking lively discussions on how this could be achieved now (during this PoC) or later.

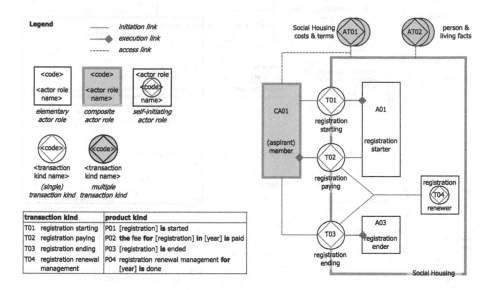

Fig. 1. Cooperation Model Social Housing/registration

In the chosen low code platform it is beneficial to start early on with a data model, for which the DEMO Fact Model (Fig. 2) constitutes the semantics. This model expresses REGISTRATION as core class, and its corresponding starting and ending as event types. Next to that the (grey-colored, because outside the *Scope of Interest*) class PERSON appears, including the property that a person may be the member and/or payer of a registration. Also the class {YEAR} is included, to express (a) the event type of yearly registration renewal, (b) the variable in the (Cartesian product) class REGISTRATION × {YEAR} for the payment event type, and (c) several decisions taken yearly, such as the standard registration fee. In deciding upon starting a registration, the existence of active registrations for and the age of a person are important; therefore the Derived Fact Specifications of the model include algorithms for calculating those.

The team then decided to focus on the process for registration starting (T01 and T02), for which Fig. 3 shows the DEMO Process Model. The model expresses that after having requested the starting of the registration, the (aspirant) member is requested to pay. For the next steps in the process, two variants were envisaged: having successfully paid the registration enables (a) actually *executing* starting the registration (Fig. 3a), or (b) only *promising* to start the registration (Fig. 3b). For this PoC, variant (a) was chosen.

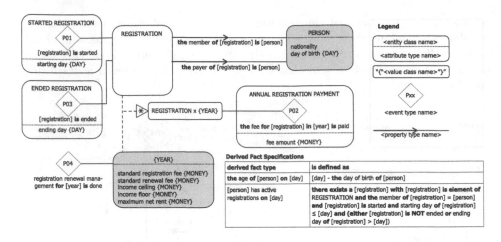

Fig. 2. Fact Model Social Housing/registration

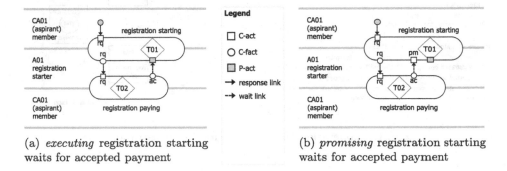

(a) *executing* registration starting waits for accepted payment

(b) *promising* registration starting waits for accepted payment

Fig. 3. Process Model variants for Social Housing/registration

To guide actors in their decisions in the process for registration starting, action rules were formulated in a DEMO Action Model, of which Fig. 4 shows the action rule to settle the agendum kind *registration starting is requested* (T01/rq). This rule assesses that the participants are authorized to play their (performer and addressee) role in this request, that the (aspirant) member is at least 18 years old and Dutch, and that (s)he doesn't have an active registration already at this moment. In that case, normally the registration starter can proceed to request the (aspirant) member to pay the registration and also to promise that his/her registration will be started; otherwise the registration starter normally should decline to do so. Note that the action rule is not deterministic; the registration starter remains free to responsibly deviate from this rule.

Organizational Variability for the Social Housing Domain. Having explored the (stable and implementation independent) DEMO model for the (registration part of the) Social Housing domain, we will now explore the organizational implementation and its desired flexibility. In the domain of Social

when	registration starting **for** [registration] **is** <u>requested</u>		(T01/rq)
	with	**the** starting day **of** [registration] **is some** day	
		the member **of** [registration] **is some** person	**Legend**
		the payer **of** [registration] **is some** person	event part
if	rightness: **the** <u>performer</u> **of the** <u>request</u> **is the** member **of** [registration]		assess part
		the <u>addressee</u> **of the** <u>request</u> **is a** registration starter	response part
	sincerity: * no specific condition *		
	truth: **the** age **of** member **of** [registration] **on** starting day **of** [registration] ≥ 18		
		nationality **of** member **of** [registration] **is** Dutch	
		NOT member **of** [registration] has active registrations **on** starting day **of** [registration]	
if	performing the action after **then** is considered justifiable		
then	<u>request</u>	registration paying **for** [registration] **to the** payer **of** [registration]	[T02/rq]
		with the <u>requested</u> fee amount **of** [registration] **is equal to the** standard fee amount **in the** year **of the** starting day **of** [registration]	
	<u>promise</u>	registration starting **for** [registration] **to the** <u>performer</u> **of the** <u>request</u>	[T01/pm]
		with <u>promised creation time</u> = starting day **of** [registration]	
else	<u>decline</u>	registration starting **for** [registration] **to the** <u>performer</u> **of the** <u>request</u>	[T01/dc]
		with * reason for declining *	

Fig. 4. Action Model Social Housing/registration – action rule for (T01/rq)

Housing, it is important to be able to easily shift accountabilities and responsibilities between organizations and functionary types. In terms of organizations, roles can shift from one social housing association to an umbrella of social housing associations, or to a municipality, or may be in the future as a collaboration of municipalities. The assignment of roles to functionary types shifts regularly, due to changes in required education and competence level, compliance requirements and labor market opportunities or constraints. Finally, it is common practice to authorize persons to fulfill functionary types (and not directly to fulfill actor roles, as defined in the DEMO CM). Therefore from the collection of OIVs [7], *Organizational Unit, Functionary type* and *Authorization* were chosen.

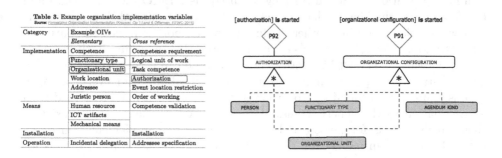

Fig. 5. Fact Model for selected Organization Implementation Variables

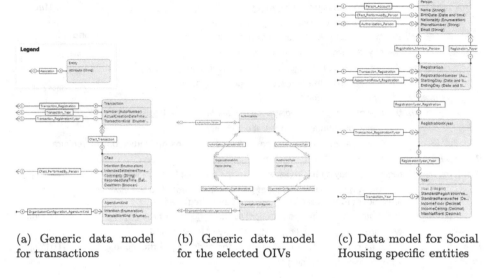

(a) Generic data model for transactions

(b) Generic data model for the selected OIVs

(c) Data model for Social Housing specific entities

Fig. 6. Mendix data models

To comprehend the organization world that establishes those selected OIVs, a separate DEMO model was drawn up, of which Fig. 5 shows the FM. It clarifies that starting an ORGANIZATIONAL CONFIGURATION is a separate transaction, in which a certain FUNCTIONARY TYPE (e.g., *Civil Servant Social Housing*) in a certain ORGANIZATIONAL UNIT (e.g., *City of Amsterdam*) is assigned the right to settle a certain AGENDUM KIND (e.g., act upon *registration starting is requested* (T01/rq)). In starting an AUTHORIZATION, a certain PERSON (e.g., *George*) is assigned the right to act as a certain FUNCTIONARY TYPE in a certain ORGANIZATIONAL UNIT –e.g., as *Civil Servant Social Housing* at *City of Amsterdam*, and/or as *Customer Contact Manager* at *Woningnet*.

Mapping to the Mendix Low Code Platform. To build a Mendix application for registration for Social Housing, we used the DEMO FMs (see Fig. 2 and Fig. 5) to create the Mendix data models (see Fig. 6). The Social Housing specific part was implemented in another module than the more generic OIV part and DEMO parts, to enable reuse over multiple cases. The mapping itself is rather straightforward: every DEMO entity class is mapped to a Mendix entity, every DEMO attribute type is mapped to a Mendix attribute, and every property type is mapped to a Mendix association; the event types are implemented with an association to the generic transaction entity. As we could not use existing (base) registrations for person and year, we choose to implement them ourselves, by adding an integer for Year and a name and some contact details for Person. Type choices were made for all attributes, and an identifier was added to the Registration. Next to that, 2 Mendix actions were defined, based upon the derived facts in the DEMO FM: one for calculating a person's age and one to check for active registrations.

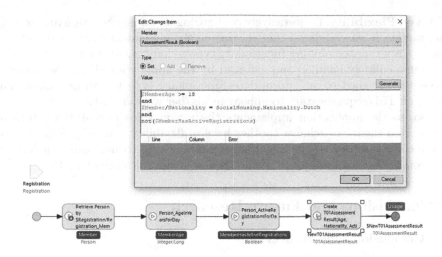

Fig. 7. Mendix implementation of the "truth part" of the Action Rule T01/rq

Additionally, using the calculations for the derived facts, an action was defined for the "truth" part of the AM (see Fig. 7). As actors can deviate from the action rules, a screen (Fig. 8) is created for the actor to act on the agendum kind *registration starting is requested* (T01/rq), in which the result of (the truth part of) the assessment is shown to the actor, combined with all other relevant information, in order to take the decision to promise or decline the starting of the registration. After expressing the decision, a note can be added, especially when the decision differs from the result of the (truth part of the) assessment.

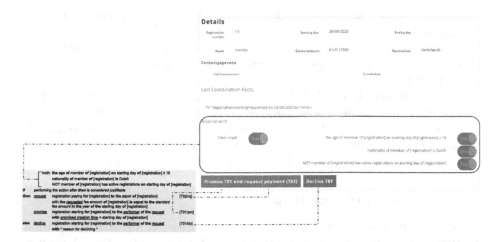

Fig. 8. Mapping Action Rule T01/rq "truth & response part" to Mendix interface

Achieved Flexibility. By iteratively configuring an implementation and testing it in practice, it was validated that changes in the implementation – e.g., adding a functionary type, combining functionary types, changing an authorization, etc. – were immediately handled and enforced by the application. E.g., the moment a person is assigned to an appropriate functionary type for an organizational unit, open T01/requests start to appear in his/her working list.

Also, as the application implements the action rules but allows actors to deviate from them, we achieve another level of flexibility – usually applications enforce these rules, by which an employee cannot decide otherwise, or a (potential) member cannot even perform the request if the rules aren't met.

5 Conclusions and Future Research

5.1 Conclusions and Reflection

In terms of RUN-time enterprise adaptivity, we found that any change in terms of the selected required Organizational Implementation Variability (OIVs) immediately became active in the application without any need to reprogram software. Additionally, the application explicitly supports the autonomy for human actors to (responsibly) deviate from action rules. Also, since the mapping from DEMO and selected OIVs to working software is now made more explicit, if changes occur at the essential model (e.g., adding a transaction kind) or in the required flexibility, it is clear what changes in the software need to be made. With Mendix, it is even possible to automate this process, with the usage of its model API.

Reflecting on the case, we found some other conclusions and questions:

- the DEMO Process Model is not necessary to build the application – indeed, all information in the PM is covered in the AM;
- the achieved organizational flexibility also raises new questions, e.g., who should be allowed to view C-facts recorded by a former employee: someone with the same functionary type, or any functionary type when authorized to act upon the corresponding agendum kind, or someone from the same organizational unit, or . . . ?;
- currently the person details have to be captured manually, resulting in data duplication and, worse, a lower degree of quality and reliability; ideally the citizen consents to use all relevant data from Base Registries, following NL (e.g., *Regie op Gegevens* [13]) and EU legislation (e.g., the Tallinn Declaration on eGovernment (2017)), and the notion of Self-Sovereign Identity [1].

5.2 Future Research Directions

Future research should clarify to what extent the achieved intrinsic application adaptivity can be increased to further enhance RUN-time enterprise adaptivity.

A first means is to systematically embed the use of APIs. To let the citizen effectively exercise his right to share his personal data from Base Registries for a certain purpose and period, it should be easily possible to give – and withdraw – his consent to a party to access these data via public APIs. In the example of Social Housing, this would mean that the aspirant member agrees with a statement such as "Hereby I grant my permission to <party> to use my data solely for the handling of my registration and renting. After ending my registration and renting, <party> will destroy these data." The moment a party is accessing his data, he receives a message on his smartwatch, such as "5 min ago, <party> requested your income data, based upon your consent of <datetime> for handling your registration and renting". This mechanism could be demonstrated using (method) stubs for the data according to standard protocols, e.g., on income (Tax Service) or persons (Base Registry Persons). And it would improve the accessibility of digital government services, also for less digitally skilled citizens, and improve the quality and reliability of the data.

Secondly, the automated support of using the universal transaction pattern should be strengthened. Examples for standard mechanisms, usable for any transaction kind, independent of its specific product kind, include (a) monitoring the sequencing and time-outs of C-acts, (b) marking an agendum kind as "picked up" or "dealt with" by an actor, (c) differentiating between the reason for deviating from the action rules and the reason to be communicated to the addressee, (d) providing insight in (not only current, but) all states of the transaction for all actors involved – e.g., aspirant member sees that he has to pay, and also that registration starting has been promised – and (e) changing the P-fact during the course of one transaction – e.g., allowing the declared P-fact to intentionally differ from the promised one.

Thirdly, more understanding is needed in the effect of more organizational flexibility by parametrizing more OIVs in the same application. This could also provide insight in how the complexity of this – probably $\mathcal{NP}$ – problem is increasing, and to what extent immediate activation of OIV changes in an application can be expected. Additionally, this might ask for other methods like simulation to provide insights in choosing between different organizational implementations.

Another helpful result would be a formal specification for the full transformation of DEMO and chosen OIVs to a low code platform, such as Mendix.

Finally, it would be great to connect our approach with formalisms for product variability, such as in the financial (RISLA [2]) or public (Legops [8]) sector.

Acknowledgments. For this inspiring collaboration of industry with academia, we want to acknowledge Giulietta Marani, Program Manager Discipl, and the Board of ICTU for their sponsorship of this Proof of Concept *Reference Model and Generic Application based on DEMO*. We also want to thank Olaf Kruidhof (EU Agency), Han van der Zanden (Shell), and Hans van Zanten (Capgemini) for being a member of the steering committee.

References

1. Allen, C.: The path to self-sovereign identity (2016). http://www.lifewithalacrity.com/2016/04/the-path-to-self-soverereign-identity. Accessed 31 Aug 2020
2. Arnold, B.R.T., van Deursen, A., Res, M.: An algebraic specification of a language for describing financial products. In: ICSE-17 Workshop on Formal Methods Application in Software Engineering Practice, Seattle, pp. 6–13, April 1995

3. Bockhooven, S.v., Op 't Land, M.: Organization implementation fundamentals: a case study validation in the youthcare sector. In: Complementary Proceedings of the Workshops TEE, CoBI, and XOC-BPM at IEEE-COBI 2015. CEUR Workshop Proceedings, Lisbon, Portugal, vol. 1408, July 2015, http://ceur-ws.org/Vol-1408/paper3-tee.pdf

4. Creatio: Low code. https://www.creatio.com/page/low-code. Accessed 31 Aug 2020

5. Dietz, J.L.G., Hoogervorst, J.A.P.: Enterprise ontology and enterprise architecture - how to let them evolve into effective complementary notions. GEAO J. Enterp. Archit. **2007**, 1 (2007)

6. Dietz, J.L.G., Mulder, J.B.F.: Enterprise Ontology — A Human-Centric Approach to Understanding the Essence of Organisation. The Enterprise Engineering Series. Springer, Cham (2020). https://doi.org/10.1007/978-3-030-38854-6

7. Krouwel, M.R., Op 't Land, M., Offerman, T.: Formalizing organization implementation. In: Advances in Enterprise Engineering X, EEWC 2016, pp. 3–18. Funchal, Madeira Island, Portugal (2016). https://doi.org/10.1007/978-3-319-39567-8_1

8. Lokin, M.H.A.F.: Wendbaar wetgeven: De wetgever als systeembeheerder. Ph.D. thesis, Vrije Universiteit Amsterdam, October 2018. https://research.vu.nl/en/publications/wendbaar-wetgeven-de-wetgever-als-systeembeheerder

9. Medium: What is low code development. https://medium.com/swlh/what-is-low-code-development-f45550c3243d. Accessed 31 Aug 2020

10. Mendix: Low code guide. https://www.mendix.com/low-code-guide/. Accessed 31 Aug 2020

11. Mendix: Openness: API en SDK. https://www.mendix.com/evaluation-guide/enterprise-capabilities/openness-api-sdk. Accessed 31 Aug 2020

12. Mendix: What is model driven development. https://www.mendix.com/model-driven-development/. Accessed 31 Aug 2020

13. Ministerie van Binnenlandse Zaken en Koninkrijksrelaties: Kamerbrief visie Regie op Gegevens (in Dutch), July 2019. https://www.rijksoverheid.nl/documenten/brieven/2019/07/11/beleidsbrief-regie-op-gegevens-nadere-uitwerking. Accessed 31 Aug 2020

14. Oosterhout, M.P.A.v.: Business agility and information technology in service organizations. Ph.D. thesis, Erasmus University Rotterdam, June 2010

15. Op 't Land, M.: DEMO as instrument for clarification in large enterprise transformations - industry talk. In: Enterprise Engineering Working Conference 2015 (EEWC-2015), Prague, June 2015. https://doi.org/10.13140/RG.2.2.21908.53125, Presentation

16. Outsystems: Benefits of lowcode. https://www.outsystems.com/blog/posts/benefits-of-low-code-platforms/. Accessed 31 Aug 2020

17. Overby, E., Bharadwaj, A., Sambamurthy, V.: Enterprise agility and the enabling role of information technology. Eur. J. Inf. Syst. **15**, 120–131 (2006). https://doi.org/10.1057/palgrave.ejis.3000600

18. Reiter, R.: On closed world data bases. In: Gallaire, H., Minker, J. (eds.) Logic and Data Bases, pp. 55–76. Plenum., New York (1978). https://doi.org/10.1007/978-1-4684-3384-5_3

19. Scaled Agile Inc.: Scaled Agile Framework (2018). https://www.scaledagileframework.com. Accessed 31 Aug 2020

20. Wikipedia: Low code. https://en.wikipedia.org/wiki/Low-code_development_platform. Accessed 31 Aug 2020

Author Index

Printed in the United States
by Baker & Taylor Publisher Services